DATE DUE

I'm the Teacher,
You're the Student

I'm the Teacher, You're the Student

■ ■ ■

A SEMESTER IN THE UNIVERSITY CLASSROOM

Patrick Allitt

University of Pennsylvania Press

PHILADELPHIA

10   9   8   7   6   5   4   3   2   1

Published by
University of Pennsylvania Press
Philadelphia, Pennsylvania 19104-4011

Text design by Ellen Beeler

Library of Congress Cataloging-in-Publication Data

Allitt, Patrick.
    I'm the teacher, you're the student : a semester in the university classroom /
Patrick Allitt.
        p.   cm.
    Includes bibliographical references and index.
    ISBN 0-8122-3821-4 (cloth : alk. paper) — ISBN 0-8122-1887-6 (pbk. :
    alk. paper)
        1. United States—History—Study and teaching (Higher).   2. Allitt,
Patrick.   3. College teachers—United States—Biography.   4. Teacher-
student relationships—United States.   I. Title.

E175.8.A505   2004
378.1′2′092—dc22   2004042047

For James T. Fisher

Contents

Preface

It's a great life being a college professor, and the best part of the job is the teaching. I've been teaching history to undergraduates for more than twenty years and have always loved it. We professors, however, are expected not only to teach but also to write. The books we write to get tenure and advance our careers are about our disciplines, not about our lives as teachers. It's strange, isn't it, that of the tens of thousands of books produced by academics in recent years, hardly any have been about our actual work? As far as I know, there aren't any about the daily life of a history professor. I mentioned this odd fact to Peter Agree, my friend and editor. "I've often thought about writing an account of one semester's teaching, to record what actually happens in class." He encouraged me to try. I did, and here is the result, based on a history class I taught at Emory University, entitled, "The Making of Modern America: 1877–2000."

Professors disagree about the proper relationship between teachers and students, about how to lecture, how to lead a seminar, how to teach writing and use writing assignments, how to give and grade exams, how to counsel students, and how to evaluate class participation. I have opinions on all these subjects, and here I'll explain and try to justify them by putting them in the context of an actual college course. In addition to describing what happened with a typical class in a typical semester, I'll throw in some how-to advice and a few "What would you do?" ethical dilemmas based on situations that arose as the weeks went by. A few of these points were debated during the culture wars of the 1980s and 1990s but much of the day-to-day activity in class bears little or no relation to that debate's great controversies.

"I'm the teacher, you're the student." There are all kinds of implications. First, as the teacher, I know more about the subject than the students do, which is why they have come to class in the first place. They want to learn things they do not yet know. As their teacher, I have power over them because part of my job is to evaluate their work and give them grades. Second, some students are more talented than others and some are more hard-working than others, which means that their achievements—and their grades—will differ. Third, despite the steady temptation to make friends with the students, I have to resist it lest it compromise my judgment and impartiality. Professors and students must not be friends (friends don't give each other grades that have a vital effect on their futures). It's certainly OK to be *friendly* toward students, and to try to make studying a pleasure, but there must be no special friendship beyond a generalized affability. When you first become a college teacher, you're anxious to be liked and admired by the students, and you tend to approach them with an exaggerated sense of how much you can do for them. As a beginning teacher I had the fantastic delusion that I could literally change all the members of a class for the better, meanwhile creating a miniature ideal community in the classroom. Experience wears away the first few layers of illusion, but the tendency to want students to like you persists.

I don't mean that the students should dislike you, of course. If they like you, so much the better; it contributes to their wanting to come to class and learn. One thing I always hope to show students is that what at first glance seems dry, technical, and dull is really absorbing, exciting, and entertaining. There are moments when students, like anybody else, can be disappointing. Not most of the time, though; what makes the job such a pleasure is *them*. Treated well, they respond. Many of our students at Emory, with the right incentives, are captivated by learning things they did not know before, especially when they are presented in an interesting or engaging way. My whole teaching life has convinced me that nothing works better as a classroom technique or gets a better response than simple enthusiasm.

A book like this can, I hope, give teachers some useful advice, but the way to improve as a teacher is by actually teaching; hypothetical situations or abstract discussions are too different from the real thing. The best you can hope for, short of actually getting down to the job, is to learn a handful of principles, on the one hand, and a handful of useful techniques, on the other. Also, it helps to think of what your own favorite teachers did and to watch the best of your contemporaries at work. Among my favorites here at Emory—always a pleasure to see in action—

are Ben Arnold (music), Shalom Goldman (Middle Eastern studies), Tom Lancaster (political science), and Frank Lechner (sociology). They read and made useful comments on this book in its early stages, as did Carolyn Forestiere (political science), Richard Roesel (a lawyer), and my former graduate student Christine Rosen, all of whom I want to thank for their help. They, along with Dan Gordon (history) at the University of Massachusetts, pointed out the many places where I didn't live up to my own standards. They also pointed out, in the nicest possible way, that the book is, in a sense, the story of how I didn't put my ideas into practice! The dedication is to my friend James T. Fisher (Fordham), the single best lecturer I've ever heard in America.

1

■ ■ ■

The Introductory Course

I'm an American-history professor with a difference—I'm not American. My vision of American history is inevitably a little different from that of my native-born colleagues. I was born and raised in England and came to America for the first time as a twenty-one-year-old college graduate. My intense love affair with America has been going on ever since, and a little of its rosy glow has colored my version of the nation's history. My approach is comparative; I look at the history of America through the eyes of someone shaped by British history and its legacy. Even though I have now lived as long in America as in Britain, and even though I feel equally at home in both countries, I'm still aware of being an outsider and of having an external point of comparison. America doesn't always come out on the sunny side of these comparisons but it often does. I say to every class when I first meet it, "It's a bit odd, isn't it, that I, a for-eigner, should be teaching you the history of your own country? You must stop me when you think I'm being unfair, or when you think I'm wrong on facts or points of emphasis." They usually look politely noncommittal but long experience has shown me that I will, from time to time, tread on a few all-American toes. Students don't want to think of George Washington as a traitor to Britain, for example. On the other hand, they have often told me that they never before considered how outsiders thought about America and are pleased to hear a verdict that is, on balance, so upbeat. I tell them never to underestimate the blessings of political stability, freedom of religion and speech, due process of law, and a society geared to high standards of honesty and hard work.

If I had to summarize in one sentence the course I am about to teach, it would go something like this: "The United States between 1877 and 2000 attained world dominance, by extensive and efficient industrialization, by extending its commercial, military, and diplomatic reach around the globe, and by trying to live up to—and universalize—its benign ideals." One way or another, every lecture and discussion class will be linked to this central theme, though the digressions will sometimes be lengthy. Throughout the semester I will offer plenty of critical insights into aspects of the American past, but I will also try to ensure that students don't lose sight of the general picture, or of its overall brightness.

For example, I'll talk often about the harsh process of industrialization, which in the short run caused a lot of dislocation, misery, and suffering, but in the long run made America the wealthiest society the world has ever known, with benefits for nearly all inhabitants. America is much wealthier and much better by having been industrialized than it would have been otherwise. I'll try to be sure, therefore, that the students learn not only about the awful working conditions endured by late nineteenth-century steelworkers, but also about the advantages of building with steel and the widespread benefits that have eventually accrued to the members of all social classes. Similarly, I'll teach them about the benefits of democracy and the ideal of human equality. The ideal has often been violated in practice, and we'll study dozens of examples, but the fact that it was widely shared often helped end violations, as the study of the civil rights movement (for instance) can show.

I also plan to demonstrate how the students themselves are connected to the great changes they are studying. In learning about American immigration history, for example, it's worth taking a moment to read off the list of the students' own names (this term my list, sent over by the administration, includes students named Andersen, Chung, Ercak,

Flores, Kim, McKinnon, Pacini, and Steinberg, among others), to emphasize their ethnically diverse origins, and the "melting pot" character of the contemporary middle class from which they come. I want to make them *feel* the contingency of history. It is so easy to think, when you look back on history, that it was bound to happen the way it *did* happen, that it was all more or less inevitable, and that history has now finished. One challenge confronting history teachers, I think, is to show students that events were *not* bound to happen the way they did, and that intelligent people whose ideas did not prevail were nevertheless reasonable in thinking they might. All the way through the course I will be trying to get students into the frame of mind of people whose ideas and values were different from the ones they themselves hold, and to give them at least a provisional, sympathetic hearing.

2

■ ■ ■

Getting Ready

Preparing the Course

I wrote the syllabus the other day, and tried to make sure that I included the complete list of threats and warnings (you'll find a copy at the end of the book, page 233). It's a list that gets longer from year to year as new technology gives bad students new opportunities for deception. In the days when I was a graduate teaching assistant, even plagiarists had to do a certain minimum of work. They had to go to the library and find a book to copy from, or go to their fraternity's file of tried and true papers. No such exertion is required today. Instead, without leaving their rooms, they can browse the Web and find something suitable in a matter of minutes, often from sites with names like College Sucks that were designed to help them cheat.

On the syllabus this time, after writing my name, office number, office hours, e-mail address, and phone number, I write, "Please do not call me at home." Otherwise some of the students will call me, especially ones I least want to hear from. One of the sorrows of being a college teacher is that there is an inverse correlation between your willingness to see or talk to students and the actual time you spend with them. The good ones, the ones who do their work well, try hard, understand the readings, and write stimulating papers, would be a pleasure to entertain. They rarely phone or drop in during office hours, however, because they have no need to—I keep giving them good grades and they keep feeling thoroughly satisfied. Some are scrupulous too and don't want to look like brownnosers. Now and again there's a mournful pleasure to be had from talking with the obsessive types, students who are so thorough and meticulous that their work is already fine, but whose self-confidence doesn't match to their ability. They come by with four or five drafts of a paper, each more magnificent than the last, and agonize over word choice and the sequence of ideas while I murmur soothing phrases. By contrast, the ones who won't do the work or can't get the point seem to spend hours with me, explaining themselves.

Next on the syllabus comes, "No eating, drinking, or wearing hats in class." Isn't it dreadful to be addressing a group of people while one of them is trying to unwrap a sandwich? It's particularly horrible if he is trying to do it quietly, which simply has the effect of prolonging the torment. Not that I like the brazen ones either, who boldly set about their lunches as though the classroom were the perfect setting for a hearty meal. I used to be a bit more permissive and said nothing about the cans of Diet Coke. But I've stiffened up in recent years—the popping of the cans is annoying and the spillages are awful. It's usually some well-meaning character who, having spilled her can while trying to take notes on a folding table much too small for the job, self-consciously cleans up the mess. She borrows Kleenex from her friends, gets down on all fours, and noisily mops the floor, drawing the interested glances of all around her.

What about the hats? You might think I'm high-handed in requiring hats off in class. I am. The baseball caps have always been an affliction. It was bad enough when they were worn with the bill facing forward. Students had an artful way of slumping down in their chairs so that their eyes gradually disappeared from view. Were the eyes open? I would suddenly ask someone a difficult question, singling him out by name. Usually this had the effect of causing a sudden flurry of alarm and a great deal of muttering. Sometimes the student requested that I repeat the question; occasionally his silence confirmed that sleep had descended. Then came the trend, starting around 1994, to wear the hats backward, with the bill sticking out behind and the adjustable plastic tabs defining a semicircle of forehead. The reversed student hat makes a statement about its wearer, something like, "I am dull."

One day a year or two ago a woman in class protested when I asked her to take off her hat. She said, "I thought that was just for the men." I said, "Don't you believe in gender equality?" She answered, "Not with something like this!" I walked over to her desk, asked her to give me her hat, then sent her to the front of the room. I pulled the hat down over my eyes and sagged into her chair, then said: "Now, I want you to talk to the whole class on a subject about which you care deeply and which you know to be complex and difficult. Watch me closely as you speak, and try to gauge how well I am grasping the subject matter." Her blush was one of the reddest I've ever witnessed.

Am I encroaching on students' rights by asking them to take off their hats? It's a fine point. No one has yet downright refused to do it, but I've had a few mutinous stares and plenty of questions. Sometimes one of them asks something like, "Isn't it up to us, as students who have paid the fees, to listen or not listen as we choose, and to do it dressed as we please and in the physical position we choose?" To which I respond, "I can't make you listen but I can at least require you to look as though you might be listening, rather than accepting the aggressive detachment implied by eating, drinking, and the hat! I want you to regard the classroom as somewhere special, set aside for teaching and learning, and free from as many of the contaminations of the outside world as possible. Whatever you do beyond the classroom is your own business, but so long as you are here, I am going to assume that you came here with the intention of learning. I am the teacher, and I am doing everything I can to put you in a position conducive to learning." We go round and round like that and I am usually able to prevail, though not on the strength of my arguments. It is because I have influence over them: the influence of grades. Only the most temerarious student would deliberately and repeatedly antagonize the person from whom they wanted a good grade.

Another prohibition on the list these days is against cell phones and beepers. The cell-phone plague also began in the 1990s. They're bad enough out on the street or in the quadrangle. There seems to be an inverse relation between having something to say and using the cell phone in public. Have you noticed how many users are saying things like, "Now I'm on Main Street and I'm walking toward Grove," or "So I said, like, whatever, and she said, like, no way, and I, like, freaked out."? Somewhere around 1996 students' bags began beeping and trilling during class. By now ownership of phones is so common that when one rings, nearly everyone starts fumbling with his or her bag to see if they're the guilty party. Only once has a student actually taken the call during a class I was teaching, and even then it was in a whisper. Indignant, I told her to stop. She said it was a very important call. I said it was a very important class. She left the room and did not return that day. Next time I saw her I made her promise that she would turn the phone off before she entered the room. These days I begin every class with the general declaration: "Cell phones and beepers off? Then we can begin!"

Among the demands on the syllabus is that the students must not be late. There was a time when senior professors used to station their teaching assistants (TAs) at the door to bar latecomers from entering the classroom at all. When I was a grad student at Berkeley, legends about those autocrats used to circulate, with the implication that their conduct was a disgrace. To myself I used to say, "Those were the great days!" In every class of forty there are two or three perpetually tardy students. After they have done it once or twice, I ask them to stay behind after class for a moment, and I say to them: "Look at the reading list. It actually says that you must not be late, and yet you come in late every time. As a result you always miss the assignments that I give out at the beginning of class, and what's worse, you disrupt the class by coming in late, opening and closing the door, squeezing past others' desks, and then rustling your bags and papers as you prepare to take notes. Will you please promise not to be late again?" I rarely get promises. Instead I get excuses, about overcrowded parking lots, having come a long way from the previous class, having overslept, or having had to cover for someone at a job. The list of excuses is long; some of them are quite persuasive. All the more reason not to accept them, especially from the chronic villains. I answer, "Don't tell me the reasons for your lateness. Just stop being late, if necessary by changing the other things you do on the day of our class." Off they go, muttering words like "uptight" when they think they are out of range.

Our professor of Brazilian history, Jeff Lesser, told me that when he taught at Connecticut College he used to lock the door when the hour for starting class arrived. When someone tried the handle and couldn't get in, he'd ask the class to vote on whether to admit the latecomer. At first, he says, they'd vote yes, but after a while they'd get sick of the way the stragglers interrupted the rhythm of the class, and begin to vote no. If only Emory's doors had locks, and if only it weren't so vexing to the fire marshal! The closest to democracy I ever get on this issue is to say to everyone who's already there, "Does any of you have a watch that says it's not yet ten o'clock?" If the answer is no, then it *is* ten o'clock and we begin.

The syllabus's second paragraph has a long and detailed warning about plagiarism, a subject I'll talk about later on. Then there's a passage about how to do the reading assignments: "Read them [the assigned books] carefully, so that you are able to discuss them intelligently." History classes always come as a shock to students who are concentrating on sciences and mathematics, because we ask them to read plenty every week. For freshmen I assign 100 to 150 pages a week and for upper division students 200 to 250 pages a week. When discussion begins, it doesn't take long to discover who has read the work seriously, who has skimmed it, and who has done nothing at all. There are always those who join in eagerly right at the beginning of discussion and summarize the first three or four pages of the reading, hoping to convince me that they took the assignment seriously. After that they fall silent, and if, later in the class, I ask one of them to summarize an issue that came up on page 50, they are nonplussed.

At the beginning of every semester I say to students, "I will be calling on you by name during discussion and I will expect you to be able to talk about these works on the basis of a careful reading. Don't try to read all of an assignment in one sitting or at the last minute. Work on it a chapter at a time throughout the week, and keep notes on what you read." There can't be many who follow this advice. I admit, moreover, that the night before a discussion class I too can be found frantically working through the book in question. While the students, scattered around campus, are asking, "Oh, why did he assign so much?" I am sitting in my office or at home, asking, "Oh, why did I assign so much?" It seemed obvious on that distant day when I was drawing up the syllabus that they must read all these chapters to grasp adequately the author's main themes, but it doesn't seem quite so necessary now!

My paragraph on the reading assignments also tells them to use a dictionary, to look up every word they do not know, and to keep a notebook of the words they have learned during the semester. When class begins I draw their attention to this passage and emphasize how much I mean it. I've often had the experience of asking a student to explain a central concept in one of the readings, only to discover that he or she didn't know the key word and didn't bother to look it up. Last term in my environmental history class, for example, I said to one, "What does *lacustrine* mean?" She said, "I don't know." "What definition did your dictionary give?" "I guess I didn't look it up." "Have you got a dictionary?" "Oh, yes." "Why didn't you look it up?" "I guess I just got a general idea of the word and went with that." "Tell me about the general idea." "Er . . . I don't really know." I've also endured generations of student writers who won't pause to use the dictionary when they don't know how to spell a word. In about 1993, one student handed in a paper which had sixteen spelling mistakes on one page. When I returned it with each of them circled in red, he said, "You know, professor, the problem is I don't have spell-check on my computer." I said, "Do you have a dictionary?" Unfazed, he answered, "No, I don't have a dictionary either," in a tone that implied: here are two ways in which fate has dealt me a tough hand!

Last term, in a freshman seminar on the history of the American west, I began giving vocabulary tests, drawing words from the assigned readings. For the first test, which came unannounced after a couple of weeks in which I'd been stressing the importance of the dictionary, I wrote a list of ten words on the blackboard, all taken from assigned readings, when there were about ten minutes left in class time. Each student had to write out the definitions, and could leave when they were done. The words were *riverine, isohyet, bovine, meridian, vigilantism, preemptive, cooper, forbs, transhumance,* and *fifth column.* Several of the students left almost at once because, as they admitted, they couldn't get any of the words. A few stayed long enough to write one or two definitions, and then a couple of the conscientious types lingered and agonized until long after class time had finished, and were finally forced from the room by the arrival of the next class. The best grade (from a class of fifteen freshmen) was two out of ten, but the most common grade was zero. I admit the words were a challenge, but since I'd been nagging them about discovering and learning the definitions, and since these were words necessary to an understanding of that week's assignment, I had hoped for someone to get maybe a grade of four or five.

There was a wonderful sequel to this test, however; several of the students, learning of their low scores, did get notebooks and begin to keep lists of new words and their definitions. The next week I got a panicky e-mail from a student who said he'd looked in three different dictionaries but couldn't find the definition of the strange word *Picassoesque*. Knowing nothing about the artist, he'd assumed it had something to do with *pica*, for which he had found the definition: "an abnormal craving to eat substances not fit for food, as clay, paint, etc."

The Books

I assign different books every term, even though the titles of the classes tend to stay the same. It's a good way of keeping up with new books coming out, and it makes sure you never get stale while teaching the same course over again. I've also discovered through the years that if I do reassign a book, I don't have the confidence *not* to reread it before class, so I spend just as long going over it again without really learning anything new. There's no question, incidentally, that the person who learns the most from a class is the teacher, because he or she is so much more conscientious than anyone else in preparing for it.

One of my rules for teaching undergraduate classes is: don't assign many books by academic historians. It is sad but true that most academic historians, especially of the last twenty or thirty years, have been bad writers, and their overspecialized, jargon-heavy, laborious prose sends most undergraduates into a deep sleep. If the students decide to become professional historians later on, they are going to have to get used to it, but I know that the majority of history majors (let alone the miscellaneous non specialists in an introductory course like this one) won't be able to deal with it.

There are several things I try to keep in mind when assigning the books. First, I assign good historical narratives by journalists or professional writers, and plenty of primary sources. Students love to read biographies, autobiographies, fiction, and eyewitness accounts, and they're willing sometimes to read works in an unfamiliar idiom, like the text of legal decisions, provided they are not too long. Even the conscientious students won't read overly long assignments carefully to the end. One hundred pages by an academic historian is the limit in an introductory class, or 200 pages by an author more alert to the audience's sensibilities. With a page-turning novel, maybe 250 pages once or twice in the term will succeed.

Memoirs are ideal. This time I'm using Theodore Roosevelt's book *The Rough Riders* (1899), about the troop he raised to fight in the Spanish-American war in 1898, recruiting partly among his old Harvard classmates, partly among his New York and Washington political friends, and partly among his cowboy friends from the Dakotas, where he had been a rancher in the 1880s. They go into battle and he writes a gripping account of the Battle of San Juan Hill, the bravery of his men, the high casualties they suffered, and the strangeness of beholding the dead bodies of men to whom you were talking moments before. It's a great book for the introductory course because TR's personality and attitudes come blazing out on every page. Nearly all his attitudes are wrong by our standards; he's virtually the personification of all that is *not* politically correct. He's lovable and admirable anyway, or at least it's possible to imagine why he was lovable and admirable to many members of his generation. The students and I have the chance, therefore, to go over passages of the book together and unravel his attitudes, why he holds them, how he applies them, and why it should be that we now think so differently.

Also this term we'll be reading volume 1 of Emma Goldman's autobiography *Living My Life*. She and TR were contemporaries, more or less, but it's hard to think of two people more different. Like him, however, she's a lovable crackpot. I'm hoping the contrast will work well and serve as a reminder that at any one time, widely different people and attitudes are abroad in the world. A third memoir on the list is *Black Elk Speaks*, as written down by the poet and amateur anthropologist John Neihardt. Black Elk was also a contemporary of the other two but he was a Sioux Indian. He describes his family's traditional way of life, how it was brought to an end by the arrival of the whites, how as a teenage boy he fought at the Little Big Horn and later at Wounded Knee, and how he toured Europe as part of Buffalo Bill's "Wild West" exhibition. Historians aren't sure how much of it is his own words and how much the words of Neihardt, who interviewed him as an old man, but as a glimpse of the Plains Indians' last independent days it's ideal for this course.

In addition to history, memoirs, and historical journalism, I often assign novels that have something to say about a particular historical time or place. We'll be using two novels this term: Anzia Yezierska's *Bread Givers* and Tim O'Brien's Vietnam story *If I Die in a Combat Zone*. You've got to be careful with assigning novels. Occasionally the students don't realize that they are fictional. Once, in a course on U.S. religious history, I assigned John Hersey's *The Call*, a terrific novel loosely based on Hersey's parents' lives as missionaries to China in the early twentieth century. During discussion in class, one student referred admiringly to Hersey's invented characters and to how he blends them seamlessly with actual historical characters. Another student gave a sudden sharp intake of breath and said, "You mean it's not all true?!" She had been completely taken in by the pseudodocumentary style and was only now discovering her mistake. I realized while talking with her later that she never read fiction. An experienced reader would have known just from the book's cover, not to mention dozens of other internal clues, that it was a novel.

It's striking to see how many students do not even know what the word *novel* means. Many use the word as a synonym for *book*. Students' papers will often include phrases like this: "Perry Miller, in his novel *The New England Mind* . . ." I said to a student last term: "Do you know what a novel is?" "Like, the books we read in class every week." "Is this one a novel?" I asked, holding up Rachel Carson's *Silent Spring*. "Sure," she replied. "Is it possible for a book not to be a novel?" "Oh yes, you know, like, the book of instructions for a washing machine—that's not a novel." When I explained her mistake, she was surprised but admitted, on further questioning, that she never read fiction.

Most students today do not read much and many have gone through school hardly ever reading voluntarily. There has been a lot of discussion during the culture wars of the last decade or two about what books we should assign to students and what (if anything) we should regard as part of the canon. What makes the debate so intense is perhaps the participants' awareness that the *assigned* books in school and college are often almost the *only* books many of the students are ever going to read. If it's a choice of just one, then reading Toni Morrison's *Beloved* really will make you come out a bit different than reading just Steinbeck's *Grapes of Wrath.* I would like students to read both (and a lot more besides) but I know that unless I and other professors use our authority on the point, the vast majority of them will never read any.

As a novice teacher in the late 1970s and early 1980s I used to say, "Do you remember that brilliant passage in *Middlemarch* where . . . ?" Everybody gave me a blank look. Then I began to put it this way: "Has any of you read Dickens's *Tale of Two Cities?*" One or two hands would go up and I'd explain to the others the incident from that book that struck me as a useful analogy. Nowadays I say, "I hope you'll all read *Moby-Dick* one day. You'll come across a passage that will make you think of this issue, where . . ." The students do have a fund of ready references, however. If I want to make a comparison with something they know about, I can rely on it. "Do you all remember the episode of *Seinfeld* where George's father decides to abandon Christmas and hold his own celebration, Festivus, instead?" To a question like that, seven out of every eight know what I mean, and similarly with *The Simpsons, Friends,* and other popular shows or movies. Or I can say, "Remember that Chevy Trucks commercial during the Superbowl?" and then the answer is a confident yes.

Many professors blame the schools for the fact that students are not well read by the time they get to college. The schools certainly haven't done a good job of teaching them to write, but surely we should blame the students' *families* for the great reading deficit. Or maybe blame is the wrong way of thinking about it. I wish students would read more books. It would help them in finding their way around in the world, give them an immense fund of moral education, and captivate their imaginations. If they have not read many books, it is probably because their parents did not read many either, making the idea of a reading as an activity altogether distant.

Now and again good students tell me that they've kept a record of the books I have mentioned during the semester and that they plan to read them later. This is gratifying, and I am even more gratified when, a year or two later, they drop by my office to report on having read a book they first heard about from me. They don't always like my suggestions (the other day an ex-student told me he'd found it impossible to progress through Norman Mailer's *Of a Fire on the Moon*), but at least they're getting used to the idea that reading can be a pleasure as well as a duty. When all is said and done, the students who read a lot are going to become the best educated. When they hear about a topic or a book on a particular issue, they should follow up by reading it or reading about it. If they don't, their knowledge will always be scanty. Teachers can do a lot but students who rely mainly on their teachers are never going to shine. They must learn (from the teachers, I hope) to rely on themselves.

For this course I am not going to assign a textbook, even though dozens are available on today's market. My reasons are partly that textbooks are far too expensive, partly that they are far duller than the assigned books I've already mentioned, and partly that their tone jars against some of the things I want the students to learn. These days, college-level textbooks on recent American history are unremittingly gloomy and doomy. They hammer away at examples of injustice, prejudice, discrimination, and repression, as if designed to induce in readers a sense of shame and regret. From them you could easily get the impression that no one in America had ever had any enjoyment, any justified sense of purpose, or any pride in their nation, their lives, and their accomplishments.

The textbooks are fragmentary, too, because their authors have learned not to "privilege" any one group over all others. Therefore they have to deal with a growing list of previously neglected citizens. Pick up any of them and you will find that a general passage on the Great Depression and the politics of the New Deal (for example) is followed by one on how the Depression affected women, how it affected African Americans, how it affected Hispanic Americans, how it affected Native Americans, and how it affected the disabled. As the number of interest groups vying for attention in the contemporary world keeps growing, so does the number of little passages in the textbooks that must be devoted to their predecessors. No one has succeeded, so far, in combining these little bits into a satisfactory overall narrative.

I don't want to imply that America has *not* been the scene of injustice, prejudice, discrimination, and repression, or that the history of many particular groups in the past is unworthy of study. There certainly is plenty in American history about which citizens today have good cause to feel shame and regret. But that's only half of the story. There is also much about which they and their children should feel pride and gratitude. For example, there has never been a powerful nation in the history of the world so generous, so idealistic, and so dedicated to the principles of democracy and human equality. The glum textbooks unwittingly bear witness to this point. Their authors sound disappointed because they *share* these high ideals, and feel shocked at how far short of them America has fallen in practice. Still, historians—with what ought to be a deeply anti-utopian view of the world—should know better. If they compare American experience not against their ideals (by which it looks rather shoddy) but against the experience of other societies in world history, it comes out looking pretty good.

3

■■■

Early Class Meetings

First Day of Class (Wednesday)

Off we go to meet the class itself. This semester it's a Monday-Wednesday-Friday class with a good midmorning time (10:40–11:30), when the students should all be alert, cheerful, and talkative. Class times are much disputed among faculty members. If you teach at 8:30 A.M. you'll be lucky to get enough students to forestall cancellation of the course. Even 9:30 is no cinch, and for any pre-noon class you can see prodigious yawning and hear students discussing how they weren't in bed before dawn and "isn't it *early*?!" Not to me: I used to be just like them, but now, with a child to get to school, I'm up by 6:00. At 10:40 I'm deep into the day's work. As a department we've discussed at faculty meetings the possibility of switching all the graduate seminars to morning times, on the grounds that the grad students are more of a captive audience and will just have to put up with it. The other big issue, among teachers and students equally, is the matter of which days their classes will meet.

Most professors covet the Tuesday-Thursday schedule because it means fewer class meetings in all and a spacious four-day weekend. I'm not immune to these allurements, admittedly, but I don't think longer classes are so good in terms of getting the students to actually learn. Their eyelids seem to gain weight after a while and they can't stop looking at the clock. I once had a student who told me, "My sociology class is a real MEGO!" "What?" I asked. "You know: my eyes glaze over." I usually spend the last fifteen minutes of those Tuesday-Thursday eighty minute classes showing slides or getting students to draw diagrams on the blackboard, so that they can look at things and move around a little. Anyway, this term it's three fifty-minute sessions per week, which is really the best option.

I go to the room slightly ahead of time and find about thirty-five students already waiting. I have brought along a carousel with fifteen slides that I plan to show in the second half of this first meeting. I hand out syllabi and give each student a note card on which to write name, phone number, and e-mail address. While they're doing that I try to make the motorized projection screen descend, but it won't. To my dismay I find I'm in a classroom that's had a high-tech makeover. They even call it a "smart classroom." I'm a low-tech person, so the auguries are bad. I have to dash across to the audio-visual headquarters, which luckily are just next door, and find out how to make the screen work. Returning, I'm just in time to catch the stragglers, get the screen working, and begin punctually.

The great challenge in the first few meetings of any new course is to learn the students' names. The more there are, the harder the job. This time there are thirty nine. I always hated being in a class where I knew the teacher didn't know my name, and I assume it's the same with everyone else. I require attendance and I call the roll each time. Repeating the names out loud is an aid to learning them, and as students answer to my call I give them a hard stare and try to remember them, putting faces to the names. I'm not great at it, but I've usually got all the names down by the sixth or seventh class meeting and it makes everything run more smoothly thereafter. Before long the students are calling each other by name in discussion, too, which helps take the impersonal edge off it (though there are always a few who point and say, "what she said . . . what he said . . ")

Every new class is unattractive. Teachers who've looked out over any particular sea of faces for the first time will agree, as will students who have found themselves sitting in the middle of a crowd of previously unknown people. Sure enough, this lot conforms to the pattern by looking pretty awful. But I know from years of experience that they won't remain that way. With the passage of each week in the semester they will become more of a pleasure to behold, until, at the end of term, I'll think of them almost as eerily radiant. Why does it always happen this way? Because most of us don't look so great at first glance—we have to become familiar to one another (only in Hollywood classroom scenes is everyone handsome or pretty straight away). And when we're doing something for the first time we're anxious. Once we get to know one another, our habitual speech, smiles, idioms, and moods, we will seem less alien and less threatening.

Teaching has always made me nervous, especially teaching a new, unfamiliar, and unattractive group. The first time I did it, back in 1979, I was almost sick with anxiety, and the class must have been nearly as grueling for the students as it was for me. By now I've got my feelings under control. Even so, I always have butterflies of anxious anticipation, which I try to overcome by preparing carefully. This term Regina, one of our graduate students, has been appointed as my teaching assistant. She will sit in on all the classes, participate in grading some of the quizzes, papers, and exams, and later in the semester give a couple of guest lectures. She frankly admits that she's terrified at the prospect, and I sympathize because I still remember how it felt.

The first few times you try lecturing, you discover that your body does things over which you have no control. In the early days I used to have a rather acute sway, backward and forward and from side to side. The effect brought to onlookers' minds the old song "What shall we do with the drunken sailor?" Mrs. Allitt caught sight of it once and brought it to a hasty stop. Then for a while my left arm used to curl itself strangely so that the top joints of my hand were folded against the front of my left shoulder. Meanwhile my right hand took excursions across the top of my head, giving audiences the impression that I was actually holding my head in place. Occasionally the haze of lecturing anxiety would clear sufficiently to let me know about this state of affairs, and I'd try to rearrange my extremities into more conventional positions, but then a verbal stumble would distract me and the limbs would take off on their own once more.

One effect of nervousness which has never abated is getting a hot head. I'm not hot headed as a rule, I think, but somehow an hour of lecturing brings massive quantities of blood to the head, and as class ends I find it boiling hot. A cooling-off period needs to follow, so students who stay behind for a moment to ask questions find me strangely warm, with radiator-like face and neck.

My father was a teacher and he used to say that he didn't like teachers who had mannerisms and gestures. He himself, when speaking in public, was effective, but only because of his mannerisms and gestures, of which he had an immense and varied repertoire. When my brother and I pointed this out to him he flatly denied it and said he just spoke straightforwardly, and without affectation. We've all got mannerisms and gestures, of course; the issue is to make reasonable ones and to know what you're doing. Sometimes now when I teach seminars or training sessions to beginning teachers, I spend quite a lot of time on anxiety management and physical self-control. To the arm wavers I sometimes say, "repeat that sentence without moving your arms or hands at all." They find it physically difficult at first but gradually learn that it can be done.

We work on verbal tics too. Nothing is easier than to fill up every empty space with an "er" or an "um." Once students latch on to the tic they'll sometimes count. A statistics-minded student told me last summer that one of my colleagues, when he taught her, had "ummed" 104 times in half an hour. Worse is getting into the habit of "sort of," "you know," "kind of," or (the great devil word of the new millennium) "like." Sometimes an entire class will utter almost no word except *like* for minutes on end, and the temptation to give up and join in is powerful. Resist it! It's the verbal equivalent of the reversed baseball cap.

I experimented last semester with actually prohibiting *like* altogether during discussions in a freshman seminar. Students for whom it had become a crutch became speechless, or had to fumble along so slowly, carefully, and artificially, that they forgot the point they were trying to make. I'd love to have carried on with the experiment but after a few minutes a visitor would have thought the class was made up of adult literacy students who were slowly and methodically sounding out their first written words. Half-annoyed with myself, I relaxed the rule and *like* came flooding back, never to depart again. I can bully my own child about it but bullying entire classes, especially when I actually want them to be talkative on the subject of the course, is more difficult. Just after this failed experiment I saw a cartoon in the *New Yorker* that showed two middle-aged men talking at a bar. One says to the other: "I, like, wonder how she, like, knew that I was, like, having an affair with, like, a college girl."

Teaching gets easier with practice. I've been through the cycle enough times by now that unpleasant surprises come up less often. Dismaying circumstances these days bring to mind *other* dismaying circumstances from years gone by and, usually, an idea of what to do about them. There's no quick fix for nerves, but experience helps a lot. In fact one of the advantages of being middle-aged is that it creates plenty of distance between you and the students around you. There's no question now that I'm very different from them. We're not far from being members of different species (in their view), and the roles each has to play are clear.

This matter of distance is central to teaching. Let the students know by verbal and body language that you're the teacher and they're the students, and that the relationship creates a space between the two. The classroom situation underlines this message. They've come to this room to learn from somebody. You are that person. The students attribute to the teacher all the relevant knowledge of the subject and regard him or her as quite different from themselves. Most teachers never feel quite ready to take on the assignment; we're always aware of how much we don't know about the subject. But from the students' point of view we're omniscient—their assurance that we know what we're talking about helps to maintain the distance. Don't let this sense of distance and difference break down; it's your ally in nearly everything you do.

As the class begins, I summarize the difference between high school and college-level history courses, like this: "In high school you were probably asked in history classes to learn who did what, where, and when. Those things are still important—without them you can't get far in history at all. But now we are introducing a second set of questions. *Why* did these events take place? Usually, historians find that events and trends can be explained in different ways, and that the evidence they are trying to interpret is ambiguous. For example, we are picking up the story of American history just after the Civil War. Everyone agreed that the Union had won, but there were lots of opinions then, and there are still lots of opinions now, about why they had won. Was it because they had more people? Or because their armies were better led? Or because their soldiers were more motivated? Or because their soldiers were better fed, armed, and transported, thanks to the North's superior railroad network? Or is it because, deep down, the Southerners knew they were defending an unjust system and therefore could not fight for it heart and soul? Or was it a combination of these factors, and if so, in what proportions? These examples are just a few of the ones offered by intelligent and persuasive historians, and the question continues to be investigated.

"Here's another thing we have to do," my speech continues. "We have to get back into the frame of mind of people living in different times and places, and try to think, at least provisionally, in the same way that they thought. We need to remember, for example, that people living in 1862 did not know how the Civil War was going to turn out. It's easy for us to assume that just because it did turn out in a certain way, it was *bound* to turn out that way. In fact, of course they didn't know that, any more than we know the important events of the twenty-first century.

"Harder still, we have to take seriously their beliefs, even when those beliefs are quite different from our own. It's easy to fall in with them when they think more or less what we think. The challenge of doing history well is to accept that they were sincere in their beliefs, even when we disagree with those beliefs completely. We will not be able to understand them if we are unable to think their thoughts along with them, at least provisionally. That doesn't mean that we have to regard them as right. In the end we can certainly judge them harshly if we want to. But our main job as historians is to understand, and if we're too quick to judge, our judgment will get in the way of our understanding.

"Even with issues like slavery, we need to understand that many slave-owners did not think they were acting wrongly. In 1877 (our course's official starting date), the South was full of people nurturing a burning sense of injustice about the recent loss of their slaves and the defeat of the Confederacy. They didn't feel ashamed of their beliefs; they felt proud of their convictions, and now we need to struggle to understand them. On the whole," I say in conclusion, "you should try to keep your moral opinions far in the background while trying to understand history. It's OK once you have understood someone to judge them, but first you must understand them in all their strangeness and difference from our own world."

After that rather abstract passage I come down to earth and talk about America in the 1870s. I tell them about what sort of things Americans read. I ask one student, Simon, whose name I have chosen at random off my list, "What was the most widely read book in America during the 1870s?" He gives me a look of stark horror and can't even bring himself to say "I don't know." I encourage him, "Here's a clue: it was the most widely read book in every decade of American history up to that point." Somebody else blurts out, "the Bible," getting him off the hook, and I say, "Yes, the Bible." I ask Simon, "Do you ever read the Bible?" and he answers: "No, I'm Jewish" (!). "But at least three-quarters of the Bible was written by Jews. Have you never read any of it?" "Well, yes, I guess so," he says, in such a way that it's clear he's trying to placate me with the answer he thinks I want to hear, rather than with the truth.

Students are quirky about religion. Normally, their teachers don't raise the point and there seems to be a tacit First Amendment agreement to leave it alone. Now the subject is coming from an unexpected source: the history professor. I tell them, "One of the best ways to get started with American history is to read the Bible, because it's the book that generations of Americans knew far better than any other, and it shaped their view of what the world was like. They got their kids' names from it, and used examples from scripture to justify their moral conduct. They compared themselves and others to its characters. When Lincoln freed the slaves many of them compared him to Moses, who led the Children of Israel out of slavery in Egypt. When he was assassinated many Northerners compared him to Christ, dying for the sins of others."

In a typical class at Emory nearly everyone has a nominal religious allegiance of some kind, with almost a third being Jewish. The Protestants and Catholics are vague about what it is that keeps them apart, except for the handful of evangelicals who've got a keen grasp of doctrine but an equally keen grasp of the fact that it's bad manners to discuss your religion with others, let alone advocate it to them. I want them to discuss it but they're reluctant.

I finish this first meeting by showing the slides. I get students to come to the screen and describe what they can see in the pictures, again drawing names off my list at random. Their comments are straightforward, but that's OK for the moment. The process gets them accustomed to the fact that I'm going to be calling on them by name and that they must try to be ready with something to say. It's amazing how much some of them cannot see in a picture. Sometimes a big object is right there, like a cow or a horse, but if I ask, "What is in the picture?" they seem unable to perceive it. Or the picture might be a great, didactic image of benevolent Abraham Lincoln freeing the slaves, but they can't recognize him or grasp the artist's message. These aren't dull students either; they got 1300 or more on their combined SAT, but they're unequipped for this kind of work because they've never done art appreciation and no one ever has asked them to stand in front of thirty-nine others and be perceptive about old photographs.

One of my favorite first-day-of-class slides is a mid-nineteenth-century advertisement for a telegraph company. It shows an angelic female form, scantily but strategically clad, floating in midair. Coiled in her arm is a loop of wire, and as she floats from right to left across the picture the wire trails out behind her, being attached neatly to successive telegraph poles. The right side of the picture, from which she has come, is light and bright. There's a city, ships, trains, sunshine, and bustle. The left side of the picture, by contrast, is dark and gloomy. Into the darkness run a group of American Indians and a handful of buffalo. In the middle of the picture, around the ethereal figure, come farmers with plows and covered wagons, all like her facing left. It's the single best Manifest Destiny picture I know of, in which the dawning of American civilization pushes away the darkness of savagery further and further to the west. To new students, however, its meaning is obscure. They don't notice the wire, for example, or don't get the point of the light-dark contrast, or can't understand why everyone's moving in the same direction. Some think it's all about time zones, others think it's an expression of sympathy for the poor displaced Indians, and others again are just stumped by the whole thing. "What's this picture all about?" "It's just a woman floating in the air." "What compass bearing is she following, do you think?" I ask. "I haven't the faintest idea . . . north?" By the end of the semester, if nothing else, they'll know what to make of a picture like this.

Second Class (Friday)

Today I lecture on farming. Not one of the forty or so students in this class grew up on a farm (I asked them last time), and not one of them has ever milked a cow, plowed a field, driven a tractor, scanned the sky anxiously in search of much-needed rain, or cursed a hailstorm for beating down the crops. Yet to understand American history you have to understand farming, without which the society would neither have come into existence nor continued to exist. It's a challenge to make them realize that throughout much of American history, farming wasn't simply the remote activity of a small minority (as it has become today) but nearly everybody's central concern.

This is an ideal lecture to accompany with slides, too, and I have a good selection, showing farms in different parts of the country and their characteristic problems. The focus today is on the Great Plains, which were opened up to settlement in the 1860s, 1870s, and 1880s in the wake of the Homestead Act of 1862 and the completion of the transcontinental railroad in 1869. The act gave 160-acre farms, almost free of charge, to anyone who settled them and improved the land for five years. First I show a picture of a primitive house on the wide-open Dakota plains and a family of Norwegian immigrants standing in front of it. They have brought out their table and chairs, butter churn, and baby's cradle, while beside them stands a yoke of oxen and the family's horses in the wagon traces. Behind them a slightly blurry windmill turns in the wind.

I ask Kathleen (just a name off the list again), "What can you see in this picture?" To her, when she gets over the surprise of being asked out of the blue, it looks like a vision of unrelieved misery and privation; there's nothing in the background except flat, empty space, and everyone looks solemn. She says, "There's a father and mother and five children, and then some farm equipment all in front of the house. It just looks depressing and lonely." Unprompted, she adds, "It would drive me crazy to live in the middle of nowhere like that."

"Why are the table and chairs outside, do you think?" I ask another one, Curtis. He's more upbeat about the scene, and says (rightly, I think), "In those days you couldn't afford a photograph very often so when you got one, you brought out your possessions as well as your family, as a way of showing how you were getting on. I think it's actually a picture of pride, rather than misery, even though they don't look like my idea of a good time" (laughter). I praise him for this shrewd answer, then ask a third student, Charles, about the house itself, but he has no idea what it is or what it is made from. I explain that in the early days of settlement in the treeless plains, settlers cut bricks of the thick prairie sod, dried them, and built them up to make sod houses. They weren't very comfortable (worms and snakes sometimes slithered out of the walls, and the roof would leak after rainstorms), but you could stay alive in one for the first couple of winters because they cost nothing but your manpower, and were thick and well insulated. Then, when your crops began to flourish, you could afford to import lumber for a frame house and start to live better.

A fourth student identifies the windmill as the power for the family's water supply, and a fifth, when shown another picture, explains that the woman with the wheelbarrow is collecting buffalo chips for stove fuel, adequate for heating and cooking. In the early nineteenth century, the standard wisdom had been that the plains would never be settled because lack of wood meant no building material and no fuel. By the 1860s, settlers were solving both problems with sod bricks and buffalo chips. Lack of wood also meant there was nothing for fencing, but Joseph Glidden invented barbed wire in the early 1870s and helped crack that problem too. Above all, the arrival of railroads in the late 1860s made it possible to bring out to the plains whatever you lacked locally, and to pay for it by shipping back east high yields of crops, grown on land that had never previously been plowed. Lack of trees was a bonus as well as a problem, because it meant that the settler could plow straight away rather than spending years in the back-breaking job of cutting down trees and removing stumps.

My next slide, emphasizing that point, shows a settler's cabin in Oregon from the 1880s—his problem is too much wood. He's got material for a cabin and fuel, but the stumps are going to make plowing impossible until he's removed them—an extremely difficult job in the days before tractors. Until then he will have to plant around them—something American farmers had done for decades as each new forested area east of the Mississippi was settled. I turn on the lights. Another student, Britney, named at random and summoned to the board but reluctant to take the chalk, says shyly, "I can't draw; I never did art!" "Well, now's the time," I tell her; "it's vital to your education." After a bit of cajolery she draws a simplified version of a tree's root system below ground level. On the ground, she adds a comical yoke of oxen straining on chains to pull the stump. None of the other class members is eager to try drawing draft animals, and one chivalrous young man, with a grin, calls out, "No one's going to improve on those beautiful oxen, Professor, unless you can draw some for us."

After the slides and blackboard art I tell the class about the importance of the seasons. Today, we urban and suburban dwellers can regard the climate as mere background, a minor irritant when it's too hot or too cold, but for American farmers it was the difference between prosperity and adversity, success and failure. When the rain stopped falling in the high plains in the late 1870s and 1880s, many settlers had to give up ("In God we trusted, in Kansas we busted!"). The round of farm chores for everyone was different in summer than winter, depending on what stage the crops had reached. Even hours of wakefulness varied— longer on long summer days, shorter in the cold, dark winter.

I end by urging them not to romanticize farming, a point I underline by reading a couple of paragraphs from Hamlin Garland's unsentimental memoir, *A Son of the Middle Border.* Garland blew the whistle on farm-life nostalgia by describing its brutal and monotonous side—it's a terrific book. Falling in with his view, I tell the class, "Farming was a life of perpetual toil and constant anxiety. You were always at the mercy of the elements and the seasons. Sun, rain, hail, wind, fire, and grasshoppers could all be catastrophic, quite apart from Indian attacks (still a hazard for settlers in the 1860s and 1870s) and from the mysterious operation of the agricultural commodities markets in Chicago, which set the price farmers' crops would actually bring." It's a pleasure to see some of the students thinking over the nature of this way of life, previously almost completely unknown to them.

Third Class (Monday)

It's just the third time we have met and Emory College's drop-add period is in full swing. Students, having tried several classes, are entitled to drop the ones they don't like from their schedules and add ones about which they have heard good things. As a result, the actual people in the classroom are slightly different from the ones I saw there last time and the time before that. I call the roll and already I'm beginning to recognize the more distinctive or unusual faces, and to recall the names of students I brought to the blackboard last time. With the semester still young, I am following my custom of wearing a shirt and tie and entering the room in a jacket, as a visible way of distancing myself from the students and underlining the fact that I'm the teacher and they're the students. The jacket does not stay on for more than a minute or two, however. It was new once, a long time ago, but now it's something close to a mere theatrical prop, always hanging on the back of my office door and just picked up a few times each term for moments like this. Knowing I'll soon be too hot, I always take it off and roll up my sleeves when I get into the classroom. Apart from anything else, a certain widening has taken place in various parts of my body, from which this coat used to hang loosely. The looseness is all gone now, and if I tried to button it ripping sounds would be heard. Observant students perhaps say to themselves as I enter, "He's borrowed a smaller man's jacket." In a couple more weeks I'll dispense with the jacket, then the ties will go, and by the end of the semester, when I've established some authority by other means and it's getting hot outside, the long sleeves will disappear too.

The substance of lectures matters more than the clothes I wear, in any case, and today's substance is railroads. I grew up loving trains and never got over it. One of the many benefits of being a history professor is that it gives me the chance to incorporate this first love into my actual work. The introductory class always gives me scope for a set-piece lecture on railways. I have so many slides on railways and know the subject so well that I just load fifty pictures into the carousel and, without any notes or prompts, start the class. I begin, "Who knows why 1869 is the most important date in American history?" One student has watched me setting up the projector and focusing the first slide, so he guesses it's the year the transcontinental railroads joined up. "Exactly!" I go on to qualify the big claim but also explain how radically the existence of the railways shrank the time it took to get from the East Coast to California, and back.

Next I ask Karen to come to the board and draw a diagram of a steam locomotive. She comes forward confidently and takes the dry-board marker, but with it she simply draws a box on top of two circles, with a chimney, from which pours a cloud of wiggly-line smoke. She smiles at me and hands back the marker. "Is that a diagram or just a picture?" "Well it's a mixture, really," she says. "Tell me what happens to make the engine go along the track." She gives me a delightful beaming smile but can't think of anything to say, so I ask her to sit down again. "Anyone else?" Martin says he understands. He comes to the board and points to the picture. "What happens is that the fire makes the engine light, and the vapor pours out of this funnel." "How does that make the locomotive move along the track? Surely if an object becomes lighter it just tends to move up into the air rather than along the ground." He can't answer that one so he sits down too. A third volunteer, Roy, draws a little turbine halfway up the locomotive's chimney and gives me a hopeful glance, as he says, "Smoke goes up the chimney and turns the turbine on its way—it's connected to the wheels somehow." I give a gentle shake of the head. By now they all know they're confused, and flutters of laughter at their lack of knowledge and their bad art spread through the room. Finally one of the women whose name I still don't know says (very astutely, I think), "I'm not coming up to the board there but isn't it something about rods and pistons?" She illustrates by moving her arms in vigorous back-and-forth motions like the Little Engine That Could. "Yes, that's right; well done."

I then draw a simple diagram of what actually happens inside the engine, and another diagram of the low-friction contact between wheel and rail which makes railroads so efficient. Then down comes the screen, off go the lights, and the picture show begins. The problem with lecturing entirely from slides is that the room is dark and the students can't always see to take notes properly. The notes they do make aren't always intelligible later, because they depend, for their coherence, on the presence of the pictures. To cover this problem I have handed out a summary of the lecture and, for the moment, just tell them, "Don't worry about taking all the details down. You'll get the main points from the handout, so for now just look at the pictures as carefully as you can." The pictures show tough Irish crews laying the rails of the Union Pacific, and tough Chinese crews laying the Central Pacific, laborers digging the tunnels, blasting the cliff faces, constructing snowsheds, and digging locomotives out of snowdrifts. There are pictures of white passengers attended by black waiters in Pullman cars, of robber-barons in their private cars surrounded by friends and family, and of bustling city depots. There is plenty to talk about with nearly every one. Sometimes I narrate, explaining what is going on in a picture, in cases where they're unlikely to know (like the old steam-driven pile driver). Other times I ask the students: "What is happening here?" and they make guesses based on what they see, sometimes wrong but plausible, quite often right.

I'm always aware, teaching, that I must not deflate those who get it wrong. With students whose diagrams are hopeless or whose suggestions about what is in a picture are miles off the mark, I look for phrases like "I'm afraid not—there's no reason why you should know this but let me help you through it a bit at a time." With a series of leading questions I'm usually able to get them describing much more accurately what is happening. I hope and intend that the question-and-answer is enabling everyone else in the room to learn from our exchange at the same time.

When 11:29 comes around, we're in full flow and I'm enjoying myself, trying to communicate my pleasure in trains to the class. Before today I expect it had never occurred to many of them that the building of a railroad across America was something to enthuse over. Now the possibility exists. Even those who really don't care about trains will be able to think to themselves, "Oh yes, the professor loved those railroads," and that in turn will help them remember at least some of the things I said.

My impression of the students we get here at Emory, who are far above the national average in wealth, intelligence, high school records, and test scores, is that they have the capacity to learn a great deal but (at least in history) don't come in knowing very much. Many of them are good company, and being in class usually puts them on their best behavior. They are young, healthy, and (for the most part) sensible. They are old enough that they can do most of the basic things involved in living independent lives; they don't have to be mothered. So I have a steady feeling of pleasure in being able to spend time among them, especially in a role that can actually win me their respect and interest. It's much better, surely, than being a lawyer, whose bread and butter is conflict, or than a doctor, who is always in the midst of sick people. I'm glad others do those jobs but glad also that I don't have to.

Fourth Class (Wednesday)

A delightful early-morning surprise to confirm that someone has read my list of instructions. A student calls to say she is sick, is going to university health services, and will try to get to class afterward if she feels well enough. I always write, among my reading-list threats, "If you are unable to come to class for medical reasons please let me know in advance." Years pass in which no one heeds this request, but now and again a rule-follower does what I have asked. I commiserate, "Get well soon, and only come to class if you're sure you're well enough." Later on, I see her there.

Student illness is a ticklish matter. There are some students who, with a small ailment, turn it into something monstrous and use it as justification for not doing any more work that term. On the other hand, there are some who, in desperately ill health, stagger along to class anyway and show signs of being about to expire during the lecture. The most dramatic example I ever had of this devotion came from a student who was in a nasty skiing accident. He hit a tree and, among the multiple bruises, cuts, and abrasions, cracked a vertebra in his neck. To assure complete healing, the doctors had to make sure that his head did not move from side to side relative to his neck. To achieve this result they actually screwed a kind of metal halo into his skull, through his forehead, and then attached it to an elaborate framework that sat on his shoulders. He was good-natured about what must have been a hellishly uncomfortable and awkward contraption, and referred to himself as "robot-man." The part of the story I liked was that within hours of the accident, while lying on a hospital bed, groggy with painkillers, he thought ahead to the probability that he would have to miss class the next day, and actually phoned in to say so.

This morning is our fourth meeting and, on entering the room, I am able to recognize about twelve of the students and mark their names down on the class roll without asking. I respond to Simon (the non-reader of the Bible) who asks why, since this is an introductory class, we haven't got a course textbook, "You know how, when you buy books for the new semester, you sometimes faint dead away at the prices and, other times, just turn pale and feel weak?" "Yes!" "When I discovered that the U.S. history text books now cost forty-five or fifty dollars, I just didn't have the heart to make you buy one. Besides, they're so depressing. But let me ask you, before I justify it further: which of you here loves textbooks?" Nobody raises a hand but there are plenty of grins. "There you are then. I want you to read books that are intrinsically interesting, not to drag your way laboriously through textbook prose. There are lots of readings in the course, and those, plus what I say in the lectures, will be sufficient to give you a pretty good introduction to the last century and a half of American history. The books I've actually ordered are, I hope, readable as well as informative. However, let me also draw your attention to our massive library. If there is ever an issue about which you want to learn more, please use it—you'll find hundreds of appropriate books, and you don't have to feel confined solely by the ones I assigned."

Since I didn't manage to finish with the railroads last time, I just pop the carousel back into place and carry on where I left off (rotary snowplows). There's so much to talk about! A photograph of a steel bridge leads me into a discussion of the superiority of steel over wooden bridges, and then to talk about the rapid development of the American iron and steel industry itself in the late nineteenth century, and Andrew Carnegie's rise to fame and fortune. Next comes a photograph of a rural railroad depot manager, sitting in his office and working the Morse-code key on his telegraph, with timetables and a big clock behind his head. American railroads had to develop methods of sending trustworthy employees all over the place, sometimes a thousand miles from where their employers worked. They had to be devoted to the ideal of punctuality, and to show the right blend of obedience in following company rules and deviating from them creatively in case of an emergency. The railroad companies adopted uniform time zones in 1883, standardizing what until then had been a chaotic situation, in which each company had its own time, with big variations. I tell the class, "You often hear people say, 'Well, we can't turn the clock back?' The truth is that you can turn the clock back. It happens every year, and it happened in a big way when the clocks were standardized. Clock time is an entirely human invention, after all." I elaborate. "Punctuality had to be invented—there is nothing natural about clock time. Isn't it an astonishing achievement that all of us here today, having never previously met, were able to show up at almost exactly the same time, in the same place, on the same day, when the semester began? Before long we can eliminate the 'almost' by persuading you latecomers to actually arrive on time."

Another slide shows an advertisement from about 1900 for the Lackawanna Railroad. It depicts an elegant young woman dressed all in white, first showing her buying a ticket, then being helped onto the train by a smartly dressed black porter, then standing on the observation platform at the back of the train as it rushes through a sylvan landscape. The text of the ad consists of little verses beside the pictures, the first of which tells us that her name is Phoebe Snow. One of them reads:

Each passing look
At nook or brook
Unfolds a flying picture book
Of landscape bright
Or mountain height
Beside the road of anthracite.

I choose a student, Meredith, and ask her to read the poem aloud. She reads it haltingly in a flat, monotonous voice and stumbles over the word *anthracite*. "Do you know what *anthracite* means?" I ask. "No." "Anybody?" After a minute Bill says he thinks it's a kind of coal. He's right, and a few more questions establish the fact that anthracite burns at a high temperature and is less smoky than other forms of American coal. I say to Meredith, "Come on, now. Imagine you're in charge of this ad campaign. Read it with feeling." She tries again and reads it a shade better. Now I ask her to explain what's going on in the ad. With occasional verbal nudges she gets the point. Phoebe Snow . . . Snow is white . . . she's wearing white . . . the anthracite is hot-burning and makes less ash and soot . . . therefore she can travel in white without getting her clothes filthy . . . through a landscape that's attractive and unsullied by smoke. She suddenly catches on: "OK, they're advertising it like the commercials we see for Delta Airlines having more legroom in business class. It's their way of saying their railroad is better than its rivals." "Exactly!" Then we talk about the black Pullman porters too and the completely unself-conscious racial separation depicted in the ad.

I show some pictures from the Santa Fe Railroad's campaign to link Southwestern tourism to its cross-country journeys. If you were going across country to Los Angeles on their line you could get off the train at Santa Fe, New Mexico, and take a tour to the Indian pueblo at Taos, a few miles north. The railroad company had persuaded the Indians to dress up in feather headdresses, to make pots and turquoise jewelry, and to dance for the tourists. (Feather headdresses were actually an import from the Plains Indians, but the publicity men weren't concerned with anthropological accuracy so much as a good spectacle.) A few miles further along the route passengers could get off the train again, at Flagstaff, Arizona, and take a trip to the Grand Canyon, driving in an early motor car and then riding on horseback through the canyon itself. My final slide in the set is a picture of Albert Einstein, wearing a feather headdress, surrounded by Indians at Taos Pueblo, and looking distinctly sheepish—he took the tour soon after coming to America in the 1930s.

A new student is waiting to see me at the end. He's one about whom I had a memo yesterday from the college office, asking me to enroll him late. The building in which he and his roommates lived burned down last week and he's just now getting back on his feet. He tells me how it happened: the cheapskate landlord, the faulty wiring about which they'd often complained, the sudden horrifying discovery of smoke and flames, the vain effort to put it out with an extinguisher, and the eventual need to grab a handful of personal treasures and flee the house. Everything that has survived is water-damaged or stinks of smoke. While he's telling me all this, we walk back across the quadrangle and into my office. I give him a reading list, tell him to get settled and then do what he can to catch up on the first assignment, and off he goes. In principle I always try to stay out of the students' lives as much as possible. I discourage them from telling me what's happening to them (because it's so often the prelude to an excuse for failing to do assignments on time or to pleas for an extension). But the truth is that real-life situations come surging at you all the time in great waves. My theoretical commitment to hard-heartedness keeps breaking down.

Almost the only topic on which I manage to hold the line consistently is that of boyfriends or girlfriends. If a student utters the word *boyfriend* or *girlfriend* in office hours, I respond, "I can't talk about your personal relationships with you, and I can't permit you to mention them. If you are too upset to discuss history you must leave now and come back when you are able to do so." This speech has the effect of causing some to leave the room weeping, but others straighten up and discuss the work.

It's a bit more difficult if the work itself is the thing *causing* the student to weep. Last term, for example, I (in my capacity as director of undergraduate studies in history) had a difficult half-hour with a study-abroad candidate who wanted to get Emory credit for a French history course she was going to take in Paris. Unfortunately for her, the class would be taught in French and she said she was afraid she didn't speak it well enough to be able to understand what was going on. "Don't take it if you don't think you can pass it," I said. "But I need the credits for my graduation, and won't be able to get them if I don't do the class." "Perhaps you should consider staying here or studying abroad at an English-speaking place." "But," she cried, as if I was being unreasonable, "I want to go to Paris. I've always wanted to!" Then, with a sudden rush of emotion, she started to cry, with great heaving sobs. I don't have any Kleenex, but I do have a grimly utilitarian toilet roll handy, and this I passed to her without comment.

Just then, another student poked his head around the door (which I always leave partly open during office hours), beheld the scene, and withdrew sharply, as if electrocuted. I hurried outside to greet him, saying to the weeper, "Stay here as long as you need to. I'll be outside." I then advised the newcomer on some routine matter, while standing in the hallway, as my office continued to emit sorrowful sounds. Back in the office the Parisienne returned the toilet roll and said, "Oh my God! I can't believe I cried in the professor's office." "Never mind," I said, "go and think it over or chat with the people in the foreign study office, or with your parents, and decide what to do." "Oh, no! In the professor's office!"

4

■ ■ ■

The Discussion and Lecture Routine

Fifth Class (Friday)

Today for the first time the class is discussing an assigned reading. It is *Black Elk Speaks*. The book is an autobiographical account by an Ogalala Sioux medicine man, as told to John Neihardt in about 1930. Black Elk was born in 1863 and was about thirteen at the Battle of the Little Big Horn, in which he participated. As a nine-year-old he had an elaborate vision of his destiny, to restore his conquered nation, and as he grew, he realized that he had unusual spiritual powers. He became a healer and holy man, traveled to the east and to Europe with Buffalo Bill's Wild West show in the 1880s, but was back in the Dakotas in time to join the Ghost Dance cult and witness the massacre at Wounded Knee in 1890. He felt his life to have been a failure because he had not been able to restore his people's independence and integrity.

Last night I got busy rereading the book, which is two hundred pages long but really engrossing. I finished it early this morning then went through it again, noting page numbers of the principal events and passages I wanted to get students to read aloud or discuss. I told them on Monday to select three passages each from the book: one they particularly liked, one they particularly disliked, and one they just plain couldn't understand; we could use these passages as the basis for discussion. Rather than starting class with these readings, though, I begin by selecting a name off the list, David, asking him, "What sort of personality is Black Elk?" David says, "He's very spiritual and takes his religion more seriously than ordinary people." "More seriously than you?" "Much more. He gets all the people in the village to act out his vision and believes that everything has a spirit." After that students chime in one after the next in quick succession, pointing out various aspects of his character: his feeling of failure, his blending of action with contemplation in life, his grisly role in the battles (he describes how he and his boyhood friends went around scalping the wounded and twitching bodies of American soldiers, then ran to show the scalps to their delighted mothers), his sense of fun, and his occasional skepticism.

The pace and shrewdness of the students' remarks in reaction to this and my succeeding questions please me, though now and again we come to an awkward point. For example: "Why do the old people have spiritual power in the Sioux village?" Michael, probably a *Dances with Wolves* aficionado, says that "the Indians knew how to treat the old with respect, not just to throw them away like we do in our society." "Do we really throw them away?" "Yes, and we need to learn a more humane way of living from the Indians." Barbara, luckily, hasn't let the mystical haze get the better of her. "No, it's just that they couldn't read or write, so the elders preserved the memories of the whole tribe. We have writing to do that for us." Another student, Flora, grasps a second point of contrast. "In those days it was hard to become old because lots of them, especially the men, died fighting or hunting, so old age was unusual and special." I talk about the need for balance in our judgments. It's appropriate to have a sense of shame at the Americans' mistreatment of the Indians. But it is important, too, not to sentimentalize their way of life. As Black Elk shows it was a bloody, visceral, vulnerable life, and one in which there was no end of gods and spirits to be propitiated. He lived in a state of constant anxiety about offending one or another of them.

As the class continues I try to recognize everyone who raises a hand to speak, but I know from long experience that some will not speak un-less called on and others will want to dominate the conversation. So I single out one of the quiet ones and ask her my next question. "First, tell us your name." "Sarah." "Okay, Sarah . . ." and with luck I will re-member it from now on. Ever since I began teaching I have debated with fellow teachers the rights and wrongs of calling directly on students in class discussion. The consensus at Berkeley, where I was a grad student and TA, was that it is wrong, because it seems too much like an exercise of power over the students (in those days we were all reading Foucault and learning that power is pervasive and sinister). I was half-convinced for a while but soon changed my mind. Ever since, I have always called on students directly, by name, and tried to make sure that in every dis-cussion class, every person present will participate.

Of course it's a power issue. I am using my power to induce them to speak up, even those who would rather not. That's what the power is for. I want, first of all, to be sure that every student has read the book. Asking direct questions on points of fact is the best way of finding out who has read it. This morning I ask Neil to explain Black Elk's ideas about the four points of the compass. He tells me flat out that he hasn't read the book but then I remember that he's the one whose house burned down, so I grant him a plenary indulgence and make a concilia-tory remark so that he knows I know why he hasn't read it.

A bit later on another student can't answer my question about the Fetterman Massacre because she says she only skimmed that bit. But a couple more questions make it quite clear she didn't read it at all. Then I say, "You must read each of these assignments carefully before the rele-vant class meeting." She feels embarrassed because she knows she has been caught. But it's a benign form of humiliation; I doubt that she'll let it happen again. The memory of that little exchange will live with her throughout the semester and prompt her to do the reading carefully and thoroughly. I can practically see her thinking, "Next time he calls on me I'm going to be ready." What's more, the others have been watching this incident, and many of them are thinking, "It could have been me caught out there. Thank God it wasn't me! I must make sure it *doesn't* happen to me." With luck there will only be a few moments of this kind in the semester and most students *will* do the reading.

Another reason for calling on students directly is to help the shy and quiet ones. Lots of people do not enjoy speaking in public, but part of becoming educated consists of overcoming your fears and finding that you can do things you earlier thought you could not. It may be a bit jarring at first for the meek to have me suddenly demanding of them, "What did Black Elk think of Crazy Horse as a leader?" But although I'm imposing on them, I'm also empowering them. They have probably gone through lots of situations in which they would have liked to speak up but never got the chance to squeeze a word in edgewise among their chattier chums. Now the floor is theirs. At first they may not make distinguished contributions to the discussion, but they usually get better as the term goes on. Once they know it is going to happen, each new demand is less of a shock than the previous one. Besides, they quickly see the merit in volunteering. That way they'll have a chance to discuss an issue about which they feel confident, rather than getting stuck with a hideously complex question on an aspect of the reading they had never previously considered. As the semester goes on, I usually find less and less need to single people out to participate.

A third reason for calling on students directly is as a way of controlling the garrulous ones. Nearly every class has someone who just won't shut up, and it isn't long before you catch sight of others rolling their eyes as the talkative one just keeps talking. I used to see it often enough and think to myself, "There's some thoroughly justified eye-rolling." It wouldn't be so bad if there were a straight correlation between having a lot of intelligent things to say and wanting to talk all the time. Alas, the world isn't like that. The worst case I ever saw was just a couple of years ago. From day one a certain young man had his hand up all the time, even during lectures, and would chip in constantly with bits of additional information. "That's when the army got Springfield breech-loading rifles . . ." "He killed Garfield because he'd written a speech and didn't get paid for it . . ." "He was blind in one eye . . ." "Her father had fought in the Mexican Revolution . . ." The first two or three days I would pause periodically to let him speak, but when it became clear that he just wanted to hear the sound of his own voice I began ostentatiously to ignore him. Undeterred, he would make the same kind of comments without being asked, just nudging them in when I paused to draw breath: "Roosevelt knew the attack was coming." "Lennon said they were more popular than Jesus." "There had to have been at least one guy on the grassy knoll." I took him aside after class in week two and asked him not to interrupt during lecture. I didn't want to be too harsh, because he was enthusiastic, but he was driving everyone else crazy, me included. In discussion class, however, I was able to keep him more or less under control by saying to myself, "I'm the teacher; he's the student," and then by saying to the class, "Please don't speak until I recognize you—and raise your hand if you want to join in." He spent the entire semester with his hand up but I was able to restrict him to just five or six interventions per hour, which was bearable. He certainly made the most of them. "I have a theory about that, which is that the manufacturers had wrongly imagined that supply was declining when actually it was still going up and that . . ." Once or twice I actually cut him off in midtheory and said, "We must stick to the information we've got in front of us, at least for the purposes of this class. Now Rachel, how did the Securities and Exchange Commission actually operate?" Teachers: if a student annoys you, he's almost certainly annoying the other members of class too, and the others are thinking to themselves, "What's the matter with this teacher? Why doesn't he just tell motormouth to shut up?!"

One problem with discussion classes is keeping them on track, so that the experience is actually educational. When I was a beginning teacher (and still to some extent now) I had a dread of the room falling dead silent and no one having anything to say. Only strong-minded people can bear more than a second or two of complete silence, and I am weak. I was so eager to encourage students to speak up that I was reluctant to say "no" even when their remarks were wrong and misleading. I used to say, "Well, not entirely," giving them the impression that they were more or less right. I've stiffened up a lot since then, and now I say, in the most benevolent and avuncular voice I can find, "No, I'm afraid that's wrong." I can usually find some phrase to explain why it's an *intelligent* wrong answer, in order to soften the blow. Or else I will say, "Let's go over it together," and ask a series of leading questions to tease out the truth.

Before a discussion class begins I usually write down the three or four main points I want the students to learn. As the clock draws towards 11:30 today I summarize them. I wanted them, first, to get a clear sense of Black Elk living in a world inhabited by a multitude of spiritual beings, and of his belief that dreams were a powerful medium of communication between this world and the spirit world. Second, I wanted the students to understand that the Plains Indians lived lives of chronic insecurity, vulnerable to natural and supernatural forces, dependent on the buffalo for their continued existence, and completely unable to measure up to the whites in technology or warfare, except when their numbers were overwhelming, as they were at the Little Big Horn. Finally, I wanted them to de-romanticize the Indians. If *Black Elk Speaks* has a weakness for a course of this kind it is that Neihardt himself is a bit too reverent toward the grand old man, and renders many of his phrases in an English of almost biblical grandeur. There's a scholars' controversy (which I don't mention in class) about how much we are hearing from the Indian and how much from the transcriber. Despite this problem it's a good book for the introductory class because it embraces so many of the main themes—the hunter's way of life, the battles, Buffalo Bill's Wild West, the Sun Dance, and the fate of the post-Wounded Knee Sioux.

How much will they remember from the book? Most of them will go over their notes before the midterm and final and recall quite a lot of details. A year from now they will probably recall that he was a Sioux holy man who had a vision when he was still a boy, became a healer, fought at the Little Big Horn, scalped dying soldiers, and later danced with the Buffalo Bill show. That's enough, especially if they recall some of the passages where he matter-of-factly describes gruesome scenes: how, as soon as a buffalo is killed, the men leap off their horses and begin butchering, eating the animal's raw liver while it is still steaming; or how, at the Little Big Horn, his relatives, enraged by the death of a cousin, retaliate by butchering a fat U.S. soldier ("The wasichu [white man] was fat, and his meat looked good to eat, but we did not eat any").

Sixth Class (Monday)

I usually spend an hour before class going over that day's lecture, even if it's one I've often given before. Familiarity with the material is an immense asset because it means you can extemporize confidently from an outline. This morning's subject is women in late nineteenth-century America. I first wrote the lecture about ten years ago and have tinkered with it ever since, deleting a few passages and incorporating new ideas and illustrations from subsequent reading. Like all the others, it is heavily dependent on the specialist historians' works that I have read and mined over the years. A fellow professional could sit in the classroom and, listening to what I say, identify the names of the authors whose ideas and interpretations I am summarizing. That's OK; history is a community enterprise and we stand on each other's shoulders. In the same way, I sometimes read summaries of historical issues that are clearly derived from my own books. One of the pleasures of doing an introductory course like this is that it gives me the chance to teach about a dozen subjects I wouldn't otherwise have the chance to mention. I know less about them than about my areas of ostensible expertise, and often haven't taught them or thought much about them since lecturing on them the previous year. Again that's OK; I'm still far ahead of the students and can introduce them to the basics. Besides, to teach subjects in which you are an expert can be disabling; you are so aware of contradictory evidence and historians' disputes that you feel unable to make the kind of bold generalizations that are necessary to persuasive introductory teaching.

First comes a section on the domestic ideal of middle-class American women, about which there is now a massive and fascinating literature. Next, Frances Willard and the Women's Christian Temperance Union (the first public reform organization to have large-scale participation by women), a passage on Matthew Vassar and other pioneers of education for young women, a section on Victorian gynecology, and a section on Susan B. Anthony, Elizabeth Cady Stanton, and the suffrage movement.

Frances Willard advocated not only abstinence from alcohol but also abstinence from sex outside marriage. She called it "the white life." Generations of students have scoffed at her for what seems like an aggravated form of Victorian prudishness; there's a bit of tut-tutting in our room too. That gives me the opportunity to talk about the history of venereal disease and to make what has become another set-piece speech. "Frances Willard may not seem an altogether likeable figure, but you need to remember how different sex was in those days. The contraceptives they had were not reliable, so any woman who had sex was in danger of getting pregnant. Nineteenth-century women knew that pregnancy often led to death in childbirth. Look in any nineteenth-century graveyard (there's a good one here in Atlanta, the Oakland Cemetery) and you will find lots of graves of women aged between eighteen and thirty five who died giving birth to children. Usually the mother and child both died. The women in this class don't have to worry about that prospect. Most of you will probably have children some time in the next fifteen years, but when you learn that you are pregnant, whether or not you are pleased by the news, you are not going to have to face the fact that it may well kill you. Advances in obstetrics have made childbirth safer than it has ever been. Just as infant mortality is now so low that we regard the death of a child as a tragic aberration (it was once extremely common), so is death in childbirth. Imagine having sex and thinking to yourself, "This act may be the direct prelude to my death." This little speech always draws anxious glances around the room and turns on the light of comprehension for several students. They are, besides, a generation that has grown up with AIDS-awareness education and are better disposed to get the point than the "sexual revolution" generation of students I taught in the 1980s.

To finish the lecture I throw in a couple of vignettes about women with axes. One was Lizzie Borden. I ask if anyone knows the poem, and Brianne is able to recite it straight off:

Lizzie Borden with an ax
Gave her mother forty whacks
When she saw what she had done
She gave her father forty-one.

Lizzie Borden was the daughter of a New England manufacturer in the late nineteenth century and lived comfortably. She taught a Sunday school class and was supposed to be the embodiment of dainty, decorous Victorian womanhood. But then she murdered her parents. Her defense attorney was able to convince a credulous jury that such a young woman simply could not have committed the crime, and although there was no other suspect, Lizzie was acquitted. She lived on to a ripe old age, widely believed by citizens not taken in by the "domestic angel" defense to have gotten away with a double murder.

The second ax woman was Carry Nation, the Kansas prohibitionist who had a far blunter approach to stamping out booze than Frances Willard and the WCTU. She led prayer meetings outside saloons, sometimes kneeling with her friends in the mud or dust by their doors. Then she took to smashing up saloons with her ax. She was in and out of prison, became notorious, attracted a lot of press attention, and even hired a publicity agent, who suggested that she autograph and sell model axes as a fund-raising device for her cause (and her legal costs). The students are delighted by these stories, as I am, and it's possible to illuminate the serious substance of the lecture, and brighten the mood, with the help of such anecdotes.

In lecturing, repetition is good. It's always worth repeating the main theme of the lecture four or five times in the course of an hour. Students are taking notes (even when I have handed out an outline), and the repetition gives them a chance to write themes down more than once, making it that much likelier that they will come to recognize the central points. I try to vary the delivery by throwing out questions too, such as the one about whether anyone knew the poem. If I mention a city I'll generally ask someone what state it is in. If I mention a river, I ask what river it flows into or where it reaches the sea (when we were doing *Black Elk* on Friday I asked Barbara what river the Little Big Horn flows into. I'm glad I did because until then she hadn't know it *was* a river, and this was a chance to go over the geography of the Dakotas and eastern Montana).

Seventh Class (Wednesday)

I decide to rewrite this morning's lecture, whose subject is racial ideas in late nineteenth- and early twentieth-century America. The first time I did it I was nervous and wrote a lot of it out in more detail than I now want, so I go through the old typescript, compressing paragraphs down to one line, and cutting the whole thing from twelve pages to four.

I arrive in the classroom a few minutes early to give myself time to write on the blackboard the names of the principal people about whom I am lecturing. When that is done, and we are still a minute or two short of 10:40 I ask Paul, "If you went west from Colorado, what state would you be entering?" He doesn't know, and neither do two others, but I finally find one who answers, "Utah," with confidence. I ask another, "If you went north from Tennessee what state would you be entering?" and so on. With states close to the Atlantic most class members can answer correctly. Beyond the Mississippi most cannot. I ask Faith, who made three wrong guesses about what state lay south of Nebraska, "Don't you wish you knew all these answers?" to which she gives a noncommittal shrug.

After taking the roll and checking for cell phones and beepers, I begin, talking about Darwin and the way in which evolutionary ideas changed Americans' conception of the Earth's age and the nature of life. No longer did everything fit together so marvelously because God had designed it that way, but rather because this was the outcome of the endless competitive struggle for existence. Some species found an ecological niche but eventually lost it to a superior competitor, and went extinct. Extinction can happen—nineteenth-century Americans were forced to face up to it in a way their eighteenth-century predecessors had not.

Under the influence of Darwin some late nineteenth-century scientists began to reason that if they were not careful, they too might head down an evolutionary blind alley. "Race suicide" was their phrase; the eugenics movement and various actions to protect the Anglo-Saxon race were the outcome. I quote some passages from William Z. Ripley's *Races of Europe* (1899). According to Ripley, the further south you went in Europe the poorer the racial stock you found. "Teutons" in the north were good, "Alpines" in the middle less good, and "Mediterraneans" in the south poor. A passage from Madison Grant's *Passing of the Great Race* (1916) illustrates the point that it was entirely socially and academically respectable a hundred years ago to believe in racial hierarchy, and to take seriously the idea that the Anglo-Saxon peoples needed to protect themselves against the "scrub races."

I describe the eugenics movement, the eagerness of asylum managers to sterilize or castrate their inmates, the Supreme Court's upholding of the practice in *Buck v. Bell* (1927) and the curious research that led to support for these schemes. One of my favorites is Elizabeth Kite's study of the Kallikak family. Ms. Kite, a turn-of-the-century Quaker-turned-Catholic, became fascinated with eugenics research and studied a family in the New Jersey Pine Barrens. Tracing it back to Martin Kallikak, a Revolutionary War soldier, she discovered that he had seduced a simple-minded barmaid while on campaign, and that their brief union had led to the birth of a villainous degenerate whom she named "Old Horror." From him were descended a long line of prostitutes, madmen, criminals, and pauperized cretins. On the other hand, Kallikak later married a decent upright woman, and from that union sprang a line of sober judges, good businessmen, and pillars of the community. Kite's conclusion was that failing to maintain absolute sexual rectitude could have ruinous consequences down through the generations, and that the simple-minded had better be restrained from reproducing.

I move next to black-white race relations, talk about the end of Reconstruction and the era of the "Redeemer" governments, the way they put in place the racial segregation laws, and the way the Supreme Court upheld those laws in *Plessy v. Ferguson* (1896), making "separate but equal" segregation constitutional until the *Brown* case of 1954. Last year I had my class read a little anthology of articles about *Plessy v. Ferguson*, and in it I discovered a delightful and unexpected example of the way the segregation laws could cut both ways. In about 1907 a white drunk got on a train in Tennessee but made such a nuisance of himself in the "whites only" carriage that the conductor put him into the "blacks only" Jim Crow carriage instead. The black passengers protested, too, sued the railroad for violating the segregation laws, and won! I also found there, and pass on to the class today, the fact that the railroad managers themselves hated segregation because it made their operations more complicated and costly—every train had to have at least two carriages, even if the trade could really only support one, and that meant increased fuel and rolling-stock costs and a great policing headache.

Five minutes before the end of class I spring on the students a little surprise, of which my questions earlier were an augury. I hand out blank maps of the United States, marked only with the state boundary lines, and tell the students to write in the names of the states. There is a great collective groan and a lot of sheepish looks as they set to work. Most students seem not to care about maps and never think about or look at them unless forced. Lucas complains that he hasn't done stuff like this since fourth grade. I say, "In this course I'm telling you about events that happened all over the United States. It is a huge area and I need to be confident that when I mention an event that took place in Wyoming you know where it is and its characteristic landscape. Is that unreasonable?" He knows enough not to answer that question. I soften the blow by adding, "I'm not going to give you a grade on this quiz. I just want to know whether you know where all the states are. If you don't know them you should spend a bit of time with the atlas over the next few weeks, and become familiar with them. Being able to read maps is such an asset."

One of the women comes up to the front almost at once, her eyes big with imminent tears, and says, "Professor, I have only just arrived in America from Pakistan. I have only been here for three weeks altogether and I'm so sorry but I just cannot do this test." "All right," I reply, "but can you show me on this outline map what state we are in now?" She points to Georgia at once. "And how about this one?" "That's Florida." "This one?" "Alabama, I think." "That's right." She knows more than she thinks, but I excuse her. When she's gone, another shouts from the back, "Hey professor, I'm a foreigner too. I come from Canada. You can't expect me to know about all these states." "I'm a foreigner too and I know them," I tell him. Some of the students are writing furiously, and before long come up and hand in their right answers with a proud flourish. Others come up furtively, put their maps on the pile face down, or even tuck them into the middle of the heap so that I won't catch a glimpse until they have left the room. One asks whether she got New Hampshire and Vermont the right way round. Laughter at the back as the room empties, and another one says, "Look, I've got Kansas in three different places now. And I'm going to need at least two Minnesotas to fill all these northern areas."

I often ask students to look at maps if they are included in the readings. In the environmental history class I hand out a big bundle of maps which I ask them always to bring to class every time, and we spend class time going over them together. Now and again I give them a more difficult challenge. Later this semester, when we are studying the First World War, I will probably ask someone to draw a map of Europe on the blackboard so that we can see the main areas of fighting. Last year this exercise degenerated into hopeless laughter because they were so awful at it. The first one drew a series of blobs and then looked hopefully at me. "Which one of those is Germany?" He chose one blob more or less at random and pointed to it. "Which one is Belgium?" He chose another, unconnected. "What's the area in between Germany and Belgium?" "The sea." "Which sea?" "The North Sea." "But you've just read a book about how the German army marched into Belgium. How could they do that if there was a stretch of sea in between?" With his cuff he then erased part of "Belgium" and part of "Germany" so that he could draw a couple of lines joining the two countries together. Another student came up to try her luck. She did a fantastically detailed Norwegian coastline, having once been there on a cruise, but otherwise gave simple blockish outlines to everything and couldn't work out where the Mediterranean was. I didn't really expect them to do a good job—outline maps from scratch really are tough. In fact the whole exercise served as much as a source of light relief as a serious attempt to get it right. Giving the class a chance to "breathe" and stretch after the first half-hour is always a good idea, and maps is one of the more educational ways to let them do it.

As I look over the U.S.A. maps after class, I find references to "Ken-tuky," "Oregen," "New Hamster," "Whyoming," and a marginal letter from another of the foreign students, who writes, "OK, so I'm Colom-bian and never taken an American history or geography class in my life, so I feel kind of ignorant right now. I've only been in the U.S. for one year. I can do Europe and South America, though." On the margin of her map Tricia has written: "Hmm . . . shamefully embarrassing? Perhaps . . ." The confident ones have gotten all the states right and have then drawn an arrow pointing northwest to the word *Alaska* and an arrow pointing southwest to the word *Hawaii*. Two-thirds of them have gotten forty or more states right and are vague only about areas remote from where they live. They're worst on the Great Plains. Southerners get muddled about the intricate New England pattern, and there are lots of wrong answers from everyone in the Arkansas, Missouri, and Iowa zone. Still, these answers are better than they were a few years ago, when nearly everyone got half the states wrong—that's a measure of the im-proving quality of Emory students, I think. The first time I tried it here, in the fall of 1988, the only right answer came from an exchange student out of Russia!

This afternoon I get a visit from Molly Cobbs, a student from last term's environmental history course. Molly has come to invite me to be her guest at the "Outdoor Emory" theme house, where she lives, on "fac-ulty appreciation night" next week. We'll have coffee and desserts, she says, and see some films of recent Emory expeditions. I accept and feel glad to be "appreciated." "Faculty appreciation" is a growing thing around here. Students who want to take professors out to lunch or din-ner can get funding for it from various groups on campus. The protocol is to go with students you taught previously because current students don't want to seem to be groveling for grades. As I said at the beginning, it's wrong to make friends with students who are members of a current course, but sometimes it's OK to develop a mentoring relationship afterward. In fact it is one of the pleasures of the job. In any year there are ten or twelve students around campus, former members of my courses, with whom I got along particularly well, for whom I am an informal advisor, and whose educational progress I watch with interest and pride.

Eighth Class (Friday)

Our second discussion section. Last night and this morning I was desperately trying to get the book read in time. It is *Does the Frontier Experience Make America Exceptional?* (1999) edited by Richard Etulain, composed of nine essays. The centerpiece is Frederick Jackson Turner's "The Significance of the Frontier in American History," the talk he gave, in 1893, that shaped several generations' conception of why America developed its particular characteristics. According to him, the existence of the frontier between civilization and "free land" as the nation moved westward gave rise to a distinctive form of thinking, inventiveness, democracy, egalitarianism, and ambition. It is well-written and fun to read, even more than a century later, but has come under increasingly heavy attack in the past three or four decades, as historians point out what a lot he missed or got wrong. The plains weren't "free"—people like Black Elk lived there. California and the Southwest were not empty either—Indians and Spaniards had been living there for more than three centuries. Women as well as men migrated to the frontier, though you wouldn't know it from what Turner has to say about rugged individualism.

As I mark the attendance roll we have a minute or two to spare, so I say, "The maps! I haven't brought them back but I did enjoy looking through them. Thanks to those of you who wrote me little letters in the margin explaining your situation. You all know whether you did well or not. If you did poorly you must spend some time learning. Which of you hangs out in the map department of the Woodruff Library reference section?" I give them an eager glance as though expecting that many will say yes. Really I know that most of them haven't the remotest idea where the place is. No one raises a hand. I tell them where it is and continue,

"You must go there, especially those of you who did badly on the map quiz. Browse through the many different types and different scales of maps we have, and you will learn to love them. Maps are a pleasure. It's a dry, quiet pleasure, but none the less real for that, and you learn so much from doing it. Tell yourself, 'Tonight I'll go to the map room instead of watching *Survivor* on TV.' Okay?" I give them the eager smile again, pretending to be more naive than I really am about the likelihood of anyone actually doing it. "Who knows they did badly on the map?" Half a dozen hands go up, and I say to Nathan, one among them, "Will you be spending some time in the map room as I have suggested?" He looks back, not sure whether I'm kidding, and settles for a docile "Yes, sir," which carries absolutely no conviction at all. "After all," I say, "think how you'd regret it if there was a map section on the midterm and you did badly because you hadn't followed my advice." Nervous glances all round, and Nathan just can't restrain himself, though he knows he shouldn't ask: "*Will* there be maps on the midterm?" "I'm thinking about it. It would be good—perhaps we could have the courses of the fifteen major rivers" (collective groan).

Now it is exactly 10:40, time to begin discussion of the frontier book. I rebuke one young man for eating a granola bar in class and make him put it away, despite his scowl, then ask him what *frontier* means. Next I ask students to list what things, in their experience, create character. They talk their way through the Turner article bit by bit, finding the way in which it misses out all kinds of important issues, like the survival of the Indians' societies, the whole Hispanic aspect of the Southwest, the Asian immigrants, and the gold rush.

Having mentioned Darwin on Wednesday, I am keen to bring up Turner's use of evolutionary ideas. I ask Chris to read this passage aloud from Turner's essay, and he does it very well.

Loria, the Italian economist, has urged the study of colonial life as an aid in understanding the stages of European development, affirming that colonial settlement is for economic science what the mountain is for geology, bringing to light primitive stratifications. "America," he says, "has the key to the historical enigma which Europe has sought for centuries in vain, and the land which has no history reveals luminously the course of universal history." There is much truth in this. The United States lies like a huge page in the history of society. Line by line as we read this continental page from west to east we find the record of social evolution. It begins with the Indian and the hunter; it goes on to tell of the disintegration of savagery by the entrance of the trader, the pathfinder of civilization: we read the annals of the pastoral stage in ranch life; the exploitation of the soil by the raising of unrotated crops of corn and wheat in sparsely settled farming communities; the intensive culture of the denser farm settlement; and finally the manufacturing organization with city and factory system. (23–24)

I ask Chris to explain the geological metaphor in the first sentence with the help of a diagram. He draws his diagram of a mountain on the blackboard, and does a pretty good job of showing how the different strata yield up their fossil evidence and bear witness to the evolution of different species through time. Then he draws a parallel list of Indians, traders, pastoralists, farmers, and manufacturers as comparable factors in social "evolution." Beside it I draw an outline map of the United States and put these layers into vertical instead of horizontal strips, and there lies the complete analogy, as conceived by Loria and Turner. When I ask: "Does society really evolve in a way comparable to the evolution of biological species?" the class has the presence of mind to say, "No, not really."

Historians in the late nineteenth century were keen on the idea of themselves as "scientists." (The delusion hasn't entirely passed off even today—the Emory history department is nominally one of the social sciences, though I would guess at least half of us don't think of ourselves as social scientists.) I mention Henry Adams, who, in the 1890s, had the idea that it might be possible to do history as a branch of physics. He even experimented with applying the laws of thermodynamics to history but never really convinced anyone else—maybe not even himself.

The class knows, from reading Glenda Riley's essay in the book, that Turner overlooked women altogether. I ask Maya, "Is it fair to criticize a historian for not doing what he never intended to do?" We talk that point around for a while, with the majority of the students sympathizing with Turner. Riley, the author, is indignant on behalf of women, but most of the women in class apparently feel protective toward Turner and don't like to see him getting raked over the coals for a sin that, in his eyes, would have been hard to conceptualize. Riley *explains* why Turner omitted women but doesn't let him off the hook. I ask Bill, "Is it reasonable to assume that some people who lived in the past don't really count as 'history'?" Like the rest of them he is learning how to fend off my questions, and answers; "It depends who's writing the history." "What is your opinion?" "Anyone who contributed to making civilization is part of history." "Give me an example of someone who lived in the past but did not contribute to making civilization." "I can't because the historians haven't bothered to remember them! That's my point." I keep pressing the point; he keeps shying away, but he eventually takes exactly the view most contemporary historians prefer: that the lives and thoughts of people who were obscure in their own day have as much to teach us about history as the lives of the powerful and famous.

As we progress through the book we find ever-more-searching criticisms of Turner and the Turner thesis. Finally, in vexation, Will at the back, asks, "So why are we bothering with this guy? He was so narrow and so wrong, from what all these other authors say, that he doesn't seem to be worth our time. Richard White [another author in the collection] says he's really just doing the same as Buffalo Bill, playing with iconography, and that it's not even dependable history." "That's an excellent question," I reply. "It's true that by now we can see all sorts of ways in which his theory is vulnerable. But when he wrote the article it was so much stronger than the theory that had gone before, Herbert Baxter Adams's germ theory, that several generations of readers found it persuasive and insightful. They wrote their own studies of Western history, taking advantage of his theoretical framework, and found all sorts of things he had said confirmed by their own research. It's true that the mood of our class this morning has been critical, like that of many of the authors in Etulain's book. But let's pause for a moment to see how brilliant Turner was as well. He managed to convince thousands of intelligent and learned people that the way to understand the development of American society was not by starting in the German forests and moving west with the Anglo-Saxons, but by starting on the frontier and moving east, as each new generation of frontiersmen contributed to building up America's distinctiveness. It's not 'true' in some permanent and mathematical way, but for most of a century it seemed to be much truer than the alternative."

I then read aloud this passage, from another essay in the book, by Martin Ridge:

A masterpiece is not merely an outstanding work or something that identifies its creator as a master craftsman in the field. A masterpiece should change the way a public sees, feels, or thinks about reality. It should explicitly or implicitly tell much about its own times, but it should also cast a long shadow. It should have a significant impact on the way people at the time and afterward both perceive their world and act in it. . . . Ironically a masterpiece must have not only these favorable attributes but also it must . . . generate serious criticism and hostility. "The Significance of the Frontier in American History" did all these things. (75)

I tell the class, "To have your ideas argued about at all, even to have them denounced, is much better than to have them ignored. The measure of Turner's achievement is that for the first fifty or sixty years people not only paid attention, but gave their assent, and only now, a century later, are the denunciations really picking up steam. Have you all heard the fuss, over the past few years, about "dead white men" and the way they tend to dominate too much the educational curriculum?" Most students nod. "Well, here's a perfect example of one of those wicked dead white men. He wasn't really wicked, and all sorts of people can benefit from what he had to say. But now they can criticize him too, and point out how much more we expect from history."

CHAPTER

5

■ ■ ■

Educators' Excursions

Summer Program

It's a great life being a professor, and one of the many privileges of being one here at Emory is our summer program at Oxford, England. I have just arranged to go again this coming summer. For the past twenty years or so, Emory has rented part of University College, Oxford, for a six-week summer school in "British studies." Just when the weather is becoming intolerable for humans here in Atlanta, late June, off we go to the U.K. where you can usually count on plenty of clouds and rain, with temperatures around seventy. There were some hottish British summers in the 1990s but they weren't Atlanta-hot—you didn't feel as though you were living *inside* the sun. I was invited to go with the program at the end of my first year here, in the summer of 1989. I accepted with gratitude and have been back with the program in ten of the subsequent thirteen years.

University College is a magnificent old structure on Oxford High

Street, a central part of one of the most beautiful views in Europe, the street's long gentle curve, which discloses an array of towers, battlements, statues, cupolas, and multicolored old shops and houses. The frontage of the college is mainly from the seventeenth century, its stonework recently restored and cleaned from a sooty black (due to centuries of coal-fire smoke) to its original warm yellow. Inside there is a clutter of older building, some of it Elizabethan and even a few medieval fragments, all cobbled together into a maze of stairways and passages. Here is the room once occupied by Bill Clinton when he was a Rhodes Scholar, the room in which he did not inhale. Here worked Clement Attlee and Harold Wilson, each of whom went on to be a Labour prime minister, and through the place have passed dozens of the most distinguished men and women in British public life.

It's hard not to be impressed by the college, and, for the first day or two, our students are on their best behavior at the sheer grandeur of their surroundings. They soon settle in and begin to notice that with grandeur come impracticalities. Few showers, an unreliable laundry room full of malicious washing machines, institutional food that many of them find inedible, and the British people themselves, who don't always conform to the ideal they have imbibed from years of *Masterpiece Theater*. It's almost as though all they had learned in life no longer mattered. The rules of nutrition are in complete abeyance on the eastern side of the Atlantic, and everybody seems to smoke heavily. England's white people, meanwhile, have a whiteness they've never experienced before,

Our students are shocked by little snippets of anti-Americanism they encounter in pubs, and surprised by how clearly they stand out from the many other foreigners in town. For one thing, Americans wear clothes that fit, whereas Europeans, especially young ones, take pride in wearing clothes that are too small. Among the ludicrous episodes at Emory in the 1990s was the idea that we were turning out not merely young Americans but "global citizens." Administrators could be heard uttering the phrase without a trace of irony. In Oxford you could watch as a crowd approached. First would come the Italian teenagers, dark, lawless, all shouting at once, entirely in denim, the women in red high heels. Next the Swedish teenagers, quieter, blond, and decorous. Behind them, a cluster of American teenagers wearing baseball caps, baggy shorts, flip-flops, and sloganeering T-shirts. "Look—here are the Italian teenagers, there are the Swedes, and do you see behind them, the global citizens?"

Each student is required to take two courses, and gets full Emory credit. I usually teach on Monday and Wednesday mornings, from 9:00 to 11:00, and give the same kind of reading and writing assignments as when we are in Atlanta. Students' desire *not* to do any academic work is extremely strong in this setting. The abundant temptations, to go to London (easy and cheap on the bus), to the pubs, to the theater, or just to hang out, often get the better of them. Our job, as professors, is to get them to do at least some work, with a mixture of cajolery, promises, and threats. As usual, the diverse characters soon appear out of the homogenous beginnings, along with widely divergent abilities and willingnesses.

Faculty live in the college along with the students. We are close together, all day and often half the night too, in the college bar or the dining room or the common room, so it is harder than usual to keep the distance that should separate students from their teachers. My voice seems not to carry its usual authority in that setting, when I announce, "I'm the teacher, you're the student." Memories of my own not-very-well-apportioned time as an undergraduate (in Oxford) haunt me, and I feel all too vividly our students' temptations, stronger for them than they were for me because to them they're abroad (many for the first time) and it's the summer vacation. It is inexpressibly enjoyable. Reader, if you're a professor, volunteer at once to participate in your own college's "Oxford experience"; if you're a parent, yield to your child's plea that it would enrich his or her education.

We share the college with students from Southern Methodist University and the University of Virginia. Simultaneously, the whole of Oxford is filling up with American students from all points of the compass, nearly all, like us, taking over rooms in the old colleges. Suddenly Yale is just down the street instead of a thousand miles away, Stanford is round the corner, Nebraska's scarcely three blocks distant, and Texas is our next-door neighbor. Someone should write a little story for the *Chronicle of Higher Education* about this remarkable compression of academic America into one square mile of old England.

Students' romantic lives are almost invisible to professors on campus back in America, but they're played out in vivid detail before our eyes when we get to Oxford. Many of them, on arrival, let it be known that they have boyfriends or girlfriends back in America and that this temporary separation is going to be a dreadful strain. The mailbox in the college lodge is brimming with letters every morning, envelopes decorated with hearts. But after a week or so, holiday-romance fever begins. One amorous Emory couple, after a few pints of beer in the college bar, wandered off to what they thought of as a secluded alley at the back of the college and began necking passionately. They had forgotten that the college, for security reasons, has TV surveillance cameras posted in every strategic spot, and that their ardent embraces were being not only watched but recorded on videotape. An appreciative crowd gathered in the college lodge to watch the scene on TV monitors, and next morning the porter thanked them for enlivening his nightly routine.

The first course I taught in this summer school was on the history of Anglo-American relations. I did it for four or five years and plan to go back to it eventually. With the obvious exception of the Revolutionary War, the two countries' destinies have been closely intertwined, and relations generally warm, for four centuries. I grew up with the Cold War and the knowledge that American power, the foundation of NATO, was the basis of Western European independence. My generation of English kids thought of America with admiration, envy, and a hint of fear. We thought of it as a place where everyone was rich but where life was terribly violent. Both these images came from imported movies and TV shows—*Dallas* and plenty of cop and cowboy shows. We also thought of America as a high-tech place, from which a steady stream of useful inventions would come to solve our daily difficulties. You would often hear people say, adults and kids alike, "The Yanks will come up with something." I usually begin the course with these memories as a way of convincing students that they must begin to think of America from the outside rather than the inside. The Fourth of July usually falls during the first week of the course, and the way in which everyday life in Britain goes on without any mention of Independence is their first powerful clue to the fact that they really are abroad.

I try to teach them, too, about a society for which democracy is an idea that generates little excitement, and in which ideas of class and social hierarchy have a much longer and stronger hold on the popular imagination than egalitarianism. Being on the spot, and being able to point to examples of it around them is a great help. Having grown up in America, it is easy for them to think that there is something natural about the idea of human equality. Actually, I tell them, it is very rare in the history of the world, and belief in human inequality has been far more normal almost always and almost everywhere. To be provocative, I also point out that the evidence of their senses and the evidence of their experiences all teach the reality of inequality. Some people are taller than others, some more beautiful, some more gifted, some more athletic, some more energetic. And despite Niagaras of rhetoric to the contrary, the gifts are not shared out equally: to some little is given, to others much. The students are uncomfortable about admitting it to themselves and each other, but as we talk it over they are forced to admit that they themselves are the beneficiaries of disproportionate good fortune. They are rich, healthy, and come from a land blessed with political stability and, as if that weren't enough, most of them come from the most privileged stratum in that country. The surprise is that they *do* believe in human equality, when so much about their experience and circumstances is a living contradiction of it.

Something that surprises them, and that we often discuss, is the fact that members of the British lower classes have not, always and everywhere, felt a sense of resentment against members of the higher classes. Underpinning the class system, rather, was the idea that each place in the hierarchy had an intrinsic dignity of its own, an idea nicely summed up in the old Tory phrase "my station and its duties." Each class had its privileges, in other words, but it also had duties to members of the other classes, and a responsibility to carry them out. People in every class took the idea seriously. How else could Conservative governments have won so many elections through the twentieth century, since there were so many more voters in the working class than in any other? In that case, why did the system ever change? That is one of the principal issues of the course. Part of the answer is that the example of America stood before the eyes of generations of Britons, and some of them took it to heart. They began to advocate a more egalitarian society and a more democratic system of government. There was a vigorous republican movement in Britain during the nineteenth century, whose supporters wanted to abolish the monarchy and move to a system modeled on the American.

It comes almost as a shock to the students to realize that people in Britain would have known about what was happening in America. Their study of U.S. history has usually been so insular that the idea of the rest of the world watching them is a surprise. For that matter, they have grown up unaware that the eyes of the world in their own times are upon them. Now the world suddenly seems like a more complicated place. They are surprised too to find just how small European countries are by comparison with the United States—the fact that you can cross Belgium and the Netherlands in a few hours, and then be off into other countries with languages of their own, comes as a startling revelation. They might have known it in theory but now it's a stark fact.

Some of the students have really woken up to the complexity of the world during these summer courses. If they grew up in Ohio, all they had to look forward to eastward was Pennsylvania, and to the west nothing more exotic than Indiana; going either way meant the same language, food, cars, cities, and standards. Now they find themselves in an intricate place where every ten miles modifies the regional accent and where, with a two-hour bus ride into Wales, they can be moving amid a population whose language is as remote as that of the Navajos.

More recently I have taught a course on Victorian Britain which includes a trip down a Welsh coal mine. The British studies program is strong on visits: our Shakespeare class goes to see several plays by the Royal Shakespeare Company at Stratford each year, we visit principal sites in London, listen to a debate in Parliament, visit the Imperial War Museum and the Cabinet War Rooms underneath Whitehall, and spend a few days in Edinburgh to get a taste of Scotland. The coal mine strikes me as the most satisfactory of these visits because it's so far off the tourist track. It is at Blenafon, a gaunt, windswept hillside site, where the mine workings are made of cinderblock and corrugated iron, and everything rusts more or less as it was rusting when the mine closed in the bitter early years of the Thatcher government. Retired miners, many of them becoming elderly now, are the guides, and they speak English in an accent almost too heavy for the students to decipher. We line up at the pithead for helmets, emergency breathing apparatus, and miners' lamps, and take snapshots amid nervous laughter. Then we hand over to the guides everything electrical, including watches, cameras, and walkmen, and anything that might make a spark, because gas and explosions are such a perpetual underground hazard. We crowd into the mine elevator and it plunges down the echoing shaft until we reach the tunnels.

Shuffling out, with only helmet lamps to illuminate the scene, the students begin to understand what it meant to be a miner and to spend all of the working day, and often all of a working life, far underground. Some of them have read Orwell's *Road to Wigan Pier*, and a couple of them D. H. Lawrence's *Sons and Lovers*, but there's no beating a hands-on experience down the pit. This mine—now promoted by the tourist board as "The Big Pit"—is a ramshackle old place. The hazards are such that it would not get insurance or be allowed to open in America, but in unlitigious Britain it makes its way. We trudge through tunnels that have buckled and twisted under the geological forces of a century. Pit props and tunnel shoring keep the roof up, flood water rushes down a channel at one side, and we move through a series of heavy doors. At one point the guide tells us about the children who often began their mine-work lives down here at the age of just five or six. Among their jobs was to open and close these underground doors to ensure proper ventilation and distribution of breathable air. They sat in total darkness because candlelight was a luxury their families were too poor to afford and the mine owner would not provide it. Occasionally a coal wagon, drawn either by older children or by pit ponies, would approach, and the waiting child would open the door to let it through before it disappeared into the gloom once more. "Turn your lights off for a moment," says the guide, and reluctantly the students do it. Then we are in a darkness that is more absolute than we ever experience on the surface. No amount of adapting makes the slightest difference, because there is absolutely no ambient light at all—it's chilling and, to some of us, frightening.

Recovering our light, we move on to the coal faces themselves, where men hacked out the coal by hand. Then we see the underground stables where the horses lived—the miners did not take them to the surface because it made them unruly when they returned. The guide tells us that being in a confined underground space all the time with the horses made the mine smell terrible. What's more, the hay brought down the mine as horse feed contained rats, and in the days when it was working, rats were everywhere, made voracious with hunger. They would eat the men's lunches if they weren't kept in metal cans, and our guide told us one of his friends had lost part of his finger, bitten off by a rat inside his glove. The horses and rats were not phased out in Victorian times either. They were still in the mine right through the 1960s.

Back on the surface, and squinting in the intense daylight, we visit the showers. They were not built until the late 1930s—before then the men had to go home filthy and bathe as best they could in tin baths in front of the family fireplace. Even when they were built, the men had to pay most of the cost. The shower house, no longer needed, is now a museum of coal mining. It includes photographs of this pit when it was still in operation, and photographs of some of the worst mining disasters that have blighted the region throughout its history. We are not far from Aberfan, where a slag-heap landslide in the 1960s buried the local school and killed almost every child in the village. The visit is a crash course into another world, or at least the memory of another world, for our privileged students.

Cardiff, the capital of Wales, is about fifteen miles away, and now, thanks to Tony Blair's decentralization, has a parliament of its own. Tom Lancaster's political science class visited it last year while I took my class to Cardiff Castle. An old medieval structure, it was owned by the earls of Bute and rebuilt in the mid-nineteenth century according to the fanciful standards of Victorian gothic architecture. Every room is a miniature masterpiece of romanticism, and with the help of an enthusiastic guide we made the most of it. What makes this pair of visits so apposite is the fact that Bute owned the local coal mines and made the money to build the castle out of the miners' sweat and blood. There are not many places where you can see the juxtapositions of voracious capitalism more starkly. No wonder the miners developed such militant unions and such a bitter hatred of the owners. Between the 1940s and the early 1980s the Labour Party, which they had helped to bring into existence, nationalized the coal mines and subsidized the working even of pits that ran at a steady loss. Margaret Thatcher put a stop to all that, shutting down the pits, throwing all the men out of work, and making the clattering, smoky old mining towns strangely quiet.

Every Wednesday at University College we have a formal dinner in a dignified paneled dining hall, the Alington Room. We sit in our best clothes along two great tables, while college servants dish up the food. There's plenty of wine too. The drinking age is twenty-one in America but in Britain it's seventeen, so suddenly all of our students find they are legal. (Since most of them are under twenty-one, I dare say that not so much as a drop of alcohol has yet passed their lips.) There's a premium on good manners and self-restraint because we are in the presence of a guest speaker, usually a distinguished figure from the British political or literary world. The best I can remember of these speakers was critic Christopher Ricks, who gave a hilarious speech on Bob Dylan, an important poet in his judgment. Ricks is small and lively—he brought a boom box, talked about Dylan's songs, analyzed the verses, then played them on his stereo. While the music was on, he would sit down on the floor. The effect for people halfway back in the hall was to witness Ricks suddenly disappearing from view and then suddenly bobbing up again, excitedly resuming his talk. We've also had Winston Churchill's nephew, Oscar Wilde's grandson, the historian Christopher Hill, and a string of maudlin Irish poets.

Tom Lancaster, from our political science department, has been in charge of the program for the last few years and has introduced the principle that each of the program's faculty members must find a Wednesday-night speaker. The one I introduced last year was David Alton, a liberal member of the House of Lords. I had heard him the previous January while visiting England on behalf of Emory to see whether I could persuade young Britons to become undergraduates at our college. He spoke brilliantly. American academics should learn a lesson from British politics. If you've ever watched *Prime Minister's Question Time* on C-SPAN you'll know what I mean. Members of Parliament from all the parties take pride in being entertaining speakers, witty as well as informative. There's plenty of rhetorical dazzle even on the most humdrum subjects, and it's a delight to listen even to those whose ideas you consider wrong. Members of Congress, by contrast, like the American professors at whose feet they used to sit, are often painfully straight-faced. Although Washington itself is full of great political jokes, the politicians are careful not to show any sign of enjoyment or any sense of fun, and are almost uniformly monotonous in the way they speak to Congress itself. Perhaps they all remember that the most amusing, wisecracking presidential candidate of the last half century—Adlai Stevenson—was also a two-time loser.

Becoming a Student

It's a great life being a professor, but I often wonder what it is like these days to be an undergraduate. Probably about the same as it was when I was a student, although I never was one in America. They've got computers and the Internet where we had fountain pens and the library, but that's not as big a difference as you might think. They've still got to find ways to persuade their brains to assimilate and understand masses of information, often in conceptual frameworks that are unfamiliar. Although I sometimes give them a hard time, I'm impressed by our students' willingness to keep going. It must seem to them sometimes that an everlasting succession of classes stretches far into the future. If anyone's an expert on education it is them—they ought to be connoisseurs of teaching style by now. They certainly know how to be brutally frank when it comes to evaluating their professors.

Britain and America have different ideas about what undergraduates ought to study. In Britain the system requires you to specialize early. I took only three subjects (English, history, and music) in the last two years of high school (the equivalent of grades eleven and twelve) and only one subject in college, history. There's no such thing as a college major in Britain, and no "uniform requirements" for every student. The last time I studied mathematics, or science of any kind, or a foreign language, was as a fifteen-year-old preparing for the O-Level examinations. What a contrast with students in the United States, who are expected to keep plugging away with a wide array of different and difficult subjects up to and beyond the age of twenty.

To my surprise, in the summer of 1999 I had the chance to become a student once more. In the name of internationalization (remember the "global citizens"?!) our Spanish department wrote a grant proposal to the administration, pointing out that it was no use trying to create international-minded students when most of the faculty was monoglot. Why not, they said, subsidize faculty visits to Spain so that more of the professors could get up to speed on at least one foreign language and culture? The administration agreed, and the program began. I was one of seven professors who volunteered and were sent off to the University of Salamanca for the summer. I was a bit apprehensive. I had never studied any Spanish and had been in Spain only briefly, as a teenager with my family, back in about 1973 when Franco was still in charge. Still, it was much too good a chance to pass up.

Karen Stolley, a delightful Emory superstar and the professor who had masterminded this entire venture, had prepped me on what to do when I arrived. I took a taxi and read to the driver, in my best English voice, the name of the Madrid bus station, which I had written on a little slip of paper. By a weird stroke of good luck he was a pretty good French speaker, and since I can speak an archaic and now much-rusted version of French, I was able to hold a halting conversation with him. What a global citizen I am! At the bus station I read off another of my little slips of paper to the man in the ticket office and was able to get a ticket to Salamanca, which is about a hundred miles northwest of the capital. If you have been to Europe, reader, you'll remember what it's like. You catch the plane from the American East Coast in the evening and it flies through the night, arriving just after dawn the next day, when your body is telling you it's way after midnight and you need a long sleep more than anything in the world. You feel queasy, alternately sick, cold, and far too hot, and everything around you is alien. It is almost as though you were coated in wax, creating a screen between you and the rest of the world. Nothing seems quite real. You'd expected it to be a wonderful lark but now you just feel alone and estranged—"so this is what existentialism was all about." That's how I felt on the bus as it lurched its way out of Madrid and climbed through mountains onto the high plains of Castile. To add a touch of the surreal, the bus showed a dubbed American vengeance movie, and through half-awake eyes I intermittently followed the plot, but not the words, of *Predator II*.

Arriving in Salamanca was great, even so. It's a marvelous hilltop town with medieval walls, splendid old cathedrals (two of them), and college buildings to rival those of Oxford, all strangely inscribed in bull's blood by young men who have successfully defended their dissertations. The approach is through miles of high, open plains—it's a little reminiscent of Wyoming—in which are scattered colorful villages. Anyone from America will be astonished by the Castilian towns, since they do not spread out. Instead, they're built in tight clusters. Abruptly the city stops, and the countryside starts again after each one, and even Salamanca, though it's big, has none of the suburban sprawl its American counterparts would display. I tottered into the town with my big suitcase and was able to locate Karen's apartment, more or less where she had predicted. What a relief to see her and to find an English speaker. She sat me down, gave me a bagel and a glass of water, then took me across a few streets to the little apartment she had rented for me.

All this scene-setting leads to the point. I was here as a student, to learn Spanish from scratch. There is a thriving industry in Spanish for foreigners at Salamanca, *Cursos Internacionales*, which has it down to a science. The next day, still feeling a bit waxy from jetlag but not quite so tired, I and my fellows, all of whom had made their way independently to Spain, took a placement test. It is one of the easiest tests I've ever experienced. I looked at each question in turn, realized I didn't have the faintest idea which of the five answers was right, checked one at random, and moved on to the next. I finished the whole thing in about five minutes, so one of the testers took me aside for an oral. She said a few things in Spanish. I answered with a few things in English. Finally she said, in slow and careful English, "You have not studied Spanish?" "Right." She made some marks in her book and shook my hand. I wandered back into the sunshine and met Karen, who awaited us. The others straggled out one by one. Some of them had taken the test as a real challenge to their knowledge of Spanish, and, sure enough, they were placed in more advanced groups.

Karen was madly overconfident about our abilities. She placed me and two other absolute beginners, Shalom Goldman and Mark Sanders, in an intermediate class, on the theory that we'd pick up the elementary stuff as we went along. The next day proved that this ambitious scheme, flattering though it was, spelled nothing but failure, at least for me. I begged Karen to have another word with the organizers and get me into a lower section; Shalom did the same. On day two, accordingly, we descended into "advanced beginners." It was anything but easy there, but at least we weren't totally out of our depth. With heroic fortitude Mark carried on with the intermediates.

Shalom's probably in his early fifties. He and I were much older than everyone else in the group. A few of them were young men from Holland and Germany who already spoke excellent English and were trying hard at Spanish. The rest were undergraduates from the University of Texas, the same kind of eighteen- and nineteen-year-olds we teach at Emory. Suddenly we and they were on terms of perfect equality—we *all* couldn't do the work! They treated us like a pair of granddads and helped us out when the lessons got particularly sticky.

One comical aspect of the program was the layout of the day. We had three hours of morning classes with the formal instructors, from 9:00 until 12:00. For us that meant we got up, had breakfast, then went to class. For many of the kids, by contrast, classes were a prebreakfast thing. Salamanca was full of discotheques that generally opened about midnight then went until dawn, and many of these kids appeared to be able to dance all night, every night. They'd come straight from dancing to class, usually much the worse for wear, yawn through their lessons, then crash around midday until sometime after dark.

Sitting there in class, it all came back to me: being a student is difficult. The class was conducted entirely in Spanish, with even the most complicated grammatical issues being explained in Spanish rather than English. I practically wept with frustration sometimes at my inability to grasp a concept due to the teachers' determination not to explain it to us in a language we could already speak. Often Shalom and I, and another Emory professor, Kimberley, who joined us a day or two later, would hastily whisper the translation to each other if one of us got the point, until reprimanded by the teacher. We had written homework every day, plus the arduous responsibility of learning dozens of verbs, first in the present tense, which was OK, but then in a wide array of additional tenses, some of which seemed then to have no English counterpart (though I later discovered that they do, really).

After these daily classroom ordeals we would go to a little cafe called the Ave, order *cafe con leche* and meet our conversation teacher for another hour and a half. It's amazingly difficult to find the words to actually speak in another language. Given enough time, I could usually dredge up the word in time to write it down, but bringing them instantly to mind for conversation, let alone fitting them together in a coherent sentence—it's more than I could manage. Pilar, the teacher, was a cheery soul, patient, good-humored, and understanding of us oldies as we fumbled along. She, like the classroom instructors, was far younger than us, and the feeling of being part of a great experiment in age inversion sometimes came over me.

What made the whole experience such an ordeal is that when I'm in the English-speaking world I literally make my living by speaking English. I love talking and love words. In Spain, suddenly, I was reduced to inarticulate babble or sheer silence. It was like suddenly becoming the village idiot. I remember my first attempt at shopping. I needed some sugar to go with the coffee Karen had given me. In the little local store I went in armed with a noun, a verb, and maybe even a preposition or two. When it came to having to speak, though, I could only blurt out the one word *azucar* to the lady behind the counter. She spotted me for a foreigner and talked with painful care and slowness as I examined each unfamiliar coin in turn. Yes, a hopeless case with a long way to go, just in order to be able to speak. Humbling!

Don't get the impression that I didn't like it, though. I found the place entrancing, the company excellent. Karen was the most wonderful helper, teacher, and guide, and my fellow struggling Emory professors were a great bunch. I also became completely obsessed with learning Spanish and didn't really want to do anything else the whole time I was there. I went everywhere with my orange and yellow dictionary, looked up hundreds of words every day, made vocabulary lists on every scrap of paper and envelope, and studied them whenever there was a spare moment. I also threw myself into the Spanish-culture seminar we had every afternoon at the "Casa Emory," set in one of the picturesque back-streets of Salamanca. Karen had given us all, before we left America, a book that outlines the whole history of Spain and the Hispanic world, *El espejo enterrado* (The Buried Mirror), by Carlos Fuentes. The idea of this seminar was that we would read a section of the book every day, and discuss it in Spanish. Never mind that in the morning class we were learning sentences like "I get up at half past six," and "I like coffee but I do not like tea." In the afternoon class we had to deal with sentences like "The indigenous population was vulnerable to a diverse and mystifying array of unfamiliar pathogens." Karen, just as she had said that we could pick up the basics of Spanish while studying at the intermediate level, took the view that by aiming high we would achieve high, and that the book wouldn't prove insuperably difficult. In fact, she assigned a string of supplementary readings to go with many of the chapters too. It wasn't long before we developed the knack of saying the Spanish phrase that means "This is a point I cannot express in Spanish," and then breaking into an English discussion of whatever theme we were on just then. She was just ever so slightly cross with us for copping out like that.

We tried to please her when we could, though. We recognized that she was our lifeline, without whom things would be grim indeed. Eating out was one of the many situations in which she showed herself to be more than worth her weight in gold. The memory of Spain is inseparable for me from the memory of hunger. They have the insane idea that lunchtime is about three in the afternoon and dinnertime about ten. I have the sensible idea that lunchtime is about eleven forty-five and dinnertime not a minute after six. Every day dreadful pangs of hunger would attack me hours before lunchtime, and when we were eating in our little apartment we made no attempt to go native.

A feature of the program, however, was that for one reason or another we were always being taken out to eat. Karen knew exactly what to say to the waiters and would usually begin by apologizing for the fact that we had come in as early as two-thirty and were already prepared to gnaw on the tables and plates if some food didn't show up really soon. Next she had to deal with our group's complicated dietary needs. Some were vegetarians, one had a yeast intolerance, two were orthodox Jews and couldn't eat ham or shellfish, and all the others had at least some rudimentary sense of what is good to eat and what bad. The rules of nutrition have been put on hold in Britain. In Spain they have yet to arrive at all, and there was a certain amount of horrified flinching from many of the dishes we glimpsed. On the first night, for example, Karen ordered a salad that sounded OK from the written description on the menu. When it came, however, it was sprinkled with ham. I loved it and began to tuck in. The Jews and the vegetarians were not so keen and asked Karen to have another word with the waiter. She told him, "We asked for a vegetarian salad but this one has meat." "That's not meat," he answered, "it's ham!" It turned out that virtually every food in this part of Spain is liberally sprinkled with ham. It's as universal in Castile as ketchup in America, and everyone thinks it's terrific. Ham became a standing joke in our group, and many photographs from the trip show me pointing to giant pieces of ham hanging in windows or on billboards. In fact we all saw a hilarious feature film, *Jamón, jamón* (Ham, Ham), whose culminating scene is a battle to the death between two young men armed with great club-shaped hams.

We were a motivated group and all made steady progress, picking up phrases, techniques of saying basic things, and learning familiar patterns of speech and writing. Then we discovered another obstacle—that no two areas of Spain can agree, even remotely, about the nature of their language. We went on a four-day trip to Galicia, visiting Santiago de Compostella, Ferrol, and other towns. There the language is Galician, and the Castilian we were struggling with in Salamanca was not quite good enough. Near the end of the trip my family and Karen's also went to Barcelona on a superb overnight train. There the language is Catalan, and the Castilian we were struggling with in Salamanca was not nearly good enough. I proudly counted out my money to the Barcelona ice-cream man only to be told I had got the numbers all wrong—he repeated a completely different set in Catalan. Portuguese is different again, not to mention Basque, and we learned throughout our course that Latin American and Iberian Spanish are sharply distinguished in many places. It's enough to make you feel discouraged.

I was eager to maintain my momentum when I left. From Spain I flew to England for the annual Oxford summer school. Every day I read another twenty pages of the Fuentes, and finally finished the whole book, a source of great pride. Back in Atlanta in the fall I enrolled in Spanish 201, the beginning of undergraduate second-year Spanish. The semester after that I enrolled in Spanish 202. What a battle! Here, too, it was all done in Spanish, there were everlasting homework assignments, and still the old difficulty of being unable to come up with the spoken words quickly enough. The undergraduates around me wondered why this old geezer was in class with them. In fact one of them, Elizabeth, is now a member of the class I'm teaching, and she must be entertained by the contrast between the hesitant blunderer in Spanish class and the know-it-all professor of her history class.

Finally, near the end of the second semester I had to stop going because of the pressure of other work. It's a year now since I was in that class. The Spanish that it was such a struggle to pack into my head has been flowing out of it with horrifying ease ever since. When I try to come up with relevant Spanish phrases now I often can't find them. I'll pick it up again one day, but I'm under no illusions about it being a simple matter. The experience has been extremely valuable, though, because it has reminded me, in the most vivid way, just how tough it is to be a student. Being a professor, especially when you've been one for a decade or more, tends to make you forget what it was like to be on the other side. It's easiest of all to forget what it's like being a student in a subject for which you have no special aptitude, because it's such a long time since you studied one. I haven't done mathematics, physics, or chemistry since I was fifteen, and I gave them up in 1972 with an immense sigh of relief. History is to some of our students what those subjects were to me, and this grappling with Spanish has taught me, I hope, to remember the difficulties faced by students working in a subject that does not come easily or readily to them. I hope it has made me more sympathetic to those who find it hard going. There's a lot to be said for getting people who are good at history to teach it, but there's also something to be said against it—they're not so likely to appreciate the nature of other people's difficulties with the subject. I wonder if I'd make a good math teacher, bad at the subject as I am; a paradoxical possibility.

CHAPTER

6

■ ■ ■

Technology and Technique

Ninth Class (Monday)

I am trying to follow my schedule for the course and avoid falling behind. Otherwise, I'll have to miss out the 1970–2000 period altogether at the end of the course. But I can't bear to omit showing my slides of nineteenth-century women—there are so many good ones. There's the page from a late nineteenth-century medical text book showing the skeleton of an "Indian woman" who has lived "in nature," side by side with the skeleton of an "American lady" who has been squeezed into corsets and had her entire rib cage distorted by them. Then there's an early advertisement for bloomers, trousers for ladies invented by Amelia Bloomer as a more practical alternative to long, flowing dresses. There is also a cartoon from the *Police Gazette*, showing how a young lady scandalized the congregation by entering church wearing her bloomers. Parishioners, men and women alike, look horrified.

The *Police Gazette* served more or less the same function in the late nineteenth century that the *National Enquirer* does today. It sniffed out scandalous stories and made the most of them, illustrating them with graphic and sometimes slightly risqué pictures. For a course of this kind it's ideal, since it shows what sorts of things had shock appeal. (Perhaps a century from now another generation of historians will show the front cover of *National Enquirer* with headlines like "Bigfoot Fathered My Twins!") Another picture from the same source depicts a young woman who, on a Long Island Railroad train, asked a man for a light and then *smoked in public*! A third shows a group of Indiana women, inspired by Carry Nation, the ax-wielding saloon smasher, breaking up a cargo of liquor barrels at the railroad depot rather than let their menfolk get drunk. I also show a cartoon of Carry Nation herself, drawn by a cartoonist who appreciated the irony of the situation. She's leading the charge of a group of clergy and temperance Christians, but the saloon keepers are barricaded behind an array of pro-alcohol biblical quotations, while bottles, Bibles, and brickbats fly both ways through the air.

Slides are becoming dated—the digital camera and the powerpoint presentation are making them obsolete. When I was an undergraduate I learned how to use a darkroom, to make high-quality black-and-white prints, and for a while was obsessed by it. I still have all the darkroom equipment but haven't used it in years. Then, in graduate school, I learned that it was possible to develop your own color slides, but that the temperature of the fluids was much more critical than with black-and-whites. I began experimenting, and at first did everything wrong, so that one batch would come out nearly all blue and the next nearly all red, due to excessive heat or cold. Gradually I got the knack, and was soon able to make them seventy-two at a time in a double developing tank (thirty-six pictures on each of two reels), of reliable quality and true color. By buying film, chemicals, and plastic slide frames in bulk, it was possible to get really good economies of scale, and for a while in the late 1980s I was making them for an effective price of about three or four cents per slide, as opposed to the two dollars per slide that the university library required for pictures that were no better.

I made the first large set of them when I was invited to teach summer school at Berkeley in the summer of 1987. Although by then I was a veteran of teaching seminars and sections, I had never given a formal lecture class. I set about writing it in the two months before summer school began. At that time I was a postdoctoral fellow at Harvard, living on the ground floor of a three-apartment wooden building on the Cambridge-Arlington border. I would spend the morning researching and writing lectures on the introduction to U.S. history since the Civil War (essentially the same course I'm teaching this term). After lunch, I would get out my camera and take it into the bright sunshine on the porch along with an armful of picture books. My camera has a "macro" lens, which enables me to focus down to within about an inch of the page. That means I can get a high-resolution copy of pictures on just a quarter of a book page. I would try to get the pages as flat as possible with spring clips, to prevent visible curvature, glare, and obvious focus faults within the frame. One early effort shows my left thumb intruding into a picture of a sod house on the Kansas prairie, but with the passage of time I got better at it. After making a set of photographs I would develop them at once, and often, within an hour of pressing the shutter, would have strips of brightly colored slide film drying in the kitchen. I'd cut and mount in frames the ones I had made the day before and make notes of the subject on the frame. In this way I soon had a collection of about five hundred, and I've been building it ever since, so that the collection's now about four thousand strong. I still prowl libraries (college and public) for new picture books and seize the chance to make new sets of slides.

Slides alone aren't sufficient for a lecture but they're a great help; they bring to life things that would otherwise seem dim and remote. The process has also had the effect of teaching me, bit by bit, about the history of picture making; the rapid improvement of photography in the nineteenth and early twentieth centuries, the perfection of chromolithography (Currier and Ives prints), the era of great mass-production illustrators like Charles Dana Gibson at the turn of the century, and their subsequent obsolescence. I've always had a weakness for the history of technology, and it's fun to be able to show pictures and tell students not only what they are pictures of but also how the pictures themselves were made and reproduced. But as I said, the time has almost come for a switch to the digital camera. I have a vision of myself heading into the classroom with a super-compact laptop computer, plugging it into some projector gadget, flipping a switch, and without further ado being able to show long picture sequences to classes. And then, as I understand it,

I'll be able to make the same set accessible over e-mail or on the Web so that the students can look at them again to help with their assignments and exam preparation. So far it's just a vision—I'm a low-tech chap—but it will be sad to say farewell to my slide collection. Someone has told me I can actually get the slides scanned into a computer. I hope that's true.

After the pictures of women (including others of middle-class women in their finery, servant women, weddings, women's cooking classes, and early department stores), I switch off the projector and begin to lecture on the growth of American cities. I have a passage on the development of street cars and the way they facilitated urban growth. Next comes a section on the hazards of horses in cities. They sometimes bolted (Emory itself is named after a Methodist bishop who was killed in a runaway horse accident); they needed to be fed; they generated mountains of manure, which caused a public health problem; and periodically they died. An epidemic of epizootic distemper among the horses in Boston in 1872 killed hundreds and brought the city to a standstill. When fire broke out there were no horses to pull the fire engines, so the blaze spread. In those days before motor vehicles, moreover, moving the corpse of a horse from the street was difficult. Almost the only thing that could drag it away was another horse, and they were suddenly in very short supply. Hence an infestation of flyblown stinking corpses. No wonder electricity caught on fast once the technology for electric streetcars was worked out. I talk a little about urban political "machines" like New York's infamous Tweed Ring, about Lincoln Steffens's *Shame of the Cities* (1904), a journalist's expose of urban corruption, and about Progressive Era attempts at urban reform. This week the class is reading a book by Theodore Roosevelt, so this is a good time to mention how he lost all enthusiasm for his breakfast sausages after reading *The Jungle*, by Upton Sinclair, with its harrowing descriptions of rancid meat and rat-dung-infested sausage vats in the Chicago slaughterhouses. One of the women in class has read the book and her description of *his* description loses nothing in the telling.

Feel-Good Education or Rote Learning?

Should we, as teachers, try to be a source of pleasure to our students? It is a question I think about when I watch my daughter's flute teacher,

Catherine Bull, who is delightful and very gifted. There's a lot to be said for it; students probably prefer classes that don't terrify them. Still, our job as teachers is not to entertain them or cater to their preferences, but to cause them to learn things they don't know yet. Sometimes there's an advantage to making them feel a little anxious. Isn't it more likely, for example, that the students in my class will read the assignment if they know I'm going to ask them detailed questions about the reading, and expose them if they haven't done it? I want them to feel the anxiety that goes with maintaining high standards and being on display. I'm not positively Victorian in my approach to pedagogy, or at least not Victorian as embodied in Dickens's Mr. M'choakumchild from *Hard Times*. He relies on fear alone, thinks that learning by rote is enough, and flogs the children. I'm slightly more enlightened than that, but I sometimes find myself wondering: a system of education that persisted for centuries, to which rote learning and corporal punishment were integral, must have had something going for it. Isn't it possible that we've lost as well as gained by jettisoning it? Just kidding.

Seriously though, one big difference between being a student now and being a student in earlier ages is that we no longer favor masses of rote learning. Radical educational theorists in the 1960s, following on from progressive educational theorists earlier in the century, said it was stifling and stultifying and that teachers should put more of a premium on stimulating students' imaginations. I wonder if the pendulum didn't swing a bit too far. Is rote learning really so bad? I remember enjoying learning poems by heart as a child, and as a railway fanatic I memorized the names and numbers of literally hundreds of locomotives. I remember a high school language teacher telling me he had memorized Latin poems as a child and had taken pleasure in reciting them to himself (not that I anticipate this variant catching on in contemporary America). Evangelical groups in the nineteenth and early twentieth centuries, and a few evangelical academies today, encourage students to learn long sections of the Bible by heart. Every kid wants to be an actor at some stage in his or her life, and being an actor entails learning the lines. When it came to learning Spanish I found there was no alternative to trying simply to memorize all those varied verb endings, cramming them into my head, repeating them over and over, and trying to make them become second nature, so that the right one would come to my lips when I actually tried to speak.

I notice in the classes I teach that the students study for exams by trying to memorize as much as possible of what I have said, and that when they're answering the essay questions they put down on paper every scrap of information they can recall, however marginal it may be to the assigned question. In other words, even in an educational culture that discourages rote learning they do it instinctively. I chide them, when returning midterms, with the remark, "You didn't really answer the question—you just wrote down everything you knew about this subject." Perhaps what I should do instead is say after every lecture, "Make sure you memorize the names, dates, chronologies, and principal themes of this lecture before our next meeting, so that, if called on, you could recite them to me. Here is a list of the main points; memorize it word for word." If they got into that habit throughout the semester they then could do a spot of creative organizational thinking in the exam itself.

Objections to this idea come bubbling up to the surface and I dare say every reader of the foregoing paragraph will find something odious in it. Something I often say to students is that history is a creative activity, and that each new generation has to rewrite history in light of its own experiences. I mean it too: black history, for example, has been completely transformed since the 1950s under the impetus of the civil rights movement and its aftermath; we know far more about the lives and culture of slaves than did historians of the early twentieth century, and we think about them in a completely different way. There's a constant tendency to read present concerns into the past, a fallacy that historians call "presentism," but even those who, at first glance, seem best at guarding against it, do it in subtle ways. That's why history books start their lives as guides to the past, but end up as guides to the society in which they were written. Even the great ones like Gibbon and Macauley are valued as much today as guides to their authors' times and frames of mind as guides to their ostensible subject. Anyway, how can we, on the one hand, tell students that history is a creative activity, and on the other hand, urge them into the rote learning of names and dates? It will have to be done right, not by insisting that the names and dates are an end product but by showing that they are the necessary minimum without which the creativity cannot even begin. Painters have to learn about the characteristics of the paint itself before they can convert their visions into pictorial form; aspiring writers have to know some grammar; and in the same way historians have to know who did what, when, and where.

There is a postmodernist objection to this kind of mechanical approach; historians have become acutely aware over the last few decades that "facts" are themselves human artifacts rather than incontrovertible lumps of truth. We know that language itself shapes and changes, or indeed creates, historical reality, and that the relationship between person, time, place, and "fact" is problematical. However, the people who understand this point most clearly are also, in most cases, the people who have mastered the conventions of historical research and writing, have actually written historical works in the conventional way, and then have become aware of strange lacunae and inconsistencies in what they have done and written. Let's make sure that students don't reach the linguistic problem prematurely—let them work through the preliminaries first and come to their own conclusions, rather than having these insights thrust on them from the outset. Otherwise they will be in the same situation as students (common enough around here) who know that fascism was bad even though they don't know what it was.

Additional Assignment (Tuesday Evening)

Tonight I showed the first film for the course, *Heartland*, made in the early 1980s and just recently released on video. I remembered it through the years and bought my own copy from Amazon.com as soon as I found it was available. It's a western with a difference. Every ounce of myth and sentimentality about the old west has been squeezed out, leaving you with the realities of farm life in the early twentieth century. I had rented the room about a week ago, and two-thirds of the class gathered there at eight o'clock. The others, who could not make it tonight, can check out the film from our video library and watch it before Friday's class.

The film follows a young widow (Conchita Ferrell) with a seven-year-old daughter, as she moves out to a Wyoming homestead farm in 1910 to work for a gruff Scotsman (Rip Torn) who ranches there. He's a man of few words and for long stretches of the film says nothing or simply orders her around with terse commands. The land is so high and remote that the snow comes early and stays on the ground late; every scene shows a bleak, windswept, treeless land. The cattle have to be branded and castrated, all of which the film shows in a matter-of-fact way. The pig is fattened and then killed for meat—we watch as the farmer, his hired hand, and the housekeeper slit its throat, strip off its bristles, and butcher it. The woman, eager to homestead an adjacent claim for herself, lays down her twelve dollars in the land office. But when she tells the rancher her plans, he explains in a few economical sentences that she will never be able to get started, because of lack of money, access to water, winter feed, and other necessities. It's land he has always wanted too, so to make her own plans viable and keep it in the family she agrees to marry him, in what must surely be the least emotional marriage proposal scene in the history of cinema. She gets married in her apron and work boots—then the grind of perpetual labor resumes.

The rancher, angered by low wholesale prices for beef, refuses to sell his animals to a visiting buyer, who potters along in an early Ford Model T. Instead he tries to feed them through the desperate Wyoming winter. A succession of scenes depicts the unrelenting misery, isolation, and hardships of winter. The woman gives birth to a son who, after a few weeks, dies from fever—events also shown in an extremely low-key way. By the spring half the cattle are dead—they have been unable to survive the winter, and the vulnerable little family is on the brink of destitution. The final scene shows them struggling together in the barn to help a cow give birth. That's pretty graphic too, as both of them are reaching in under the cow's tail to grasp the hooves of the unborn calf. They tie a rope round them, attach it to a block and tackle, then heave with all their strength. The calf finally pops out in a great rush of blood, afterbirth, and shit. A collective cry of dismay and horror arose from the class; they're not used to this kind of reality.

There isn't a better film, so far as I know, to supplement the teaching of western and farming history. Another fairly good one, though, is *Days of Heaven*, made in about 1978. I sometimes show the first ten or fifteen minutes of that one, before the melodramatic plot takes over from the documentary-like scene-setting. In this film we first see a young industrial worker (Richard Gere) in a Chicago factory, shoveling coal into furnaces. After an argument and fight with his overseer, he runs off. He, his young sister (the narrator), and his girlfriend hop a freight train and the scene cuts to harvest time in the great Texas wheatlands. As the train slows near a set of grain elevators, they and lots of other hoboes jump from the train to sign up as migrant harvest-workers on a vast wheat-growing estate. Fine early scenes show the actual techniques of harvesting and threshing in the days of partially mechanized harvesting, when lots of hand labor was still required. I usually turn off the VCR just before the first kiss (groans of disappointment from the class), but urge the students to see the rest of it for themselves.

There's a running debate about whether films harm or help in the study of history. On the whole, I come down squarely on the help side, though the particular choice of films makes all the difference. Anything by Oliver Stone seems like a bad idea to me—students are ready enough to believe in conspiracies as it is, and need no encouragement. *Dances with Wolves* is also beyond the pale. Later this term I'll probably show some of the incredible D-Day landing sequence from *Saving Private Ryan*, which is about the best fragment of war-film making I've ever seen (while granting an honorable mention to *Memphis Belle* in the air-war department and a very honorable mention to *Das Boot* in the naval war department), and I plan to show them *Doctor Strangelove* when we discuss nuclear war planning. I usually show documentaries as well, and will probably use *Rosie the Riveter* and *Atomic Cafe* later this term.

Tenth Class (Wednesday)

Here's what I like about the South. It's early February and already the days are warm. I'm in shirtsleeves, students are playing Frisbee on the quad and sitting out to study, yet cold evenings still forestall the insects. The lovely long spring here beats even the lovely long fall, and everyone is feeling good. News of bitter snowstorms in the Northeast and arctic chills in the Midwest do nothing to dampen our good spirits. My mood lifts a little further when I get unexpected evidence, in the form of an e-mail, of a student following up on last Friday's reading. In the Frederick Jackson Turner book, one of the authors mentioned that two of Turner's children had died in 1899, and one of the women in class asked me if I knew what had happened to them. I had no idea. Here is her e-mail:

Hi Professor Allitt,

I looked in Allan Bogue's book, *Frederick Jackson Turner: Strange Roads Going Down* and I found that the deaths of two of Turner's children were unrelated incidents, both happening to occur in 1899. In February his youngest daughter died of diphtheria and in October his only son died from complications of a ruptured appendix. I had assumed they had died together in an accident of some sort. Interesting!

Tricia Ercak

I never knew that before. It's a little thing, but teachers often have to be satisfied by little things, and I am delighted that Tricia kept the subject of the discussion on her mind after class finished, went to the library, found a book about Turner that I had not mentioned, and browsed through it until she found out what had happened.

I nip into the audio-visual office to complain about the way the slide projector creates an image bigger than the screen in my classroom. The last few times I've shown slides I have had to ask the student working the projector to lift the front so that we can see the bottom of the picture, or to lift the back so that we can see the top of it. The technician comes in, fiddles with it for a while, agrees that it's a problem, and says he'll try to find another lens with a narrower beam or else bring in another projector on a trolley and put it closer to the screen.

Projectors are like Xerox machines—they can sense their operator's mood. As his anxiety or dissatisfaction rises they become less cooperative. Sure enough, I've shown only five or six of the urban-history slides left over from last time before the light fades from a picture of urchins in turn-of-the-century New York wheeling trolleys of kindling wood through the streets. The bulb has blown. I recognize the problem immediately. I'm a veteran of mid class bulb changes, but now that there's a permanent projector in every room instead of a portable one in a box, there are no spare bulbs available. Instead, I have to make a joke about projectors knowing when the operator is dissatisfied, and turn to the subject of my next lecture—the election of 1896, a notoriously complicated subject.

I begin with a passage on Southern sharecropping cotton farmers, white and black, and another on the over development of grain farming on the high plains, which brought prices relentlessly downward. Then I move on to the new Populist Party's attempts to overcome sectional divisions and unite all the suffering farmers (the Republican Party tried to keep Kansans' loyalty by "waving the bloody shirt," while the Democrats sought to hold white Georgia sharecroppers' allegiance by summoning up memories of the Lost Cause). The students can understand these anecdotes and get a sense of how the People's Party came into being, but the origins, nature, and effects of deflation, not to mention the intricate blend of monetary theory and evangelical theology in Bryan's "Cross of Gold" speech, are too much for them. Every year, the most difficult issue on which to engage undergraduates' sympathetic attention is economics. Unless they're aspiring or actual economics majors they nearly all get lost in the byzantine complexities of late nineteenth-century finance, the free silver campaign, and Henry George's single tax.

CHAPTER

7

▪ ▪ ▪

Papers and Plagiarism

The First Paper

On the basis of casual remarks, impromptu in-class performances, and contributions to discussion, I have been developing a sense of who's good and who's not so good in this class, but now comes the acid test: it's time to assign the first paper.

I have assigned a staggering number of papers over the past twenty years, and graded them too. It would be nice to think that all my experience was paying off, making each set of papers better than the ones before. Unfortunately, each new group of students is as obtuse as each previous group, and there's no sign of progress at all from one year to the next. At least there is no sign of deterioration, so student writing hereby defies one of the laws of historical change, according to which nothing stays the same. The same dreary old mistakes and confusions come up again and again, remorselessly repetitive, and I sometimes have gloomy premonitions that the last thing I'll do before descending into the grave will be to write on a student paper, "verb tense inconsistency" or "disagreement of singular and plural in the same sentence."

I have a standard speech associated with each step of the course, and now it is time for the speech that accompanies the assignment of a paper. First, I write on the blackboard the question that I want them to use as the title of their papers: "How did the natural environment and human cultures combine to create distinctive ways of life in the American west of the late nineteenth and early twentieth centuries?" Then I begin the speech.

In writing this paper, or any other paper, you have to assume that you are writing it to someone who knows less about the subject than you. I know that in this instance you are really writing it for me, but you must not take advantage of your knowledge that I am the teacher and you are the students. Explain everything carefully so that someone who had not been here in class with us, had not heard the lectures, and had not read the assigned books, could nevertheless understand what you have to say. That's what writing is for: to inform people about things they don't yet know. It's quite likely that after you leave college you will get jobs which require you to write, and you'll be rewarded if you can write accurate, straightforward, economical prose, which teaches people as clearly as possible what they do not yet know. Think of someone you like and whose intelligence you respect, and imagine that he or she is the person for whom you are writing. I usually choose my father, who's an intelligent person but not a historian. When I'm writing I ask myself, "Would he understand what I have said here?" If the answer is yes, I am content. If the answer is no, I must change it. Think of one of your parents, too, or a friend who is not in this course.

When you have written a first draft give it to your friend or roommate and ask him or her to read and criticize it. You must say to your friend, "Do not praise it. Tell me only what is wrong with it." Otherwise your friend's good manners will get the better of him and he'll say, "Oh yes, jolly good, very interesting," because normally that's the kind of thing we're expected to say about each others' creative work. Ask your friend to be remorseless, to point out logical gaps in the argument, to circle places where your evidence does not lead to your conclusion, and to copyedit so that all errors of grammar, spelling, and punctuation are eliminated.

Above all do not think that this paper can be written adequately just by starting at the beginning, writing fifteen hundred words, and then finishing at the end. When you have drafted the whole thing, start editing for content, style, grammar, and continuity. If you would like me to read your draft and comment on it I'll be happy to do so. Start writing early so that you don't have to do the whole thing in one go—papers are always better if written over a period of time. Give yourself the chance to put it aside for a day and then go back to it. Otherwise you'll get so close to it you'll lose the ability to judge where its strengths and weaknesses lie.

It's quite all right to write the introduction last. Sometimes when you begin writing you find you are not sure what you are trying to show, but after going through the process you discover your own principal point. That's the time to write the introduction, declaring what you are going to show, to precede the rest of the paper in which you do show it.

They listen to this speech. The conscientious ones take notes as I'm going along, and then off they go to attempt the paper itself. I always give at least two weeks, usually three, between assigning it and receiving it, so that those who want to spread the process over many days can do so. Until now in the semester no one from the course has been to see me in office hours. Now I wait with interest to see who will turn up. It is at this point in the semester that you begin to discover who's really talented, as opposed to who can make verbal bluffs but cannot match them when it comes to writing coherently.

Helping students to write papers and to edit their drafts is rewarding work, and when the students are receptive there are few parts of the job I enjoy more. For one thing, it has to be done one-on-one; you're not approximating your points to suit the whole class. Instead you have something definite before you, just you and student, and can get down to working on it in detail. For another thing, most students are aware that they need help in this area and are pleased to get it in the form of personal attention from a faculty member.

Most Emory undergraduates are bad writers; most Berkeley undergraduates are bad writers; and I know from talking with my academic pals around the country that most students at Yale, St. Louis, Stonehill College, Colby-Sawyer College, Hiram College, Notre Dame, and Duke are also bad writers. They have not done enough writing to become good at it. They've been cursed with a lifetime of multiple-choice examinations instead, so even the highly intelligent ones come to writing as a strange and alien activity that is occasionally forced upon them. But writing is an activity that needs constant practice if you're going to be good at it. It's like being a violinist—if you once had a few lessons but then got into the habit of picking up the violin just four or five times per year, you would not make sweet and beautiful sounds on it to delight an audience. So it is with the students' papers. They haven't written much, ever, most of them, and they don't really know how to do it, with the result that they can't convey their knowledge and intellectual ability in writing.

I'm no great advocate of educational innovations, but here's one: teach students how to write and make them do it often. I have asked many student groups: "Who keeps a diary?" Sometimes one or two raise their hands but this semester there is no one at all. I say, "You really should keep a diary. It's extremely good practice to write every day, and the more you do it the more familiar you will become with the actual process of writing, which needs lots of practice. It has this benefit too: twenty years from now you'll read what you wrote in your college dairy and say, 'Did I really believe that? Did I really do that?! How weird I was in those days.'" Twenty years hence is unimaginably remote for an eighteen-year-old, but the line usually raises a good laugh. Then I get serious about this matter of writing practice.

Certain errors are so common as to be almost universal. The first one is that almost no student really knows how to construct an argument and then deploy information to support and substantiate it. Usually student papers describe what happened, more or less, then throw in an indignant moral judgment or two before stopping abruptly. I have come to expect that by now, even though I try to assign questions that will encourage them to *argue* a point one way or another. I often say, "There is no right answer to this question. You can argue that it was mainly an economic matter, in which case you need to use the information about the economic changes. Or you can argue that it was mainly a cultural matter, in which case you need to show the reader how these cultural issues led to all those complications. Remember that when you are writing a paper you are doing three things. One is to *inform* the reader about what happened. The second, equally important, is to *explain* to the reader why it happened. And third, also vital, is to *persuade* the reader that your explanation is the right one. As the reader goes through the paper, she must gain a sense of conviction that you are explaining the events and issues in the most convincing way possible.

"As a writer you are like a guide. Just as the guide who takes you around Thomas Jefferson's house, Monticello, will say, 'Look at these devices Jefferson invented to help him copy his letters and get his dinner,' so you have got to say to the reader, in effect, 'See how these economic problems made the failure of those early irrigation schemes inevitable.' You are a guide, and if you are a good one you should always be anticipating the reader's objections, questions, and puzzles, and trying to meet them with convincing writing." Just occasionally a student is really able to argue a case in this way—I tend to reward them even if the argument itself is not really watertight.

Second, they almost all use unnecessarily complicated language. Another of my endlessly repeated remarks is, "It's harder to write simple prose than to write complicated prose. Aim for simplicity." Many of them have been exposed to awful academic prose and have begun to think that making their sentences long and complicated will give them greater authority. Once I experimented with simple sentences, and required every member of a class to write a five-hundred-word paper using no sentence longer than ten words. It was an eerie and rather wonderful experience, as though the entire group had just begun to learn English and didn't trust themselves with anything ambitious. I copied a few of them and I'll give you an excerpt so that you can get the feeling. "Roosevelt was inaugurated in 1933. At once he told Congress to stop the Depression. In 100 days they passed many laws. They created the National Recovery Administration. It organized businesses. They had to stop cutthroat competition. Republicans were angered. Democrats were enthused. Then he ended prohibition. People could drink beer legally again. They were grateful." It was stultifying but at least half successful, and I called it to the students' minds next time they had to write. It forced them to get right to the point.

Third, they make elementary grammatical mistakes. One of them is the confusion of singular and plural in the same sentence. For example, "The average American would stop at nothing to beat the Japanese and they were determined to avenge Pearl Harbor." It doesn't sound too bad, but the sentence really implies that "they" is a reference to "the Japanese" (a plural noun), and not to "the average American" (singular). Equally common is the confusion of verb tenses in the same sentence. "The British aren't ready for Washington's surprise attack and when he crosses the Delaware they were overrun almost before they noticed it." Use of the present tense in writing historical narrative is common; nearly all the students do it. I think the reason is that they have seen lots of TV documentaries that use this technique to give their stories a "you are there" feeling (I'm doing it myself in this book). I always write in the margin, "Use the past tense when describing events that took place in the past." I can tolerate it if they are consistent with the present tense throughout. They are rarely consistent, however, and go jumping back and forth between present and past, often within the same sentence.

Few of them know what the pluperfect tense is, because they haven't got that far yet in their study of a foreign language (if they have studied one at all). I spent a lot of time explaining it to a student last term, and she was as delighted as if she had found a new form of communication, previously unknown. I said, "Sometimes in historical writing you find yourself looking back on people in history who themselves were looking further back in history. That's when you use the pluperfect tense. For example, 'The Confederate leaders argued that secession was permissible because the sovereignty of the states had preceded the sovereignty of the federal union.' *Had preceded* is a pluperfect. So is *had eaten,* in 'She did not want a sandwich because she had eaten earlier in the day.'"

Hardly any students know the past participle of the verb *to lead.* In a group of thirty papers twenty-five will say something like this: "Sherman was a tireless commander and he lead his army to victory." That could be a confusion of verb tenses, but it's more often just a spelling mistake. And if *led* and *lead* are rarely distinguished, even rarer is it to find students who know the rules for apostrophes. Picking up at random a paper from last term that the student failed to collect, my eye at once falls upon this sentence: "American's eagerly snatched up all the manufactured good's they could afford." Confusion is absolute when it comes to *its* and *it's* and on the question of whether the apostrophe goes before or after the s when making possessive and plural a singular noun that ends with s. I tried writing out the rules and handing them out with the paper assignment, but it had no perceptible effect on what came back. If anything, the tangles they got into were worse than ever. You sometimes hear the argument that the language is always evolving and that it doesn't do to impose hard and fast rules. If so, I'm almost ready to throw in the towel on the apostrophe and advocate its complete abandonment. But only almost. Until someone in a high place (like the editor of the *New York Times*) declares that from now on the apostrophe is out, I am going to continue my vain and bitter rearguard action on its behalf and doggedly circle in red every misused (or omitted) apostrophe on every student paper, writing in the margin: "Learn the apostrophe rules!"

Students bristle when you point out grammatical errors. One of the commonest irritable statements I get from those whose grades are rather low is, "This isn't an English course. You shouldn't grade me down for grammatical mistakes." One of my colleagues tells them, "If you want to write it in German you may do so, but it must still be grammatical." I tell them, "It's true that we should not have to be concentrating on grammatical issues now that you are a college student. This is certainly something you should have mastered many years ago. But since you have not mastered it, I must point out to you all these elementary grammatical matters and insist that you work to correct them. Do you remember me telling you that one of your jobs in writing the paper is to *persuade* the reader that your way of looking at the issue is the best way?" "Yes . . ." "Well, you know how it is: when you want to persuade someone you have to convince them that you are trustworthy and that you really know what you are talking about. If the reader finds elementary grammatical mistakes in the paper, especially ones which actually obscure the meaning, as these often do, he's unlikely to think, 'Here's someone I can trust.' To be convincing, you've got to be flawless in your writing and editing. Those are the building blocks without which nothing you say will be convincing."

Plagiarism

One of the sorrows of a professor's life, closely related to the assigning and grading of papers, is plagiarism. We have here a bizarre system for dealing with it. Professors are not allowed to confront students they suspect of cheating. Instead they must report their suspicions to the Honor Council, which sends a student representative who interviews the professor for the evidence. The Honor Council notifies the student and schedules a hearing, which often takes place several weeks later. At the hearing, the accused sits at a big table along with the members of the Honor Council, all of whom are also undergraduates. One (nonvoting) faculty advisor is also present. Witnesses are called in one by one, who give their evidence and leave. The accused makes a statement, answers questions, and brings in witnesses of his own (including character witnesses to vouch for his inner goodness). Then the accused leaves and the Honor Council deliberates. It needs a unanimous verdict of guilty to convict; if there is a conviction the council then decides on a sanction. The sanctions tend to be mild, sometimes merely requiring the student to actually do the work he or she was supposed to do in the first place, but could include an F for the course or even expulsion. Even then the sanction doesn't always stick because the relevant associate dean is permitted to reduce sentences.

It's an unsatisfactory system, disliked by many of the faculty, including me. Why? First because it prevents cases from ever being cleared up quickly. Because cheating is common the Honor Council is overworked, so cases are often pending for weeks or even months at a time. When the cheating takes place at the end of term, in final papers or final exams, the council members and cheaters all have gone, or are in the midst of going, home for vacation so a hearing cannot be scheduled until the next semester. That's bad enough, but even worse is midsemester cheating. In those cases the student and professor continue to meet in every class session while the case awaits a hearing, each of them feeling aggrieved by the other. Students sometimes spread the word that they've been accused, and allege that the professor is prejudiced against them. It poisons the mood of trust and purposefulness that normally makes teaching and learning such a mutual pleasure.

The second weakness of this system is that the accused sometimes turns the hearing into an inquisition against the accusing professor. If the professor doesn't have tenure it becomes a real ordeal—she feels she's the one on trial, even though she merely did what she was supposed to do. And since she is only in the room to give her evidence, she is unable to refute allegations made against her, behind her back, by the accused.

The third weakness is that the system, run by students, often lets the guilty get away with it by mistake. The student members of the Honor Council whom I have known have been a conscientious bunch, doing the best they can. But I've had several of them in class, and know that they cannot always spot obvious cases of plagiarism because they lack the necessary skill and experience as writers. Similarly, the evidence brought to them by science and mathematics professors is sometimes too technical for them to grasp.

The result is cynicism on all sides. Most professors I know simply deal with cheating cases on their own, reluctant to undergo the ordeal that follows from reporting a case. In doing so they're technically violating the honor code themselves, but after getting burned a couple of times when they tried to do the right thing they've drawn the appropriate conclusion. Their own sanctions vary widely, with the result that no two cases of cheating get treated in quite the same way. It's a far cry from places like the military academies, the University of Virginia, or Washington and Lee University, where honor is a central preoccupation, and where the *only* sanction for violating the honor code is expulsion, and where appeals take the form of a solemn public hearing that all members of the community can attend.

In history courses plagiarism is the commonest form of cheating. It takes various forms, and has changed with recent technological advances, but the reasons for it have stayed more or less the same. Some students plagiarize because they are lazy. It's easy to get a book on the subject of your paper, then just copy out a few paragraphs and save the otherwise strenuous labor of researching, planning, and writing the paper as assigned. The really lazy ones can't even be bothered to find a book different from those assigned by the professor, and they are correspondingly easy to catch. The tough ones are savvy enough to explore the library and find a book that's a little off the beaten track. Some subjects are small enough that a decent professor is always going to know the likely places to look. Other subjects, such as the American Civil War and the French Revolution are so massive, and the literature on them so extensive, that it's going to be harder to find the source. One of the worst feelings I get as a teacher comes from reading a paper by a student whose work has shown him throughout the semester to be idle and weak, realizing that it is plagiarized but being unable to recognize the source. The telltale sign is that the writing is much too accomplished, the analysis too cogent, and the vocabulary too rich. Students who previously couldn't get agreement of verb tenses in a sentence and didn't know how to use apostrophes are not suddenly going to write resonant prose full of artful sustained metaphors and skillful analogies.

It can take hours and hours of library research to find the source of the cheating—often you never do discover it because the plagiarist has shrewdly held onto the library's only copy of the book throughout the grading period. Without the actual source, the Honor Council will not convict, even when the internal evidence is overwhelming. Once, when I was faculty advisor to the Honor Council, we were reviewing such a case. I said to the accused student, "Define the word *hegemony* for me." She could not do so. "What made you use this word, whose meaning you did not know, in your paper?" "Er . . . it just sounded right in the context," she said. "I see. What does *proletarianization* mean?" "It means having a lot of children." "Oh! Why did you use that word since your paper has nothing to do with children?" The verdict from the Honor Council was . . . not guilty.

Another form of lazy plagiarism comes from students who belong to fraternities and sororities, which keep files of papers from all their members' courses. Stories circulate among professors about papers that have appeared in their courses year after year, unchanged. The way to forestall this kind of plagiarism is not to assign the same question twice. The trick is to make it almost more trouble for the students to cheat than to actually do what they are supposed to do. You're still not exempt from the frat paper. I've heard lots of times about students just looking for the closest key word in the frat file and handing in the same old stuff, often bearing only the faintest and most distant resemblance to the question asked.

A third form of lazy plagiarism is the straight copy, which pairs of friends quite often attempt. In a big class, say forty students or more, this is a method that sometimes works. If the professor reads the first of two identical papers seventh out of forty, and the second thirty-fifth out of forty, he's unlikely to make the match. This is particularly true if one of the two students *actually wrote the paper*. If it is plagiarized from a published source its high quality is going to make it suspicious, but if it's written in the usual student way, only a professor with almost superhuman powers of alertness is going to make the match. One of the difficulties in grading a batch of papers (all in answer to the same question) is that the stumbling, ungrammatical mess of one blurs into the fumbling unenlightened mess of the next. Much head shaking and coffee drinking is needed to keep clear where one stopped and the next started, even though you gave the first one a grade and wrote some of the usual comments on it before turning to the next.

I had a straight-copy plagiarism case a couple of years ago, with an unusual angle. One student had been in the big computer lab writing her paper. She left the computer on and the file open for a few minutes while she went to the bathroom, and another member of the course, who had a work-study job at the lab, walked by and noticed the subject of the writing on-screen. Having fallen behind with her own work she seized her opportunity and pressed the print button. She was crafty enough to stick in her own introduction and conclusion, but the twelve substantive paragraphs of the paper were entirely the first student's writing. As it happened, I read them with only one other paper intervening. The force was strong with me that day and I had a vivid sense of deja vu, flipped back from the second to the first paper, and beheld the identical paragraphs. At that stage I didn't know which of the two of them was the author and which the copier, or whether the two of them had collaborated. This was the middle of the semester and I feared the worst—a long delay. Even so I reported the case to the Honor Council. When it came time to give back the papers to the whole group, I followed my usual practice of handing them out at the end of class as the students were leaving. The two students in question were therefore left in the room after everyone else had gone. When they asked for their papers all I was allowed to say was, "I have handed them over to the Honor Council and I'm not allowed to discuss it with you." Both made vehement protestations of innocence and both continued to come to class. It's tough trying to ignore something like that, and I felt queasy every time I saw them. After a week, however, the cheater's nerve broke and she admitted to the other student, and then to the Honor Council representative, what she had done. She was given an Honor Council F for the course and I saw her no more. The other, fully exonerated, went on to get a decent grade, leaving me with a sense of shame for having doubted her.

Not all cases have such a tidy solution. A student who had been in one of my introductory classes had done badly. To my dismay he showed up the next semester in my environmental history course. He was never willing or able to volunteer a remark, never understood what he had read, was hopeless at reading aloud, and showed every sign of indifference and distraction. He could spend an entire hour picking at the frayed edge of his sweater, without glancing up or showing any sign of awareness that educational activities were going on around him. Halfway through the term he disappeared for two weeks. When he showed up again after six consecutive absences, I asked him to stay behind for a moment after class. "Where have you been?" "Something really horrible happened, and I had to go home and spend a while with my mother." "Oh, dear, what was that?" "I woke up one morning and found there was a worm on my leg." Further questions elicited reassuring information; the worm was not poisonous and had not harmed him in any way except by actually being there. But, he said, it had "grossed him out" so much that he lost his ability to work and could hardly bring himself to go back into his apartment. Mom, in Tuscaloosa, was the alternative.

I chivvied him along and tried to help him catch up with the work he had missed. That term, to avoid the monotony of reading thirty versions of the same paper, I had invited the students to choose any issue in American environmental history on which to research and write their final papers, subject only to checking in with me that their topic was suitable. The potheads in the group had chosen the history of hemp, as usual, and the rest had singled out a wide variety of different topics, but this chap said he just couldn't think of anything. "Would you," said I, "like me to suggest a topic?" "Yes," said he. So I asked him to write about the history of wind-generated electric power and its early technical development. I gave him the titles of a few books and articles he could read on the subject too. When the paper came in, however, it carried all the telltale signs. Marvelously well-written paragraphs, packed with accurate technical information, filled page after page, and all of it sounded familiar. I went to the library and got one of the books I had assigned. There were all those paragraphs, exactly as written in the paper.

"Can I bear to turn it over to the Honor Council?" I wondered. No, I couldn't bear it. Instead I called him in again and said, "Look, you've copied out nearly all this paper from the book." He looked straight into my eyes, not in a challenging way but just in a matter-of-fact, business-as-usual way, and said, "Yes, I did." "But that's plagiarism. It's forbidden by the university honor code. I can't accept this work and I ought to hand you over to the Honor Council. Why did you do it?" "Well, this guy knows far more about the subject than me!" (also said without any sense of incongruity or shame). I said he would have to do the assignment properly, read a variety of sources, think over their implications, and create a historical narrative based on what he had learned. He was indignant, "What?! Do the paper again?! I'm a graduating senior." "You haven't done it once yet." "Oh, don't be ridiculous. None of my other professors have ever done this to me." I thought that was a remarkable admission—indicating that he hadn't treated only my assignment this way but did it routinely. With much ill grace and complaining he went off, did the assignment, and handed in a thoroughly inferior piece of work, whose badness assured me that it really was his. He got the lowest passing grade and gave me a killing look when I happened to catch sight of him on graduation day.

All these were, in a sense, cases of plagiarism induced by laziness. Another form is greed-plagiarism, in which students are so hungry for A's on their transcripts that they leave nothing to chance and present the work of others, cleverer than themselves, as though they had written it. They can be tough to catch because they're often intelligent and motivated, albeit in a dishonest way. Occasionally they even intersperse their own sentences with those they have copied out, to throw the bloodhounds off their scent.

Finally come the hopeless cases, students who are in over their heads and don't really know how to write a paper but are too embarrassed to ask for the help they obviously need. I had the job of supervising one in 1995, while she did an internship with a brokerage company. I told her that to get credit for the internship she would have to write a historical research paper related to the work she had been doing. Her company traded with Mexico, so, after much uncertainty and to-ing and fro-ing, she decided to write on the negotiation of the North American Free Trade Agreement (NAFTA) back in the early 1990s. The paper came in with every sign of plagiarism. Much of it was written in the prose of international law, and it was clearly the work of a deeply informed expert. My favorite passage of the paper (remember, this was 1995) said, "This interim phase of the negotiations has settled the quota issue, but the enumerated items remain to be negotiated when deliberations resume in June 1993." I handed it over to the Honor Council but got a call from the professor it assigned to be faculty advisor. Normally he's a tiger in such matters, but this time the student's sheer bewilderment had turned him into a lamb. "We can't sanction this kid for plagiarism because she simply doesn't know what it is. When I asked her about it, she couldn't grasp the concept, and when I showed her that sentence about 1993 she couldn't see why it was incriminating." "Well if she's that incompetent can we at least give her a straight F instead of an Honor Council F?" That's what we did, but I still had to endure a long and painful session in office hours while she berated me for ignoring all her hard work and for being prejudiced against her.

The fastest-growing form of plagiarism is Internet-related. One semester I assigned a paper that required the students to consider the seven movies they had watched during the term, and to compare the version of events depicted there with the events that had actually taken place (about which they had done intensive reading). It was a tough paper assignment, since it required them to keep two chronologies in mind: the historical chronology itself, and the twentieth-century chronology of the films. Some of the students were annoyed to discover that the film directors had not obliged them by making the earliest film depict the earliest historic events. That was only one of the many conceptual tangles the assignment created.

The paper written by a student I'll just call Z consisted of a summary of the seven films' plots. I gave it a C+ and wrote something like this: "You have been studying this subject for fifteen weeks but no one would know it from this paper, in which you have hardly done more than summarize the plots of the seven films, throwing in occasional references to the history that lay behind them. Also, you have clearly used outside sources to get those plot summaries. You must footnote them" (the paper had no documentation). About two papers later another student made a mistake in his description of the events in *The Great Dictator*. To check on the sequence (I knew he was wrong but couldn't quite remember the order of events), I went on the Web and just typed in "Charlie Chaplin, *Great Dictator*." Up came a long list of relevant sites and I clicked on the first of them. After reading for a minute I realized that this was prose I had read somewhere else very recently. I checked back to student Z's paper, and there, sure enough, unchanged, were the same words. I noted the site's name and checked to see whether it offered plot summaries of the other films we had seen. It did, and I found that Z had followed the same procedure with all of them. I got on the phone to the Honor Council at once.

Plagiarism always has an effect on me—an invariably bad effect. First, it shows that the student wasn't willing to do the work he or she was supposed to do, and looked for an easy way out. That in turn suggests a lack of interest in the course. It would be nice to think that, after paying the incredible sums they or their parents shell out for tuition, they would take it seriously. Most do, but some don't. The easy way out, plagiarism, also suggests that the student doesn't expect to get caught. In other words, they think the professors aren't clever enough to catch them. That's why, when you *do* catch one, it's hard not to feel at least a little gleeful pleasure. You know: "Gotcha!!" But along with that feeling comes a queasy, unhappy feeling: "The kid thought I was stupid and that everything I'd taught him didn't really matter. It was just for a grade, and he was willing to get the grade any old how."

Discussions of Honor Council reform that suggest the professor ought to have more say in what happens to the cheater often run up against the stumbling block of professors' righteous anger. I admit it: the righteous anger is real. I've had moments of fury about it, especially when the cheat is a student to whom I have given a lot of time and attention. There aren't many feelings worse than feeling betrayed, and plagiarists can bring it on in a sharp and acid form. Actually, I suppose the last thing on the plagiarists' minds is the professor's reaction—I doubt it even occurs to one in fifty. They are usually desperate to get something finished and handed in on time, and just hope the professor won't notice. In everyday life, moreover, they are surrounded by examples of cheating—in filing taxes, in using fake IDs to get alcohol, in sexual relationships, and in sports. College cheating probably seems like fair game, too—they probably think of it as a victimless crime.

Another way in which plagiarism is sickening to a teacher (or at least to this teacher) is that it jaundices the way you look at students' work in general. When, in a pile of mediocre work, you finally encounter a well-written paper, almost the first thing you think is, "It could be plagiarized." If it's *very* good, the thought that you've got an excellent student in your class jostles against the thought that you've got another cheat. In other words, you're going to react strongly one way or another, and when what you hoped turns out to be what you feared (yet again), the disappointment is all the more nauseating.

CHAPTER

8

■ ■ ■

Treats and Tribulations

Appreciation (Thursday Evening)

Last night I went to a reception at the "Outdoor Emory" house. I mentioned it about a week ago, when Molly Cobbs invited me to be her guest. The house itself is one of several "theme houses" on campus, in which students with common interests live. There's also a Spanish house nearby in which Spanish language and culture enthusiasts gather—they've asked me to be a judge of a photography contest they're having later this term. The Outdoor house used to be a fraternity whose members were so wicked they were finally thrown off campus. They amused themselves in the farewell days of their tenancy by burning the doors off their hinges, slashing the furniture, and stubbing out cigarettes on the carpets, so the place had to have a fairly extensive makeover before the rugged mountaineering set could move in. It's a jolly little gathering this evening, and I'm no sooner through the door than I begin to see familiar faces, including many of the students from last term's environmental history class. They're dressed up and on their best behavior—Molly is wearing a dress, whereas I usually see her on campus dressed in such a way that if I were to say to her, "Let's go and save an endangered species in mountainous terrain right now," she'd be able to jump to it without a backward glance or so much as a change of footwear. We have dessert and coffee and the students I have taught in previous years gather round to reminisce. Then they show me pictures of expeditions their group has undertaken. Last weekend they went skiing in North Carolina. At Christmas a group of them camped and hiked through Zion National Park in Utah, and another set went snowshoeing in New Mexico. The trips are ambitious and the participants fearless.

Talking with them, admiring the pictures, discussing river rafting and mountaineering trips, and generally talking up the great outdoors, reminded me of Christopher McCandless, who graduated from Emory just a year or two after I got here. He had always been talented and hardworking, but he became estranged from the normal privileged young American's way of life. After graduation he drove off across America, eventually abandoning his car beside a deserted wash in a remote part of Arizona, just as he abandoned every sign and symbol of his privileged upbringing. He began to hitchhike around the Southwest instead, and sailed the lower reaches of the Colorado River in a canoe he found. He did migrant farmwork in the Dakotas, squatted in a counterculture commune in the desert, and finally set out for Alaska, resolving to live in the wilderness for a season. After hiking in and making a provisional home in an old abandoned bus, he accidentally poisoned himself by confusing an inedible plant with an edible one. Growing ever weaker, and unable to feed or keep himself warm, he finally died of starvation in the old bus and was found there a month or two later by hunters, having written a vivid and revealing diary almost up to the last day. His story is told in Jon Krakauer's *Into the Wild*, and when Krakauer came to Emory to talk about the story he drew a fascinated audience of students who looked at each other as if wondering whether another such soul was among them. If he *had* been in my classes I doubt whether I could have singled him out—I certainly have no talent for guessing what each of them is going to do, and am often amazed a few years later when ex-students come back to report on the way of life they have chosen.

Eleventh Class (Friday)

In the classroom this morning are just twenty of the students, because I have divided the group into two sections in mid alphabet, giving half of them to my teaching assistant, Regina. She is in a room nearby teaching a section for the first time, and as my section progresses I wonder anxiously about how she's getting on. Afterward I see her and it's turned out well. "They actually talked," she says, in her wry, self-deprecating way. "Perhaps it was from pity, but at this stage I'm willing to settle for pity." It's a relief to hear that all went well, and she must have been fine since pity alone would not be sufficient to sustain an hour-long conversation on the Spanish-American war.

My group is lively. I spend the first ten minutes, as stragglers arrive, asking what they thought of *Heartland*. Brianne says it was boring and disgusting. Meredith says she hates to see animals killed and thinks it is wrong. I say, "But Wyoming ranchers did kill animals in 1910. That's just a fact. Is it wrong to represent it in a film?" "It's gross!" Others thought the film was great, loved the emotional understatement, and recognized that the depiction of boredom, if not boredom itself, can be oddly fascinating. Curtis said he liked the way everything you expect doesn't show up. There's no bronco busting, no gunfights, and no soaring violins to mark the major events. I ask whether they foresee being able to use the insight it has given them into western life when it comes to writing their papers, and they look dubious. Then we discuss whether the use of fiction, in books and films, can be useful in the study of history, and they agree that for the study of social history, where it's partly a matter of getting a feel for places and eras, it's ideal.

Now we turn to Theodore Roosevelt's *Rough Riders*. What a lark. He was like a big frat boy, with all its good and all its bad qualities rolled into one and then grotesquely magnified. I reread the book yesterday and this morning in a state of high enjoyment. There aren't many books where you find every element of political correctness violated in quick succession by a man who became president just after writing it. He reels off the ethnic and racial stereotypes one after the next, loves violence, tries to kill every living thing that moves, scarcely acknowledges the existence of women, and falls constantly into unintentional self-parody.

He had an idea about purification through violence, and yearned for a glorious battlefield death. The whole book is written in a ludicrously elevated tone. To hear him tell it, you'd think that every man who joined his volunteer cavalry was obsessed with honor, never flinched in fear, faced death without complaint, and died with scarcely a murmur. The first time they go into battle, Roosevelt says that those who were shot crumpled up without anything more than a "My word!" Men who were badly wounded and had to be shipped off to the rear would sneak out of hospital in order to rejoin the regiment; one man had seven bullet wounds but fought on just the same. We debate the more obvious aspects of Roosevelt's character, the bombast, the egotism, the falsely elevated tone, and the eerie ideals of manliness and courage.

Next I ask Sarah what the Spanish-American War was all about, but she doesn't really know. Simon, who's been in a European history class, describes the imperial context: Britain, France, Germany, and Portugal had large colonial empires, and some Americans, Roosevelt included, wanted one too. They were "Anglo-Saxon destiny" types. Meanwhile, an anti-Spanish revolt had broken out in Cuba. Why not join the rebels in expelling the Spaniards, enforce the Monroe Doctrine, and get the beginnings of an empire into the bargain? "Now, Sarah," I say, "suppose I'm Theodore Roosevelt and I put these ideas to you. Why might you oppose them?" "Because America's just conquered the whole continent?" she says (weird answer; possibly a throwback to the discussion of Turner last week). "Well, possibly. Why else?" She looks puzzled and her voice keeps getting quieter, but I won't let her off the hook. "How if, today, I said to you, 'Sarah, let's invade Brazil and make it part of the American empire,' would you agree?" "No." "Why?" "Because a lot of other nations might fight against us on the Brazilian side." "OK. So there is a prudential argument against going to war. Are there any others." She gives me the I-don't-have-the-faintest-idea-what-you're-talking-about stare so I say, "Well, do you think it's OK to kill large groups of Brazilians?" "Oh, no!" "Well then . . . ?" "There was a moral objection?" "Yes, exactly. And why should some Americans feel a particularly strong moral objection about a war like this?" "Because America itself had once been a colony fighting against an imperial power, and ought not to do the same in return." "Exactly." Chloe points out that Roosevelt can use this argument in his favor—he can say he's just doing what the French did during the

American Revolutionary War—helping a colonized people get free of its tyrannical European overlord. True.

Last week I asked all of them to mark key passages in their books. Now I call on Karen to read one of her chosen passages. She reads it, and it's an excellent choice, but unfortunately she's slightly misunderstood its meaning. Roosevelt says that during lulls in the campaign he was reading a book on Anglo-Saxon superiority by a Frenchman, who nevertheless agreed with the basic principle! According to this author, the Anglo-Saxons had never had a highly militarized society, the kind, common in Europe, which robs the people of all initiative. Roosevelt chuckles to the reader that in his experience militarization has been all a matter of taking the initiative. The American expedition to Cuba was so badly organized, the food so deficient, the medical supplies and staff so inadequate, the transport so badly arranged and inferior, and the weapons so defective, that only by seizing supplies, requisitioning space on ships, and occasionally even paying for the regiment's food out of his own pocket could he keep the Rough Riders going at all.

Flora reads aloud a passage that had drawn my eye too; it's one of the un-PC bits. "No troops could have behaved better than the colored soldiers had behaved so far; but they are, of course, peculiarly dependent upon their white officers. Occasionally they produce non-commissioned officers who can take the initiative and accept responsibility precisely like the best class of whites; but this cannot be expected normally, nor is it fair to expect it." Some class members see the passage as a fairly blunt example of racism, others attribute it merely to ignorance, but others again say it's simply Roosevelt's actual observation. I urge Flora to read more lines a bit further down the page, when some of the black soldiers begin leaving the ranks while under fire.

This I could not allow as it was depleting my line, so I jumped up, and walking a few yards to the rear, drew my revolver, halted the retreating soldiers, and called out to them that I appreciated the gallantry with which they had fought and would be sorry to hurt them, but that I should shoot the first man who, on any pretence whatever, went to the rear . . . I ended my statement to the colored soldiers by saying "Now I shall be very sorry to hurt you, and you don't know whether or not I will keep my word, but my men can tell you that I always do"; whereupon my cow-punchers, hunters, and miners solemnly nodded their heads and commented in chorus, exactly as if in a comic opera, "He always does; he always does!"

This was the end of the trouble for the "smoked Yankees"—as the Spaniards called the colored soldiers—flashed their white teeth at one-another, as they broke into broad grins, and I had no more trouble with them. (87–88)

The consensus that Roosevelt is just a downright racist grows after this passage, especially (one student shrewdly notes) because of the fact that TR gives it a comic and slightly burlesque turn, even though the situation could equally be described in really horrific terms.

We have a few more passages. Chris picks out this marvelous sentence: "We drew recruits from Harvard, Yale, Princeton, and many another college . . . and from among the men who belonged neither to club nor to college but in whose veins the blood stirred with the same impulse which once sent the Vikings over sea." I end class by reading my own favorite, which comes not from TR's text but from Edmund Morris's introduction. "Modern day readers of *The Rough Riders* will notice, as did contemporary critics, that Roosevelt has a fondness for the personal pronoun that borders on the erotic. (It was rumored that typesetters of the first edition had to send out for an extra supply of the letter 'I.') But there is something engaging about the boyishness of his vanity, the force and clarity of his prose, and the acts of bravery he truthfully narrates." The class breaks up in good humor; it's been much easier and more satisfying to conduct discussion with twenty than with forty. Next week we're reading the first volume of *Living My Life*, by Emma Goldman, and I'll be teaching the other half of the class.

Another passage I meditated upon but didn't have time to discuss aloud with the class was one in which TR reminded me of myself. Just as I often say, "I'm the teacher, you're the student," so Roosevelt believed strongly in the principle, "I'm the officer, you're the enlisted man." He expressed it like this:

It is a mistake for an officer ever to grow too familiar with his men, no matter how good they are; and it is of course the greatest possible mistake to seek popularity either by showing weakness or by mollycoddling the men. They will never respect a commander who does not enforce discipline, who does not know his duty, and who is not willing both himself to encounter and to make them encounter every species of danger and hardship when necessary. The soldiers who do not feel this way are not worthy of the name and should be handled with iron severity until they become fighting men and not shams. (110)

Let me paraphrase, making allowance for our different occupations: "It is a mistake for a professor ever to grow too familiar with his students, no matter how good they are; and it is of course the greatest possible mistake to seek popularity either by showing weakness or by mollycoddling the students. They will never respect a professor who does not enforce discipline, who does not know his duty, and who is not willing both himself to encounter and to make them encounter every species of reading and writing assignment when necessary. The students who do not feel this way are not worthy of the name and should be handled with icy formality until they become industrious and not laggards." Well, I'm not a mollycoddler, exactly, but neither do I ever show much in the way of "iron discipline."

Twelfth Class (Monday)

I developed a cold on Saturday evening. It came on suddenly while I was watching an extremely depressing French film, *The Diary of a Country Priest*. The combination of the film and the miserable anticipation of illness gave me a couple of morbid hours. After a huge sleep I felt a little better but was still rocky on Sunday afternoon. I lay in bed and began reading next Friday's class assignment, *Living My Life*, volume 1, by Emma Goldman. It's wonderful, melodramatic, gripping, and a good antidote to my condition.

My health does strange independent things, just as parts of my body used to take independent actions when I was a beginning lecturer. When I'm ill but have to teach, the illness goes away, and it does not come back until that class is finished. It's almost as though it is willing to lend me the necessary health for a while, but only by charging interest on the transaction. A few years ago I was seriously ill with pneumonia. I never missed class, however, because as the time to teach approached, I would recover and do it all in the usual way. Afterward I would feel wretched and often retire to bed for the rest of the day. Confident of this pattern, I had no hesitation in going ahead with class today, and found, yet again, that so long as it was going on, I was completely unaware of the heavy head, swollen nose, coughing, and gasping I'd been suffering for the past couple of days.

This morning I had some catching up to do. I got to class early, installed a new projector bulb, and showed the rest of the urban history slides from last Monday while the students were coming in. Next I called roll and spent fifteen minutes bringing the election of 1896 to its dramatic climax (the thing I was supposed to do last Wednesday). To mark a break I then asked various students to come to the blackboard to draw bicycles. The first one, Kathleen, did a picture that made me ask her, "Have you ever seen a bicycle?" It was just two circles and three sticks, all in the wrong places. In her defense she said she didn't have a bicycle. A second, Michael, tried to modify it but added some more grotesqueries, and soon the whole class was laughing. A third, Nigel, came to the board, erased the bizarre hybrid, and drew one of his own, which was at least half-accurate. I thanked him and then moved on to today's principal subject; the development of mass production. The bicycle industry was the first American industry to achieve mass production through complete interchangeability of parts. In other words, the parts were manufactured so accurately that any set of the components would fit together into any instance of the finished product. Until then manufacturers like Colt, the gun maker, and Singer, the sewing-machine maker, had used "fitters," who tinkered with the almost identical components, filing, sawing, and fiddling until they could be put together to make one decent machine.

I showed some bicycle slides, explaining how the League of American Wheelmen had campaigned for improved roads, to make cycling easier, and how the safety bicycle had displaced the "ordinary," with its giant front wheel and tiny trailing wheel. The safety bicycle (the same basic pattern as the ones we ride today) was advertised through campaigns that emphasized ease and safety—even mothers with little babies could ride them. Another slide showed a bicycle ad emphasizing the independence a man could get by cycling to work instead of riding the crowded streetcar; his red blood would flow, he'd feel invigorated, and he would throw off the early morning blahs. It's all true—I too commute by bicycle.

Central to this lecture is Henry Ford and the way in which he brought mass production techniques to the auto industry. He was influenced not only by the bicycle makers but also by the slaughterhouses. They disassembled cows and pigs on a moving line; he assembled cars in more or less the same way. I explained how his factories became so good at it that they were producing cars at the rate of more than one per minute by the second decade of the twentieth century. To make sure that he wouldn't run out of potential buyers, Ford also had the daring idea of paying his workers a lot more than the prevailing rate. That was also a way to build worker loyalty, at a time when turnover in his plant had been 300 percent per year. He raised the daily wage for assembly-line men from $1.50 to $5.00. Although the men still hated the boredom of doing one simple repetitive task, this huge pay raise induced them to put up with it, in return for incomes which permitted them to become Ford owners as well as builders. Pictures of the Ford factory in operation brought the lecture to an end. No sooner had class finished than I felt terrible again—the debit side of my cold was exacting tribute for the hour of buoyant health it had lent me.

Teaching Grown-Ups

If I have a general criticism to make of young undergraduates it is that most of them take it all for granted. They come to class, take notes, and go out again, speak if spoken to, and occasionally throw in an unsolicited remark. What many of them never show, except the handful to whom I give a lot of personal or remedial help, is gratitude. Admittedly I'm being paid for the work, but teaching is vocational as well as professional, and it would be pleasant to enjoy, a little more often, the sense that students were grateful for what their teachers give them. Sometimes I spend ages writing a new lecture or rewriting one that has gone out of date, and yet, when I deliver it, along with the usual oratorical fireworks and audio-visuals, they sit there, calm, polite, and utterly noncommittal. Some take notes.

What a contrast with my experience in teaching adult groups. About six years ago a group of senior citizens contacted Emory's public relations office to ask if it could recommend someone to teach their evening history group. The office suggested me, and the group's leader phoned to see if I was interested. I went to visit her, and that was the beginning of a long and highly pleasurable relationship, which continues up to the present. She is a distinguished widow of about seventy-five, and lives in a comfortable gated community just off Paces Ferry Road, in the Buckhead district of Atlanta. She explained that her group met on the second and fourth Monday of every month between September and April, but with a break for Christmas, such that they held twelve meetings per year in all. The group's members, she added, were all senior citizens, all highly educated and formerly people of power and position in the city and its principal businesses. They were willing to pay a little for the teacher. I agreed to try it and began the following fall.

I was extremely nervous the first time but got such a hearty welcome, and found that my talks were greeted so warmly, that it soon turned into sheer pleasure. The meetings take place in members' houses, and so each year I make a tour of twelve opulent dwellings. A few have black servants, and over one or two the faintest whiff of the antebellum South still hangs. Even those of my hosts who are managing for themselves manage very well indeed. The usual format is that I speak for an hour, from 7:30 to 8:30, then we have half an hour of refreshments in the adjacent dining room, and finally I gather them together again for another half-hour, during which I say more on my general topic while encouraging questions. Nearly every session ends with each one of them coming up to shake hands and thank me ardently. They tell me they are amazed at what a lot I know, and that I'm bringing history to life for them. These compliments are music to my ears; it would take a stronger personality than mine to be immune to such a show of open-hearted gratitude and courtesy.

Another great difference between them and the undergraduates is the fact of their age and experience. The undergraduates now in college were born in the 1980s, so nearly all of them are too young to remember the Cold War—the huge fact with which everyone in my generation grew up, and of whose end we had no premonition almost until the moment it happened. They cannot remember the first George Bush, in many cases, and have been sentient really only since the Clinton years. The elderly members of the senior citizen group, by contrast, were born in the years between 1910 and 1930—the oldest is ninety—and they have lived through most of the events I discuss whenever I do a twentieth-century topic.

I remember a couple of years ago, when my theme was leadership in British history. I was talking about Winston Churchill in the 1930s and the way in which, at that time, he was out of favor in the Tory Party and widely regarded as a belligerent old dinosaur, a leftover from darker ages. One of the group, who is now in his eighties, said that while he was studying at the London School of Economics in 1937, he had gone to the House of Commons and heard Churchill make an impassioned speech about rearmament. Most of the men are World War II veterans with wonderful powers of reminiscence—a few weeks ago one of them told me about sailing back and forth across the Atlantic on a convoy-escort destroyer. After the war several of them worked for international banks and businesses that posted them overseas—one was head of Coca Cola Europe for fifteen years and has traveled throughout the world. Even today they take ambitious holidays, cruises through the Baltic and Mediterranean, rent houses in Scandinavia, Spain, and Britain, tour Ecuador and Peru, and live to the absolute limits of their physical strength. Some are frail in body but nearly all are of sound mind and still full of will and daring.

Teaching them (I have now done it for five consecutive years) is an unalloyed pleasure. They don't have reading and writing assignments and so don't have to be nagged about that; they aren't being evaluated so there are no irksome finals to grade; and they are there purely from choice because they love to carry on learning. As the end of each season approaches the members begin to say how much they hope I'll come again next year, and their warmth, generosity, gratitude, and enthusiasm make it hard to say no. I keep telling myself I must say no because I have so many other commitments and so many as-yet-unfinished writing assignments. But each time, the pleas have reached a climax on the last day, we're all awash with emotion, so there and then I make a firm promise to see them again in September.

There's a lot to be said for adult education. As the baby boomers age and as the general level of public health keeps improving, more and more oldies are taking a serious interest in higher education. Entrepreneurs, realizing the growth of demand, are setting in motion a variety of continuing education programs. Earlier this year I made a series on American religious history for one of them, The Teaching Company. It consists of twenty-four half-hour lectures on American religious history, and is now available on video, audio cassette, or CD. I recorded it during an enjoyable week at the company's studios outside Washington D.C., in January, and next winter I'll be doing a second series, on Victorian Britain. Reader: permit me to recommend these series—along with all the Teaching Company's work—to your sympathetic attention.

Restful Moments (Tuesday)

I'd just come back from lunch and, feeling slow and dull, decided to take a nap. Professors everywhere will confirm that ten-minute naps on the floor are reviving—some of the best sleep I ever get—and energize me for the rest of the day. You might almost call them common. Often a nap ends with a knock on the door or the ringing of the phone. When it's the phone I lurch up, shake my head awake, remind myself of who I am and where I am, then answer. Knocks I usually leave unanswered because I look so groggy and disheveled. But today I had no chance. An insolent youth knocked once and then boldly opened the door and entered. Since I was stretched out toward the swinging door, it almost cracked me in the head. He jarred to a stop and made a gargling sound. I think he thought I had collapsed and was in the middle of a medical emergency. I staggered to my feet, popped my glasses on, and said, "Oh, sorry, I was sleeping." It was the best I could come up with while making the transition from deep sleep to full embarrassment in the space of about a second and a half. "Can we do the paperwork for my study abroad?" he asked. "Not now, I'm busy—please come to my office hours instead, tomorrow morning between eight and ten." Busy! He had to accept it, and retreat.

9

Radicals and Patriots

Thirteenth Class (Wednesday)

As students are coming into the classroom, I ask them whether they are making progress with their papers. Karen says she doesn't know how to set about organizing it. I encourage her and everyone else to use chronology as an organizing principle. It's not always the best, but it usually is because it lets readers know the sequence in which events took place, and is given to us ready-made by history itself. I rhapsodize about the power of dates. "They are a wonderful shorthand way of describing many things all at once in the smallest possible space."

There's a long tradition among students of not liking dates, of resenting having to memorize them, and of thinking that history is boring because it consists so much of dates. Teachers have been too willing to give way in the face of this tradition, and the social history revolution, in which trends rather than events make the running, has enabled the anti-date forces to gain headway in the classroom. I'm teaching masses of social history in this course but I'm old-fashioned enough still to love dates. They can't tell you everything but there's no substitute for them, and without them you can't really understand history properly. To Karen I say, "Don't you find dates entrancing little things? Like jewels, almost?" She gives me an uncompromising stare, so I urge her to bring me a draft during office hours.

Today I'm talking about work in the late nineteenth and early twentieth centuries. As the scale of manufacturing grew, fewer workmen actually knew their employers. As work was mechanized, the premium on regularity, punctuality, and sobriety intensified. As production lines went into high gear, work became more monotonous and less skilled. I describe the horrors of child labor, the early struggles of the trade union movement, the bitter battles that surrounded the great railroad strike of 1877, the Haymarket anarchist bomb of 1886, and the Homestead Strike of 1892. We discuss the obstacles confronting men who tried to build trade unions; employers' techniques of dividing and separating their workmen by ethnicity; the temptation to temporary, "birds of passage," immigrants to become strikebreakers; and the use of labor spies. I give a brief summary of the early history of the American Federation of Labor and its first leader, Samuel Gompers (like me, a British immigrant), the early history of the American Socialist Party under Eugene Debs (an ex-railroad-union leader). I contrast Debs's indigenous Christian Socialism with the atheist anarchism of Emma Goldman, Alexander Berkmann, and Big Bill Haywood, the famous chief of the International Workers of the World. It's really too much for one lecture, but the imperious demands of the introductory course force me to move quickly, or I'll never finish the syllabus.

Chloe interrupts my summary description of the anarchists' ideas with a puzzled question: "You mean they didn't believe in government at all?" "Right, and many of them believed that a revolution was necessary to overthrow government, which is why they sometimes committed assassinations, like Berkmann's attempt to kill Henry Clay Frick." "But it's impossible to live without *any* government!" she exclaims. "How do you know?" "I just know what people are like." I respond, "They would have told you that the people you know, because they have grown up under the yoke of political authority, have been distorted by it, and that without government, underlying human powers of generosity and capability would emerge." She wrinkles a lot more furrows into her brow but makes no further remark. "I can see I haven't convinced you, Chloe. That's OK: I'm not asking you to become an anarchist; I'm just asking you to accept the fact that these people were anarchists and that they were wholehearted in their beliefs. Have you begun the Emma Goldman readings for this week?" Chloe answers, "Not really" (student euphemism for "no"). "Well, when you do you'll see that she's a lovable character in some ways, but tempestuous, impractical, and utopian. She's certainly vulnerable to the old charge against anarchists that they're unrealistic about human nature." I don't go on to tell her that lots of historians don't believe there is such a thing as human nature; that might be too much to swallow just now.

For the last ten minutes of class I show the early scenes of Charlie Chaplin's *Modern Times*, with its wonderful parody of life on the production line and the dehumanizing power of technology. It follows nicely from the discussions in the last two classes about the development of mass production. The film begins with a flock of sheep being herded into pens, immediately followed by a sequence showing crowds of men being herded into a factory. In a nice jab at the contrast between owners and workers, we see the men working frantically at the assembly line while the boss calmly adds pieces to a jigsaw puzzle, pausing only to order his foreman to speed up the assembly lines again. A group of inventors comes into his office to show him a new device, a machine that can automatically feed a factory worker while he continues to work on the assembly line, by shoving and tipping food into his mouth.

Charlie's job on the line is just to tighten two nuts on squares of metal as they rapidly pass by him. He does it with a repetitive lurching motion that he cannot stop even when he leaves the line to go to the bathroom or for lunch. The boss chooses him to test the feeding machine, which starts well but gradually goes wrong, tipping soup and cakes over him and forcing him to eat nuts and bolts. It's high-quality slapstick, still entertaining seventy-five years after it was made. We have to stop for lack of time, just when the automatic feeding machine is running out of control and attacking Charlie, so everyone leaves laughing.

A student who had to miss last Friday's discussion section asked me on Monday how he could make up for it. I told him to write and give me a five-hundred-word summary of the Roosevelt book. He gives it to me today as the class ends, so here is the first piece of written work from a student in this course. It's a typical piece of student writing, from someone who has obviously read the book and tried conscientiously to single out the main themes. Here's his first paragraph:

In a time when the United States was vying to be a colonial power and prove supremacy in the western hemisphere, Cuba's cry for freedom from Spain was perfect. At the first sight of risk for Americans and their property, McKinley consented to send in the troops. Roosevelt, Secretary of the Navy, having been steadfastly urging the war and craving to fight in it, rather quickly organized a team of skilled volunteers to fight under his command. When called, they joined the regular cavalry and infantry units in embarkation to Cuba. Some units were, to their disappointment, denied leave for lack of room.

It could be worse. He covers a lot of points quickly and is grammatically sound—he even used an apostrophe correctly. But like most students' writing it shows every sign of inexperience. There are too many participles ("vying," "urging," "craving"). There are too many adverbs and adjectives ("steadfastly," "rather" [in "rather quickly"], and "skilled" should go). The first sentence should begin with *At* rather than *In*, and he should tell the reader when this "time" was by using a date. I understand what he means by "Cuba's cry for freedom from Spain was perfect," but that's because I've read the book. A reader who didn't know the history of these events and had not read the book would be baffled. The sentence implies that Cuba made a perfect cry, rather than (as he intends) that pro-intervention Americans regarded the situation as a perfect opportunity to flex their muscles. You can tell, also, that he doesn't know much about the army. When in the last line of the introduction he says that "some units were . . . denied leave," he wrongly implies that they were forbidden to take a few days off from military life to visit their homes. *Leave* is an ambiguous word. If he had said, "they were denied leave to board the transports and had to be left behind," his meaning would have been clearer, but the ambiguity would have lingered. Better not to have used "leave" at all. He should have written: "Lack of space on the transports obliged some soldiers to remain in the United States, much to their disappointment." That way he could have avoided the "leave" problem and avoided the passive verb "were denied leave," which is weak because it doesn't make clear who did the denying. When he mentions the president for the first time, he should refer to him as President McKinley—nonspecialist readers today might not realize from the paragraph, as written, that "McKinley" is a reference to the president.

I do not write any of this nitpicky criticism of the paragraph on the paper—I can't possibly devote that much time to every paragraph, nor do I want to crush students to the ground with impossibly high demands and my own sometimes quirky editorializing. On the paper I write an S, for satisfactory, mark a couple of grammatical infelicities further on, and leave it at that.

Fourteenth Class (Friday)

Discussion section on Emma Goldman's *Living My Life*. What a wonderful book it is; torrid, passionate, overwrought, dripping with sentiment, self-contradictory, and nutty. I read it this time in a fever of enthusiasm and enjoyment, and when there's time I'll finish it and read volume two as well. The half of the class that was with Regina last week is with me now. Flu is going around and only fourteen out of the expected nineteen have shown up. Sorrowful e-mails have been coming in to account for the remainder. Suddenly a big class has become an intimate one, with a transformed collective personality, and I'm able to make the most of it by getting all of them closely involved in the discussion.

Our conversation about *Living My Life* revolves around two main questions: the justification for political assassinations and the perks, obligations, and duties of a "free lover." Goldman's boyfriend, Alexander Berkmann ("Sasha"), decided, after the Homestead Strike in 1892, to assassinate Henry Clay Frick, who had brought to the steel factories boatloads of Pinkerton detectives and strikebreakers. A day-long gun battle between workers and detectives along the river led to dozens of gunshot wounds and a handful of deaths. Goldman and Berkmann had been drawing up an anarchist manifesto, hampered (but not deterred) by the fact that neither of them could at that stage speak or write English. In a typical passage, Goldman describes hearing the news of the killings,

We saw at once that the time for our manifesto had passed. Words had lost their meaning in the face of the innocent blood spilled on the banks of the Monongahela. Intuitively each felt what was surging in the heart of the other. Sasha broke the silence. "Frick is the responsible factor in this crime," he said; "he must be made to stand the consequences." It was the psychological moment for an *Attentat*: the whole country was aroused, everybody was considering Frick the perpetrator of a coldblooded murder. A blow aimed at Frick would re-echo in the poorest hovel, would call the attention of the whole world to the real cause behind the Homestead struggle. It would also strike terror in the enemy's ranks and make them realize that the proletariat of America had its avengers.

Goldman and Berkmann were so broke that they lacked even the train fare to get to Pittsburgh, and they had no weapons. Berkmann experimented for a while with explosives but in his tests they did not work. Finally he scraped together the money to buy a gun and a ticket. Ordering Emma to stay behind, he went to Pittsburgh and shot Frick three times, then stabbed him with a poisoned dagger—only to have him survive! To Emma, Sasha was a hero, and she was horrified when he was sentenced to twenty-two years in prison. In her view, since Frick didn't die, Berkmann shouldn't be thought of as a murderer—she was hoping for something more like a seven-year sentence. Several of the students could understand Berkmann's logic but none of them went along with it. They're a "prelaw" crowd and don't hold with summary justice.

I want students to be able to read aloud well and confidently—most of them are extremely bad at it and try to resist me when I call them to the front of the room to read aloud to the others. Under duress, however, they make the best of it. Elizabeth selects the passage in which Emma describes how she and another man, Ed Brady, became lovers shortly after Sasha went to prison. Wasn't that a betrayal of her man? No, says David. Emma believes in free love; she thinks of monogamy as selfish and middle-class, and will have nothing to do with it. We speculate on whether Ed admires Sasha or wishes he were completely out of the picture, and another student, Barbara, reads the passage in which Ed (himself a veteran of a ten-year stretch in an Austrian jail for anarchist activities) shows his conservative colors by urging Emma to give up her career as a radical speech maker and settle down with him to have babies. He even denigrates another anarchist woman by predicting that she'll soon have babies, age quickly, and forget all about anarchist idealism. Emma refuses to be tied down and eventually this disagreement leads to a separation.

We discuss the rights and wrongs of her attitude to sex. The students keep on comparing Emma's attitude with their own, and I keep urging them to put it in historical context, mindful of the lecture I did about late nineteenth-century women a week or two ago. Kathleen brings up a comical episode in which Emma decides that she'll raise funds to help Sasha by becoming a prostitute—revolutionary necessity makes it permissible. She gets out onto the street in her cheap finery and gets picked up by a wealthy man who takes her for a beer and tells her: you're no prostitute. It's obvious from how you look, how you walk, how you dress, and all the rest of it. He gives her ten dollars, asks nothing in return, and sends her home. Goldman is amazed and baffled; he's a living contradiction of her idea about what bourgeois Americans are supposed to be like.

Fifteenth Class (Monday)

Now that I have learned everyone's name, I add a new element to the routine by starting class with music. I began this introductory course tradition three years ago and resume it today. Taking advantage of Emory's big music library, which owns seven or eight thousand CDs, I will play three or four minutes of music at the beginning of each meeting from now on, while marking the attendance roll, then talk about the selection before turning to the main theme for the day. I begin with the "Maple Leaf Rag," by Scott Joplin. Some students, to judge from their faces, already know and like it; to others ragtime is new and strange.

I lecture on the First World War; first the European background, then the nature of the trench warfare, the horrible casualty rates, and finally the way America got drawn, bit by bit, into the fighting. It traded with the belligerents (but found that the British naval blockade made it impossible to get ships to Germany, with the result that it was forced to deal entirely with the Western allies). Next President Wilson decided to permit American bankers to loan money to Britain. The German government reacted to the Americans' undeclared support for the allied cause by authorizing unrestricted submarine warfare against American shipping in early 1917. I sketch Wilson's early life and political career, summarize his idea of Progressivism, ending with America's military preparations and the utopian claims that went with them: of a "war to end all wars" and "a war to make the world safe for democracy."

A question from Chloe: why were Wilson and so many other influential Americans so pro-British, despite the legacy of the Revolutionary War? It gives me the opportunity to review the arguments about Anglo-Saxon destiny from a couple of weeks ago, and to emphasize the strong cultural contacts the ruling classes of the two countries had established over the years since the Civil War. Chloe is a good questioner—eager to know, reluctant to accept things on trust—and correspondingly an asset to the class. I want students to interrupt and to ask questions like this; the subject is dreadfully complicated, especially when you're also trying to weave into the narrative the early days of the Russian Revolution, and I'm aware that they will not all have gotten the main points, despite frequent repetition. Students who ask for clarification usually think of themselves as a bit dim; actually they're more often unusually sharp because they can see awkward issues and unresolved implications. Chloe is certainly a case in point.

I go on to discuss the Committee for Public Information and the American propaganda machine, whose representatives, the "four-minute men," gave talks at theaters and cinemas, persuading young men to join the army, young women to volunteer for the Red Cross, and older citizens to spend their money on Liberty Loan bonds. I have a super old poem from one of these propaganda campaigns. I hand out xeroxed copies, then ask another student, Marcia, to come to the front and read the poem to the whole class with the appropriate emotions. Here's what she reads:

My boy must never bring disgrace to his immortal sires—
At Valley Forge and Lexington they kindled freedom's fires.
John's father died at Gettysburg, mine fell at Chancellorsville;
While John himself was with the men who charged up San Juan Hill.
And John, if he was living now, would surely say with me,
"No son of ours shall e'er disgrace our grand old family tree
By turning out a slacker when his country needs his aid."
It is not of such timber that America was made.
I'd rather you had died at birth or not been born at all,
Than know that I had raised a son who cannot hear the call
That freedom has sent round the world, its precious rights to save—
This call is meant for you, my boy, and I would have you brave;
And though my heart is breaking, boy, I bid you do your part,
And show the world no son of mine is cursed with craven heart;

And if, perchance, you ne'er return, my later days to cheer,
And I have only memories of my brave boy, so dear,
I'd rather have it so, my boy, and know you bravely died
Than have a living coward sit supinely by my side.
To save the world from sin, my boy, God gave his only son—
He's asking for MY boy, today, and may His will be done.

Like most of her classmates Marcia is unaccustomed to reading aloud, says "disagree" when she means "disgrace," and seems unaware of the poem's actual content while concentrating on the words. The rest of the class get the point though, and wince both at the doggerel and at the emotional manipulation. I ask Barbara to talk us through the poem, and she does an excellent job of it, picking up on the comparison with Jesus at the end, the moral blackmail, and the fact that the mother, addressing her son, represents a marriage of ex-Union and ex-Confederate parents, that she's the widow of a Rough Rider casualty, and that she feels the collective pressure of military generations bearing down on the family. I recall to them a scene from the film *Forrest Gump*, in which we see in quick, ironic, succession men dressed in the American army uniforms of five different eras, falling dead to the ground, the ancestors of Gump's commander, Lieutenant Dan. With Gump it's a brilliant comic stroke—here it's all in earnest.

I spend the last few minutes of class talking about the conscription of young Americans and the army's discovery of their poor physical and medical condition. There's a superb passage in Stephen Jay Gould's book *The Mismeasure of Man* about how the army gave IQ tests to all its recruits. They were poorly conceived tests that actually measured knowledge rather than intelligence, and were administered even to immigrant illiterates who had never previously held a pencil. The army, instead of concluding that its tests measured knowledge rather than innate intelligence, concluded that immigrants were much stupider than old-stock Americans.

Time expires: I'll have to do the end of the war and the Treaty of Versailles next time. Students who missed Friday's class hand in their five-hundred word summaries and a couple of the best-organized hand in drafts of their papers for me to read and criticize.

Paper Drafts (Tuesday)

Michael was one of the students who gave me a draft paper yesterday. I read it this morning, called him, and he comes to discuss it. It is not good. He has written it in inverse chronological order. First he wrote about farms in the plains states. Then he remembered that they had been made possible by the railroads, and included a passage about trains. Then he recalled that the Indians had lived in the area before the whites took over, and so wrote a passage about them as well. When I mention to him that it would make more sense to write it moving forward in time, he agrees with a beaming smile. Other problems include a tendency to imply that everything happened at once. "The Homestead Act of 1862 allowed Americans to settle 160 acres without paying for it if they farmed it for 5 years. Immediately people swarmed out into the plains at full steam ahead." "Did they really all go at once, during 1862?" I ask. "Oh no, it was a steady process right through into the early twentieth century." "Right, so why did you put in that 'immediately,' and what's the idea with that 'full steam ahead'?" "I wanted to show that they were enthusiastic and that they used the railroad." "How about writing, 'Settlers were enthusiastic about the availability of free land, and many of them migrated to the plains by rail'?" He understands my point: "Oh, yes, OK, that makes sense." We talk about many other points of phrasing and I give him another of my standard talks: "When you and I sit here talking, there are lots of ways in which we can make our meaning clear to each other. We have body language, smiles and frowns, hand gestures, and repetition. But when you're writing you've got to be much more careful to say exactly what you mean, because the person reading won't have you there to explain things that are not clear. When you are editing you should ask yourself, about every phrase: 'Is this the clearest and simplest way of saying it?' It's also easy to be unintentionally comical, and you must make sure that your phrasing hasn't become an accidental source of merriment for the reader."

I then read Charles's draft, which also came in yesterday. My favorite bit reads as follows: "People had gone out west before the Homestead Act on the Oregon Trail, which was created in 1843 in order to be a part of the Gold Rush of 1848." How's that for defying the principles of chronology? I have a vision of the hardy pioneer saying to his friends, "Listen men, the California gold rush will be starting in five years. We'd better prepare the way by establishing the Oregon Trail, or how are those Forty-Eighters [?!] going to get there?"

Finally, I also read through a few five-hundred-word summaries of *Living My Life*, from students who missed Friday's discussion section on Emma Goldman. Some are fine but too many have a tone of vague and wandering disengagement. Here's the conclusion from the worst: "She is asked to speak at many conventions and is admired by many. She meets many new people and suddenly feels the need for a strong female bond, a female friend who shares her beliefs and her ideas. She begins working as a nurse and soon decides to go to Austria to study nursing. A very liberal woman indeed, Emma was a radical woman in her day." Horrible! That repetitious "many," the lack of connection between sentences, and the extreme lameness of the concluding sentence, all bespeak the author's unfamiliarity with her task. She doesn't really know how to summarize, which is a recurring problem. You might think that the five-hundred-word summary was an insultingly easy task, hardly more than busywork. Not really: about a third of the members of every class are unable to do it. They can't single out central from peripheral issues or link issues together into a coherent narrative. Some semesters I make five-hundred-word summaries the only writing assignment, but give one nearly every week, so that each student has twelve chances to improve. Occasionally they begin to get better, but it's vexing, with the poorer ones, to find the last of their summaries as jumbled, opaque, and off the point as the first. Although I enjoy counseling students about their writing, it eats up vast amounts of time, and with a class of forty it can reach unmanageable dimensions.

Sixteenth Class (Wednesday)

Today's tune is a march by Sousa, "The Washington Post," to hint at the mood of America's World War I militarism. Sousa has the gift of making you feel more cheerful than you really are. Probably half the students in this group were members of marching bands in their high school days, so there's no difficulty in getting it recognized. My lecture today is on the latter days of World War I, the role of the churches in boosting the war, the refusal of American socialists to participate, the imprisonment of Socialist Party leader Eugene Debs, and the expulsion of foreign-born radicals, including Emma Goldman. I tell an anecdote about Billy Sunday, who was then the most famous traveling evangelist in America. Wildly enthusiastic about the war, he declared in one sermon, "If you turned Hell upside down you'd find 'Made in Germany' stamped on the bottom." Before becoming an evangelist he had been a professional baseball player, and he would sometimes begin revival sermons by racing into his tent, sliding up to the lectern, as if trying to steal second base, and declaring, "The Devil says I'm out, but the Lord says I'm safe!"

The story of the American clergy in the war is shameful. Many of them got so carried away with excesses of patriotic fervor that they believed the absolute worst of the Germans. Atrocity stories, about how they raped and tortured the Belgian nuns, and about their brutality to all who fell into their hands, became staple pulpit fare for the eighteen months of America's participation in the war. I quote one lurid passage from a sermon by Brooklyn pastor Newell Dwight Hillis:

Why do the German soldiers cut off the breasts of French and Belgian women? Here is the secret. A syphilitic German soldier is refused access to the German camp women because the disease communicated to her would spread to other German soldiers and thus wipe out the Kaiser's army. And if he uses one of these women he will be shot like a dog. Therefore, the soldier that has this foul disease must stay away from the camp women on peril of his life. Under this restriction the syphilitic soldier has but one chance, namely to capture a Belgian or French woman, but using her means contaminating her. To save his own life, therefore, when the syphilitic German has used a French or Belgian woman, he cuts off her breasts as a warning to the next German soldier.

It and many similar passages come from Ray Abrams's book *Preachers Present Arms*, written way back in about 1930 but still a rattling good read. When the war ended, nearly all these stories turned out to be untrue, and many of the clergy felt ashamed of being taken in by the propaganda. In fact, many joined the Fellowship of Reconciliation, which pledged to live up to President Wilson's promise that this was indeed "the war to end all wars" and that a Christian peace must now reign throughout the world. By a stroke of bitter irony, many of these men, when they heard in the late 1930s and early 1940s about Hitler's persecution of the Jews, conscientiously refused to believe it. The stories sounded too similar to the stories they had let themselves believe back in 1914 and 1918, which had turned out to be lies. In consequence they were wrong twice: the first time for being too credulous, the second time for being too skeptical.

I describe Woodrow Wilson's triumphant visit to Europe and his role with respect to the Treaty of Versailles, his inability to outmaneuver Lloyd George and Clemenceau, and his dismay at the vengeful terms of the treaty. He hoped that the League of Nations could remedy its infelicities when passions had cooled, but that hope was scotched when the Senate refused to ratify American membership in the League.

How is the course going, in general? The best way to find out is to ask the students. When there are about ten minutes left, therefore, I hand out a midterm evaluation form. It consists of just two questions, one printed at the top of the page, the other halfway down: "a) What do you like and dislike about the course? Can you suggest ways in which it could be improved? b) Comment on the length, difficulty, and degree of interest you feel in the reading assignments." A few students simply write a one-sentence answer to each question before scooting off while others are still there fifteen or twenty minutes later when students for the next class in the same room are crowding in.

There is a wide measure of agreement among their answers to the first question. They like the slides that go with most lectures, they like the music that recently got started, and the snippets of film, and they like the anecdotes with which I try to enliven and illustrate the narrative. On the other hand, they don't like the fact that I am such a hard case in my attendance policy, and at least half are anxious about the upcoming midterm exam. They point out that since there is no textbook it would be helpful to them to have written outlines of every lecture instead of just a few. Then they wouldn't have to take highspeed notes all the time and would have a better sense of what is central to the course and what peripheral. They are right; I'll start with the handouts next Monday and make it a policy from now on.

Answers to the second question are more varied. Some students find the colorful readings, like TR and Emma Goldman, delightful. Others say they give only one perspective on complicated issues and that readings like the Etulain, which presented multiple points of view, are better. Several say the readings are sometimes dry (how dare they?!), but there is a steady stream of positive commentary too. Nearly everyone is delighted not to have a textbook.

Let me cite a couple of typical responses. Here's a rather anxious one:

a. I like the fact that we have no textbook but sometimes that makes me confused as to what to take notes on. I think writing key words on the board, which has been done recently, is a good way to improve my confusion [entertaining ambiguity there, surely, with the implication that the student is now suffering from "new, improved confusion"].

b. I must say that I find the reading to be a bit overwhelming, in length mostly, because all three of my other classes also require a lot of reading and I'm finding it difficult to balance. What I end up doing is slacking on my other assignments because I *know* that I'll be asked about history, and slacking isn't a good thing!

Here's another, which appears to contain a confession of latent laziness:

a. I appreciate how the class permits and even requires participation by students. This mode of teaching causes students such as myself to remain alert and attentive throughout the duration of class.

b. I feel very interested in how the books and films relate to the particular time periods discussed in the class. Yet, not all of the books held my interest like the first, *Black Elk Speaks.*

I will collate the answers and write a collective e-mail, thanking the students for their input, promising outlines, and explaining why I *won't* change the attendance policy. It's been an interesting exercise, especially the discovery that nearly everyone is concerned about what to study for the exams. It's not something that anyone has mentioned to me face-to-face, by phone, or by e-mail (nobody wants to look like a whiner).

CHAPTER

10

■ ■ ■

The Conscious Professor

Seventeenth Class (Friday)

I've had a wonderful time this week rereading *Bread Givers*, by Anzia Yezierska. It's a terrific counterpart to Emma Goldman's *Living My Life*, since both are books by Jewish immigrant women from the late nineteenth and early twentieth centuries, vividly written and brimming with passion. *Bread Givers* is just about perfect from a professor's point of view, if he wants to teach about the psychological stresses and material hardships of immigrants' lives and assimilation to America. A novel based on Yezierska's own life on the Lower East Side of New York City, it tells the story of the Smolinsky family through the eyes of Sara, the youngest of four daughters. Their father, Reb Smolinsky, is a devout student of the Torah, a holy man whose piety is so intense that he regards even the rabbinate as beneath him, because it implies trading for money on his religious knowledge.

I begin class by asking Tracy to give her reaction to the book, and she cuts right to the heart of the matter. "I hate the father; he makes me so mad!" For the next five or six minutes, nearly everyone chimes in their agreement that the father is unbearable. Finally I ask whether anyone likes him. To my surprise, Flora, with almost superhuman kindheartedness, says she feels sorry for him at the end, when he's reduced to selling chewing gum from a peddler's basket. Barbara adds, "I'm Jewish and I know some guys like him." "Well, knowing such people doesn't necessarily mean you'll like them." "True; yeah, I guess I'm just saying I know the type and it rings true to my own experience." "Have you ever known any who were as reluctant to work as Reb Smolinsky?" "No, actually I was going to say that the great difference is that the super strong Jewish fathers I have known have been family tyrants but have also been very hardworking and successful." Curtis delights me by *sounding* like me, observing that we need to get beyond likes and dislikes: "This was a different time and place. Maybe in those days it was OK for the father to act this way." Chloe says, "No, because his daughter hates him and she wants us readers to hate him too." After a few more reactions we get to a crucial point. Britney says, "What we are seeing here is a conflict of two systems of values. The father thinks he's justified in tyrannizing the family, and expects them all to do what he wants. That must be the way it was in the old country. But Sara has grown up in America and she's learning a different set of values, so to her the father's way seems unfair." "Good." I say. "Is anyone of you a recent immigrant?" Michael raises his hand and says that he came from Hong Kong when he was nine. I ask him, "Without letting me pry into your personal life, can you give a comparable example?" "Yes," he says. "My father's nothing like the father in *Bread Givers*, but he and my mom want me to go back and live at home as soon as I finish college but I don't want to. I want to live in an apartment with some of my friends, but they say it's wrong for a man to leave his family before he marries."

We move to the subject of marriage. Some of the most harrowing scenes in *Bread Givers* consist of the three older daughters each trying to marry young men they have met. In each instance the man is from the same Jewish community and seems superficially suitable. But in every case the father condemns his daughters' choices, insults the young men, and drives them away. He then becomes a matchmaker and chooses husbands for his daughters, and his choices are uniformly bad. He is unworldly in the worst sense, being easily deceived. For Masha he chooses Moe Mirsky, a man he believes, wrongly, to be a diamond merchant, who brings diamonds for the woman to wear. For the second, Fania, he chooses Abe Schmukler, a cloak dealer who has emigrated to Los Angeles from New York but is back in town looking for a wife. The two marriages take place on the same day, leading to congratulations from the community and preening by Smolinsky himself on what a clever matchmaker he is. It isn't long before the "diamond dealer" turns out to be no more than a clerk in a jewelry store, who is dismissed for taking jewels to his fiancee. Schmukler is indeed rich but he is also a heartless gambler. Fania's life as his wife drives her almost mad with regret and loneliness. Saddest of all is the fate of Bessie, the eldest daughter, who is admired and pursued by prosperous Berel Bernstein. The father refuses to let them marry unless Bernstein not only agrees to go without a dowry but actually pays the father compensation. After all, says Smolinsky with brutal honesty, she's my burden bearer, earns more than the other women, gives me every penny she earns, and does a lot of the housework into the bargain. I'll be much worse off without her. Bernstein snorts derisively at this proposal and tells Bessie, "Let's just go get married at city hall." Bessie can't bring herself to cross her father's iron will and so the match fails. Instead, Smolinsky proposes that she marry the recently widowed fish peddlar Zalmon, a sordid old man, always stinking of fish, who already has five delinquent children. She detests him and will have nothing to do with him, until her heart is softened by seeing the neglect in which the youngest of these children lives. To the horror of Sara, the narrator, and to the equal horror of my class members (and me), poor Bessie has to marry Zalmon, and is coarsened and beaten down by the new life she has to take on as a heavier "burden bearer" even than before.

In the face of these events, Sara declares her independence from the father and leaves home. As Simon points out, "It's a book all about will power." "Yes, and why is it that Sara has the strength of will to leave and go her own way?" He suggests it's because she's witnessed the dreadful fate of each sister and is determined to avoid it. Nathan adds that it might also be that she, as the youngest, has no memories of the old world and is the most Americanized of the daughters. For her, accordingly, the American principle that women should be able to choose husbands is all the stronger. A normally silent student, Paul, who speaks only when I ask him directly, volunteers a comment, saying he was shocked by the ensuing passages, which show Sara's desperate struggle to get an education and become a schoolteacher. She has to work long hours in a laundry, then go to night school, then do her homework. She lives alone in a dark and sordid tenement room, and denies herself all pleasures for several years, in order to graduate and win a place at college. Paul hadn't realized it would be so difficult for someone in Sara's position to make any progress. Another normally quiet student, Sarah, responds, saying that in America, hard as it is, there is at least the possibility of getting out of the worst ghetto existence. In Poland it would have been impossible. In effect these two students have different ideas about what "opportunity" means. The first seems to think it ought to be relatively straightforward; the second has a harsher idea and expects it to be closely linked with anguish, suffering, and self-denial.

Chloe says she had always heard that America was anti-Semitic for her Jewish ancestors and that she's surprised the book does not even mention that as an issue. The remark leads to a discussion of whether the book is realistic in its portrayal of immigrant life. Why is there so little mention of "Americans" (at least until Sara goes off to college, where she begins to meet them)? And why nothing about the Italians, Irish, Greeks, Bohemians, and other immigrant groups who were also crowded into lower Manhattan during the same years of the early twentieth century? Several students respond. Helen has the insight that life there is intensely localized and that nearly everything important to the characters' lives is squeezed into a few city blocks. The other ethnic groups are there but the Smolinskys, in their daily battle for food, shelter, and warmth, have little occasion to come into contact with them.

More than half the members of today's discussion group are Jewish, and a debate about pro- and anti-Jewish attitudes ensues. Chloe, who comes from a Reform family, says her own upbringing was nothing like this but that she once visited the Lubavitcher community in Brooklyn and found a modern-day equivalent of *Bread Givers*, in which the women were completely subordinated to the despotic men. "And," she adds, "their authoritarianism is so provoking that they often bring down anti-Jewish prejudice on themselves."

As on the previous two or three occasions, I devote the last minutes of class to asking students to read passages aloud. Rifat chooses this one, in which the father rebukes his despairing wife: "Foolish *yideneh!* Why are you getting yourself so excited over nothing? What's loss of money anyway? You know the old saying: 'Money lost, nothing lost. Hope lost, all is lost.' The less money I have, the more I live on hope. And hope is the only reality here on earth. It's hope that makes people build cities and span bridges and send ships from one end of the earth to another." She says this passage is typical of the father (she's right), and it comes just after he and his family realize that he's been swindled into buying a nearly worthless grocery store from a crafty fellow immigrant. Rather than admit his own folly and credulity, he berates the family for their dismayed realization that he has squandered their savings.

I could go on and on about *Bread Givers*, it's just so good. Reader, if you haven't read it, go and get a copy at once. Its later pages are full of interesting thoughts on education. Sara goes to college, where she finds she's still an outsider, utterly unlike the American-born students, who are easy and comfortable with money and privilege. For her it's a battle every step of the way, until she realizes her old ambition of becoming a schoolteacher. When she is in night school, trying to graduate, she describes a scene I have often witnessed among students whose intellectual curiosity outstrips that of their classmates:

Even in school I suffered, because I was not like the rest. I irritated the teachers, stopping the lessons with my questions. A bored weariness fell over the whole class the minute I started to speak. They'd begin to nudge each other by the sleeve and whisper, "Oh, Lord! That bug! Again showing off her smartness!" They didn't hunger and thirst for knowledge, they weren't excited about anything they were learning, so it jarred on them that I was so excited. To them I was only a selfish grabber of their time because I was so crazy to know too much. (180)

There's a fine line between genuine thirst for knowledge, like hers, and becoming the classroom bore.

It's a busy day because this is the last day on which I have agreed to read students' drafts of their papers. The six or seven who bring me drafts after class nearly all have the same problem; they're not chronological, having that perverse tendency I mentioned earlier, to talk first about the things that happened last. I say to Faith, who has brought her second draft for me to review (after rebukes on the first one that it was not chronological): "Do you have any posters on your dorm-room wall?" "Yes, a sunset and a picture of the beach." "Well, for the duration of this semester I want you to make a huge sign that says: '*CHRONOLOGY*' and stick it on the wall beside the sunset. Gaze at it constantly and let it always be in your thoughts." She laughs in the "I wouldn't dream of actually doing such a thing" way but admits, when I point it out to her, that there are all sorts of advantages to an historical account that talks first about what happened first, and last about what happened last. Several other students come, nearly all with the same trouble, in addition to the usual array of writing weaknesses. It's a real treat to read Sarah's paper, though. She's written it extremely well, it's grammatically almost perfect, and she has thought logically about the issues the question raises. She's a mousy little student, drab and withdrawn, almost never volunteering a remark in class discussion, and seeming almost listless most of the time, yet here she is, far outshining everyone else whose work I have seen so far. College teaching is full of surprises, and even though I've had this kind of surprise before I still wasn't ready for it.

Eighteenth Class (Monday)

Preparing for each lecture is going to take a little longer now because of the new outlines. After going over the lecture, this one on the 1920s, I get busy writing an outline, make forty Xerox copies, and then look for a suitable CD in the music library. In the end I decide on a jazz tune called "Nickel in the Slot," by Zez Confrey. It comes from a CD of the music played at Paul Whiteman's Aeolian Hall concert in 1924. "Whiteman" was a stage name, designed to emphasize that jazz was for whites as well as for blacks. His idea in giving this concert was to show that jazz was no longer the music of poor blacks but had become part of the mainstream; it could even be thought of as concert music. This was the concert at which George Gershwin's "Rhapsody in Blue" premiered. One possibility would have been to play its opening bars, with the lovely clarinet glissando, but it is so well known (from Delta Airlines ads, among other things) that it has come to sound like a piece of generic Americana rather than something specific to its original time and place. "Nickel in the Slot," not previously known to me or the students, sounds right—jazzy but smooth. The only problem is that the boom box the audio-visual office has lent me is too small to make sufficient noise for the big room. Instead of booming it seems merely to quaver and tinkle, so I will have to replace it before Wednesday. To make matters worse, the usual latecomers are thumping in, scraping desks and chairs, and chatting to each other as though the music were no more than a bit of distant background. A generation that has grown up with Muzak is used to overriding it with talk and bustle.

The first theme of today's lecture is the red scare at the end of World War I, when middle-class Americans dreaded the onset of a Soviet-style revolution. Attorney General A. Mitchell Palmer rounded up alien radicals and deported them en masse, while Congress drew up legislation for limiting immigration. Laws of 1921 and 1924 favored northwestern Europeans while keeping out southern and eastern Europeans, Asians, and Africans. My second theme is xenophobia, the generalized fear and dislike of foreigners during and after the war. I pass along the probably apocryphal story about the Nebraska legislator who spoke in favor of abolishing the teaching of foreign languages in the state's school system. He is alleged to have said, "The English language alone was good enough for Jesus Christ and it's good enough for the people of Nebraska." Third is a passage about Presidents Harding and Coolidge and their determination to minimize the reach of the federal government, shrinking it at a time their contemporaries Mussolini, Lenin, and Stalin, were building massive centralized states.

Next I talk about improving standards of living, the rise of a consumer society, the new availability of refrigerators and radios, the immense surge of advertising, and the spread of cars throughout society. (In 1929 five-sixths of all the cars in the world were owned by Americans.) The lecture continues with a passage on American writers of the 1920s. First, Sinclair Lewis, and the picture of a conformist society he draws in the character of George Babbitt. Then a section on the "exiles" of the 1920s, the literary modernists living in Paris, partly because it was cheap in those days, partly because alcohol was still legally available, and partly because they thought America so sterile, and groaning under such a heavy puritan yoke, as to be unendurable. I ask whether any of the students has read anything by Hemingway and two or three are familiar with *Farewell to Arms*. The fact that the hero is a deserter from the army, and is treated as *justified* in deserting, is something that hadn't occurred to them before, so here is an opportunity to talk about the widespread sense of disillusionment that followed the war.

The lecture ends with fifteen minutes on Prohibition and why it went wrong. It's a good illustration of the way in which the law needs citizens' assent to be enforceable. Collusion in violating it was so widespread, and violators' sense of wrongdoing so slight, that the enforcers faced a hopeless task. Al Capone said, "I make my money by supplying a public demand. If I break the law, my customers, who number hundreds of the best people in Chicago, are as guilty as I am. The only difference between us is that I sell and they buy. Everybody calls me a racketeer. I call myself a businessman. When I sell liquor it's bootlegging. When my patrons serve it on a silver tray on Lakeshore Drive it's hospitality." For the sake of a comparison I ask the students whether they would admit to driving seventy in a fifty-five-mile-per-hour zone on the urban freeways. They all admit it, and agree that it doesn't make them think of themselves as criminals. It's difficult from this vantage point to take seriously the fact that Prohibition seemed like such a good idea before the fact. There were thousands of industrial accidents every year, violence and crimes committed by drunks were widespread, as were marital rape and family neglect and impoverishment. No wonder so many people put faith in the possibilities of a world without alcohol. Who could have foreseen that the incidence of drunkenness would rise, rather than fall, and that the number of saloons would increase rather than decrease, while organized crime would flourish as never before? History is full of bitter ironies.

Class ends with high anxiety levels because today's the day for handing in papers. I meet with my teaching assistant, Regina, to discuss grading them. She's never done it before and is about to encounter with full force the shocking badness of students' writing. I xerox two of the papers, chosen at random, and ask her to grade them; I'll grade them too and we'll meet tomorrow to compare, and set grading standards. Then we can do half each and lighten the burden.

In the evening, to complete a busy day, I drive to West Paces Ferry Road to talk with the senior citizens' group. My subject with them is religion and the American Civil War, and before long I am being interrupted, especially by the ladies. Many of them, born in the 1920s or even earlier, grew up in Georgia and other parts of the deep South, learning about the heroism of the Confederacy and the savagery of the Yankees. The passage of time has in no way diminished the intensity of these early lessons. I have known most of them for five years but never before have I touched such a sore point. In my remarks I strive for a tone of detached impartiality, but in their view it's outrageous even to suggest that the Northerners were as sincere in their beliefs as were Southerners in theirs.

When we break for a glass of wine and a few hors d'oeuvres, one of the ladies tells me all about her grandfather, who fought from beginning to end of the war, was loved by his slaves, and looked after them for the rest of their lives when the war ended. "They didn't want to leave him; they loved him!" she exclaims, and gets about as close as it's possible to get in the twenty-first century to endorsing slavery itself. After a moment's pause, however, she adds, "Some slave owners were unkind, and that gave all of them a bad name." Another emphasizes the extraordinary brutality of General Sherman to her great-grandmother's family, and one of the men tells me that his grandfather suffered as much in a Yankee prisoner of war camp in Ohio as any Yankee prisoners suffered in Andersonville.

Rather than affirm or deny their protests, I give one of my standard speeches: "I'm not trying to argue in favor of one side or another. Our job in studying history is to understand what happened rather than take sides or condemn either group. Historical researchers have shown that men on both sides really did think they were doing God's work, and we know that the camps on both sides were swept by evangelical revivals. Historians can't answer the question of whether God actually took sides and favored the Union or the Confederacy, but it can show that many of the participants *thought* they could discern the will of God and *believed* they were doing His will." As always it's great to teach this group; they are so much more willing than undergraduates to stand up for their ideas, and to trust the reality of their own (very long) experience. They know and care nothing at all about political correctness, whereas students at Emory, whose ideas are even slightly irregular and offbeat, know enough to keep quiet about them on campus.

Nineteenth Class (Wednesday)

First thing this morning I take the little stereo back to audio-visual and ask if they can give me a bigger one. One of the assistants says she thinks the videodisc players might be able to read CDs. She walks over to the classroom with me, carrying a Paul Simon CD she's unearthed in their office. Videodiscs are an obsolete technology by now (DVDs have eclipsed them), but the machines can sometimes manage both. Sure enough, we find a small indentation in the videodisc player, pop in the CD, and out of the room's built-in loudspeakers comes a wonderful rich sound. I crank up the volume until it's almost at the level of aircraft noise—but musical!

Two hours later, heading off to class, I just carry the CD of Duke Ellington's greatest hits instead of all the previous clutter. It is good to have built-in machinery after all, and in a moment the exotic notes of "Caravan" fill the room. The wretched students, however, still don't get the point. You know how it is in restaurants when the music is too loud? Everyone just talks louder to be heard over it. So it is here, half of them just increase the racket as they chat with their friends. Perhaps if I lowered the lights in order to give incoming students the sense that a presentation was going on it might help. Somehow I doubt it.

Today's theme is religious history in the early twentieth century. I give an extremely quick overview of five centuries of Christian history, summarizing the various strands of the Reformation tradition in a dozen sentences, and trying to give them a glimpse, on the basis of a blackboard chart, of the lineage of the major denominations. I describe the fragmenting tendencies of American Protestant churches, and the way in which controversies over social Christianity, evolution, comparative religion, and historical-critical method engendered a further round of splits in the late nineteenth century. The culmination of this schism came with the Scopes Monkey Trial of 1925, which also lends itself to a good bit of storytelling. A year or two ago I read and reviewed Edward Larson's book on the case, *Summer for the Gods* (1997), and it provides plenty of good stories to give students the feel of the trial itself. When I ask who has seen *Inherit the Wind* (1960), the Spencer Tracy movie based on the case, and find that only two or three out of thirty nine have seen it, I resolve to show it to the whole group.

Next comes a passage on immigrant Catholics in the early twentieth century, and their bishops' strenuous activities to hasten their assimilation and allay suspicions that they were not good Americans. The best examples of this activity come from Edward Kantowicz's book about Cardinal George Mundelein of Chicago, *Corporation Sole* (1983). Mundelein, in building St. Mary of the Lake seminary for trainee priests in his archdiocese, modeled the exterior on Jefferson's designs for the University of Virginia as a way of suggesting to Protestant passers by, who were likely to see only the exterior, that it was a thoroughly American place. But to reassure visiting Vatican officials that he wasn't scanting on orthodoxy or trying to trim his doctrines to suit American tastes, he modeled the interior on the Barberini Palace in Rome. As Kantowicz says, it was thoroughly American but also Roman to the core, a beautiful example of the tightrope the cardinal had to walk between potential antagonists in America and potential antagonists in Rome. Mundelein followed up by making the outside of his bishop's palace a copy of George Washington's house, Mount Vernon.

It's difficult to convey to contemporary undergraduates the ferocity of American anti-Catholicism in the late nineteenth and early twentieth centuries. A few look shocked when I explain that many Protestants, especially Bible belt dwellers, regarded Catholics not simply as another type of Christian, but as followers of the anti-Christ, and Catholicism itself as demonic. I give the example of the Ku Klux Klan, refounded in 1915 (in Stone Mountain, Georgia, just fifteen miles from here) as an organization dedicated not just to the persecution of blacks but equally fiercely against Jews and Catholics. In Oregon its influence led to a state law against private Catholic schools. A group of teaching sisters took their objections all the way to the Supreme Court in 1925 and won *Pierce v. Society of Sisters*, which ever since has guaranteed religious schools' right to exist.

Klansmen contributed to the electoral failure of Al Smith. A former governor of New York, he was the first Catholic ever to be chosen as presidential candidate by one of the major political parties. He was the Democrat in 1928 and ran unsuccessfully against Herbert Hoover. The Democratic Party was an ungainly object in the early twentieth century, a mix of white Southerners and Northern, urban, ethnic workers. They managed to stick together behind Woodrow Wilson in 1912 and 1916, but the Southern evangelical half found Smith intolerable. He openly flouted Prohibition and was baffled when he heard the allegation that he would deliver America into the arms of the pope if elected. When asked what his policies would be for states west of the Mississippi, he is alleged to have answered, "Which states *are* west of the Mississippi?" To a question about papal authority he said, "What the hell is a papal encyclical?" He would probably have lost anyway, since the country was in the middle of a great boom and Hoover was a national hero, but his religion sealed his fate. The events of Smith's campaign preyed on the mind of John F. Kennedy thirty-two years later, when he became the second Catholic candidate for president and also had to overcome anti-Catholic prejudice. The fact that he won and didn't hand over the nation to the pope reassured anxious Protestants and contributed to the decline of anti-Catholicism thereafter, so that the whole idea just seems weird by now. I ask the class, "Which of you hates Catholics?" There are no takers.

After class, at lunchtime, Emory's Center for Teaching and Curriculum has a meeting, "The Conscious Professor in the Classroom," addressed by James Curtis, a visiting dignitary. I signed up for it mainly from a sense of obligation, since I'm a member of the CTC board and current holder of the N.E.H. / Arthur Blank Professorship of Teaching, but the event is a pleasant surprise. I don't think the title is quite right, since it implies that it's quite common for the teacher to be unconscious in the classroom. Then again, thinking about some of the professors I know (not at Emory, of course!), that sounds like a reasonable assessment. Curtis is a retired professor of Russian from the University of Missouri, and now runs Curtis Associates, which, according to its card, offers "teaching workshops and other pedagogical services." It's hard to believe such an enterprise could prosper, but there's no denying Curtis knows his stuff and is right on all the big questions.

He is a self-contained, small, polite, and positive man with economical gestures and smart clothes. In the opening minutes he goes round introducing himself to the twenty or so people in the room while they eat giant sandwiches. You know how it is in such situations; you've just taken a massive bite, hyperextending your jaws to get them open wide enough for one of those meaty items, when someone comes up and says hello, so that you have to blush and munch for fifteen or twenty seconds before you can answer, simply giving a vigorous handshake and grinning foolishly meanwhile. Among his many gifts, he seems to watch for the conclusion of a bite-sequence, shaking your hand when your mouth is empty. I warm to him. He is a good name-memorizer too, with the result that when his speech begins he can use us as examples of the points he is making, while singling us out by name.

His main points are soon summarized. To be successful as a teacher you have to be acutely aware of your audience. You cannot be fully aware of them unless you are master of the material, and unless you have no need to read from notes. The good teacher remembers with pride the first day she was able to give an entire lecture without notes. Being able to do so greatly increases the amount of energy she can bring into the classroom. *Energy* is one of Curtis's favorite words. He goes on to emphasize how much a teacher's body language enhances or diminishes this feeling of energy. He pantomimes several common professorial poses: the lean on the desk, which bespeaks boredom, and the slump over the lectern, which suggests the need for support. Both of them drain energy out of the classroom rather than pump it in. Don't bring coffee or food into the classroom, he adds—you don't want to give the students of feeling of informality or relaxation. You want them, rather, to concentrate. A man after my own heart!

He dresses up some commonsense ideas in the language of Gestalt therapy, and talks a lot about binary oppositions, but as academic talk goes, his is mercifully jargon-free. Think first, he says, of the two principal components of the classroom: the professor and the student. Next think of the two things the professor represents. One is the discipline, the other is the self. It is appropriate for the professor to introduce the discipline with reference to himself, at least to begin with. We professors, after all, are success stories. "The fact that you are professors here at Emory shows that you were successful at college, successful at graduate school, and successful on the job market. Surely this triple success is something you can turn to good advantage as you offer yourself to the class. Your life histories are the kind of thing Hollywood directors like most. Do you remember the one who said he wanted to make 'Stories about happy people with happy problems'?" Tell the students what brought you here, and try to communicate to them your love for the subject, so that they will recognize it as something that can be loved.

The students, he continues, are also two things: consumers and learners. Our job is to convert their initial frame of mind, that of consumers, into that of learners. The consumer mentality has been nurtured by tens of thousands of hours of television and movies, and is itself highly binary. He recalls an experiment in which he went around a class of new students, asking them to tell him about a film they had seen recently. The only condition was that they were not allowed to say whether or not they had liked it, and they were not allowed to summarize the plot. He timed each student. Not one of them could speak for more than fifty seconds. They are conditioned, he said, to say either that they like something or that they don't like it, to describe it briefly, and then to run out of things to say. They bring this "consumer discourse" to the classroom, saying of books or whatever else they are studying either that they do like them or that they don't. Our job is to teach them "academic discourse," in which they have to consider precedents, evidence, and context, to achieve understanding, rather than the like/dislike dichotomy in which mere emotional judgment is required. They must learn, for example, that "I worked very hard on this paper" is not admissible as evidence in discussion of a grade. If they are recalcitrant, says Curtis, we can remind our students that in the twenty-first-century workplace there is a close correspondence between "learner discourse" and "earner discourse." Ability to learn, discriminate, and weigh evidence are exactly the kind of skills most valued in middle-class careers today.

He next asks the audience to guess what adjectives students use on their evaluation forms when they want to praise a professor. Joseph Lowman, a psychologist at University of North Carolina, did it a while ago by painstakingly counting the adjectives in thousands of student evaluations. In assessing intellectual stimulation, the most positive and widely used adjective was *enthusiastic*. Just behind it came *knowledgeable* and *inspiring*. On the interpersonal skills list *concerned* came first, closely followed by *caring* and *available*, while on the motivation section of evaluations, students used *helpful*, *encouraging* and *challenging* as the three most positive adjectives. It's no bad thing, therefore, to be enthusiastic, concerned, and helpful, and when I think about how I set to work with a class, that's more or less what I'm aiming for, albeit with a certain jaundiced skepticism thrown in. I certainly get lots of *enthusiastics* on student evaluations each term. Where I'm weakest, on the other hand, is in self-discipline, time management, and pacing (because I always speed up, trying to squeeze too much into each class).

Another good part of this talk concerns the "double-point classroom." He reminds us that the normal American classroom is a secularized version of a setting originally established for the training of clergy. The classroom, in which the professor addresses the students, is similar in structure to the church, in which the minister addresses his congregation. The teacher standing at the front represents a merging of the self and the discipline. There's much to be said for teaching of this kind, formal lecturing, but it's also good sometimes to create a double-point classroom, in which the object of the discipline, a picture, model, map, or diagram, stands before the class, while the teacher walks away from it. As he passes by students he asks them questions, and ensures that none is allowed to remain remote from the center of the class's attention. With sufficient mastery of the subject he can circle the room and, at least for a while, be physically close to every student. Or, while being physically close to one, he calls on students far across the room, so as to remain at least slightly unpredictable.

Curtis urges teachers to ask students by name to answer his questions. Once he told a class of Russian language students, "You're least likely to be asked a question in Russian if you are looking at me as though you were entranced by everything I said and did." That's the way to keep their attention!

11

■ ■ ■

Long Dry Spouts and Levels Unheard Of

Grading the Papers

Thursday is paper-grading day. It's a slog, as always, and nearly all the papers are poorly organized and unchronological. But by forcing myself to concentrate on the first five or six, which are always the hardest, I break through to a mental condition of positive enjoyment. It's like the hard work you have to do when you begin running, but then, eventually, you attain the euphoria of "runner's high." "Grader's high" is comparable. The job has to be done; it's self-contained, you can see the pile of papers diminishing steadily over the course of the day, you try to put useful remarks on the papers, which will actually help the students understand what they did right, what they did wrong, and how they might more profitably set about the task next time. Also, more than at any other time in the course, you have access to the students' minds. They cannot hide when they are writing. Even the tough guys in the class-room seem almost pathetically vulnerable when they are writing, and it feels as though you have a chance to glimpse their minds as they struggle to write. Most are so inexperienced as writers that they cannot hide behind the protective shields used by more experienced writers. They certainly use overworked and cliched phrases, but usually in the wrong places. They're full of Freudian slips, or else they get quotations slightly wrong, so even with tired old phrases they reveal themselves. The disparity between teacher and student is at its maximum point now, and it's hard not to feel protective toward them, even those you suspect of being lazy or villainous. Incidentally, that's another reason plagiarism is so painful—you realize that you have been denied the chance of this visitation.

In addition to the pedagogical (and slightly voyeuristic) element of paper grading, there's the occasional gift of unintentionally comical statements. Loads of these statements circulate on academic e-mail lists, and there are some great ones, though you sometimes think they're a bit too good to be true. With this paper assignment on the American west I get a pretty good haul and can vouch for their authenticity.

Remember that I urged students to act as guides to the reader? Here's one student taking that advice a bit too much to heart as he strives to explain the development of a distinctive western character.

First, we must discuss the natural environment of the West itself. Second, we will turn to a discussion of the cultural characteristics that the settlers brought with them to the West. And after we have laid this ground work, we will turn our discussion towards the ways of life on the American frontier. It is my belief that when you finish the journey which is this essay, you will realize that these things, the natural environment and the human culture of the frontiersmen, helped to facilitate the development of a new type of American. This "new American," you will see, has always been present. He just needed help finding his way to the surface.

It's a lovely image of the archetypal American beginning life as something like a mole, but eventually digging up to the surface and turning into a cowboy. The same student's paper also provided the following sentences:

Unlike the plains, the northwest was not flat at all. On the contrary, it was very rigid.

The great plains were characterized by their extremely long dry spouts.

Many did not survive the harsh journey west, but they still trekked on.

If one looks at the theories of Charles Darwin, they will realize that this new American came about for its own survival.

This last one reminds me of another of my oft-repeated remarks, which I forgot to mention when I made the paper assignment. It's the issue of separation of voices. If a student agrees with an idea voiced by someone in the past, she often incorporates a bit of advocacy in the paper, rather than making it clear to the reader that she is just reporting what the character said. Here's one I copied down a few years ago: "The Continental Congress in writing the Declaration of Independence used religion to say that our justification is because of our Creator. Our Creator is above any laws that man can construct, and the King has clearly violated the laws of the Creator. Therefore we are justified in revolting against the king." The writer's point is clear enough in that one, and I dare say she was keen on the principles embodied in the Declaration of Independence. There's so much going on in the Darwin sentence, though, it's more difficult to unravel. I explained to the class a few weeks ago that some American intellectuals in the late nineteenth century had applied evolutionary theory to sociology, and thought that societies evolved in a way analogous to the evolution of organisms. Frederick Jackson Turner drew on this idea of social evolution when he described the development of each new frontier into a settled and civilized part of the United States. In a compressed and jumbled way, and mindful of the phrase "survival of the fittest," the student seems to have been making something like the same point.

Here are some other students' contributions. One seemed excessively preoccupied with the west's low rainfall, but was also toying with themes from social Darwinism.

The summer days were hot as could be, often drying the land around you, for miles and miles. When the sun went down the day turned to night and the air became frigid . . . When fall turned to winter fear spread among those living in the west . . . You were at God's mercy with huge accumulations of snow and temperatures falling to levels unheard of.

Whites in general moved west because it was human nature.

The whites knew that they for one had much better technology in the form of weapons than the Indians. In their minds they couldn't see how these primitive creatures could even put a dent in their military.

Another had the common problem of struggling for the right word in the right place, and turned his prose a shade purple.

The frontier proved itself to be a fierce monster that wrestled with thousands of those who dreamed of succeeding in the wild, undeveloped American west.

Water has proven, even today, to be an extremely necessary resource in sustaining life.

For those not fortunate enough to live by a river, other methods of water obtainment were necessary.

An unfortunate strong difference in culture caused the two societies to butt heads in a collision that drove the Indians out of the big picture in America.

As farming communities grew in the midwest, schoolhouses and bridges erupted.

For many of the Indian tribes, the buffalo was a scared animal.

The best grade among the whole set of papers, the only A, went to a paper written by Chris, almost the only student who really has a feel for the nuances of language and a logical way of setting it out. The worst papers got Cs—none was bad enough to fail. Actually I'm so soft that if I get a paper that deserves only an F, I usually assume that the student didn't really know what to do. I give him or her an intensive counseling session and a second chance, and that usually brings forth a weak but passable paper. I did notice, however, that one young lady had not handed in a paper at all. When I wrote her an e-mail asking why not, she wrote back indignantly saying she had a lot of work to do and would get to it as soon as possible. That was on Monday, four days ago, and there's still no sign of it, and no evidence of penitence. She rarely comes to class, despite the attendance policy, and is about to get a "you are failing this course" e-mail.

Twentieth Class (Friday)

As usual I haven't kept pace with the syllabus I distributed. In my last lecture, I meant to describe the boom and bust of the late 1920s but got too carried away with the religious issues and never got onto the economics at all. Browsing through the slide boxes I also realize that I haven't yet said anything (beyond a passing mention) about advertising. I therefore get out fifteen of the best advertising slides as a way to begin, even though today was originally slated for discussion of Nicholas Lemann's *Promised Land*.

The students come in to the sounds of Count Basie, then I show the advertising pictures. The earliest ones are of nineteenth-century corset advertisements. In one crudely drawn ad, a pair of angels brings a corset to a grateful group of women, who raise their arms in salutation and thanks. The idea is that this one is so much more comfortable than normal corsets, it's almost as though angels had brought it. There's an interesting early soap advertisement too, in which the celebrity endorsement comes from Elizabeth Cady Stanton, who is pictured, very wrinkly and aged about seventy. It seems not to have occurred to the advertisers at that point that a fresh-complexioned woman might be a more appealing model. I move through the first twenty-five years of the twentieth century, showing how advertisers quickly realized, and developed, the main techniques they have relied on ever since: creating a psychological anxiety, then offering a consumer product to alleviate it; suggesting that you'll be more like famous and glamorous people if you consume an item; and offering sheer groveling flattery to customers. A 1927 ad for Palmolive soap, in striking contrast to the Stanton ad of thirty years before, shows a young bride, saying, "And I promise to keep my schoolgirl complexion," as though it were one more of the wedding vows. Another one from about 1923 is an ad for an early deodorant called Odorono (geddit? "Odor? Oh, no!"). It shows a group of pretty young women with bobbed hair, straight from a Fitzgerald story. The headline is "Flappers they may be, but they haven't forgotten the art of feminine appeal," and then a lot of blurb about making themselves delicate and fragrant. A Quaker oatmeal ad from the same period shows slum houses, and in pseudosociological jargon declares that only one in ten slum houses serves Quaker for breakfast, whereas nine in ten among strong, racially advantaged households eat it. It's a wonderfully misleading allegation of cause and effect.

I lecture about the Florida land boom, the hurricane of 1926 that ended it, the stocks and shares boom of the late twenties, and the Wall Street crash of 1929 that brought this bigger bonanza to an end. I try to summarize the historiographical debate that still surrounds the causes of the Great Depression, but it's hard to do so because one of the students, a graduating senior and economics major, is eager to join in and he challenges almost every generalization I make. It seems from his remarks that he's a radical libertarian, who takes the view that government intervention in the economy at any time, for any reason, is always wrong. He's well read and knows how to pick holes in my oversimplified explanations. This is the kind of situation that terrified me when I was a beginning teacher, and can still be troublesome. I have the advantage of experience, however, and ask him to talk with me for a minute afterward about some of the details, since constraints of time oblige me to round out the lecture in the remaining few minutes. He's pleased to be asked, and when we do discuss the issue afterward I'm able to convince him that I'm not advocating New Deal policies; I'm merely describing them. He, in turn, convinces me of something I know well: that I ought to spend more time studying economics.

At the end of class I hand out the graded papers, and give to each student, in addition to his or her own paper, a copy of a model paper I wrote in answer to the assigned question. In this way they will have a point of comparison when (if) they go over their work and my comments.

Rebuke (Saturday)

E-mail to the negligent student:

Dear X,

You have still not given me a paper. Late papers are penalized one grade per day, so I regret to inform you that your grade on this assignment is now an F.

You joined the course late, when the class had already met six times. You have been to class a total of seven times and missed it a total of eleven. You will note from the course reading list the statement: "Attendance at all class meetings is required." The only acceptable reason for missing class is illness, which must be documented.

In addition, you have almost always entered the room late on the days you have come. If final grades were due today you would get an F for the course.

From now until the end of the semester I require you to be in class for every meeting, to be seated in the room before we begin, and to do every assignment promptly and thoroughly.

That should do the trick!

Twenty-First Class (Monday)

A surprising lack of visitors to office hours this morning. I expected a handful of malcontents about the paper grades. Perhaps my connivance at the nationwide plague of grade-inflation has satisfied them that I've been more than fair.

There's nothing special about my lecture on the New Deal, and I dare say professors all over America about now are giving ones pretty similar in content and character. I used to be a wholehearted believer in the essential rightness of it—now I'm not so sure, and doubts take a bit of the bounce out of my presentation. Aware as I am that the libertarian student from last time is listening hypercritically, I veer between wondering if his sighs are aimed at me or at Franklin Roosevelt's ideas about how to run the economy. Strong-minded professors aren't supposed to quail, but I've never been good at facing down disapproval.

Despite these distractions, there's a certain amount of vitality left in my remarks, I think. There's the story of Roosevelt's triumph over polio, for example. It means a little more to me, at any rate, because my father was a polio victim too. Students are amazed to hear of the White House press corps' willingness to cover up the fact of the president's disability and to avoid showing him being helped to walk or stand, so that most ordinary citizens never knew of it. They enjoy tales of Roosevelt's fireside chats, too, and the way in which he manipulated the new medium of radio, appealing over the politicians' heads directly to their constituents, by persuading them to lobby on his behalf for controversial legislation. The stories of the era's eccentric reform advocates, Huey Long and Charles Coughlin, are fun too, and I always dramatize the sit-in strikes at the General Motors plants in 1937. There's something disheartening about having to rush through the New Deal like this, though. The quicker you do it, the more bare-bones it feels, and the less interesting. The Tennessee Valley Authority, for example, deserves more than half a dozen sentences, as does the comparison with the Soviet Union and the temporary surge in enthusiasm for Communism among American intellectuals, but nagging imperatives of clock and calendar won't let me slow down.

At the end of the class, as expected, the student who got the warning e-mail, stays behind to have a word with me. She's a real innocent, or at least plays the part of one. It never occurs to her that I am teaching not just her but thirty-eight others and that I am going to put her weak excuses in the context of the other students' ability to do the right thing. "I couldn't hand in the paper on the day you said. I had a midterm." "Did it last all day?" "No, but I guess I was distracted by studying for it." "I assigned the paper seventeen days before it was due. I know that students have to juggle various responsibilities—that's why I gave you plenty of time. Everyone else managed." "I've written it now," she says. "But now is too late—everyone else gave in their papers a week ago." "Will you read it now that it's here?" "I'll read it and make comments, if you like, but I'm not going to give you a passing grade." "Will you give me an extra credit opportunity later in the semester?" "I doubt it—so far you haven't show any interest in getting the *available* credit."

Then she denies that she is a latecomer on the days she comes at all. "Yes you are; we've started, and then you come in and disrupt the class." "It isn't ten-forty yet." "Yes it is; I ask the whole class: 'whose watch says it's not yet ten forty?' and if anyone says not yet, I wait for the slowest watch. You're not telling me that all thirty-eight of them have watches that are fast?" She says, "Last Friday, I'm sorry I wasn't in class then. My alarm didn't go off." "You must get a new one or ask a friend to wake you." "I woke up and said: 'Oh man, it's twelve o'clock. I've missed Allitt's class again.'" "Don't give me the details of your personal life. Just tell yourself that getting to this class every time, on time, is a priority. That's the thing you've got to put before everything else from now until the end of April." "I really need to get a grade on that paper . . ." And so on. I don't know for sure, but I wouldn't be surprised to find that she's a graduating senior, hoping to get away with the absolute minimum and willing to get a low grade as long as it isn't actually an F. Perhaps she's taking it S/U (Satisfactory/Unsatisfactory, such that any passing grade is S).

CHAPTER

12

■ ■ ■

Mid-Term Misconceptions

Twenty-Second Class (Wednesday)

Last night I played the part of a good Emory citizen by giving a speech to a group of alumni. It was entitled "America Has Its Advantages." In it, I describe the odd fact that I find myself, a foreigner, teaching young Americans the history of their own country, and I explain why I, like generations of immigrants, have felt such pleasure and gratitude at the life America offers. It's a speech I've given many times to Emory alumni here and around the country; its upbeat tone and feel-good mood make it popular with the alumni office. During questions, as often happens, a member of the audience asks me to predict America's future. I tell him, "Historians don't know anything about the future. The more we study the past the more we become convinced of how unpredictable the future really is. History teaches us a few lessons about ways in which we ought to act and ought not to act. It gives us occasional warnings, but it says nothing at all about what will come next. The world is far too complicated for us to be able to predict it, and if we try, we'll just be making ourselves into figures of fun for the next generation. Have you ever looked, for example, at ideas from the 1930s about what the year 2000 is going to be like? They tell you a lot about the 1930s, when they were written, but nothing at all about 2000 itself. The authors only have their own frame of mind and their current interests to work with, and are hopeless at predicting what will come next. Here's another example: think about 1970. No one then was talking about personal computers, and yet between then and now, they have transformed our world in totally unforeseen and unforeseeable ways. Students sometimes say to me, 'What's the point in studying history?' I tell them it helps them to understand themselves, where they have come from, and why their world is set up in this particular way. But if they ask me whether it will help them predict the future, the answer is no. History isn't useful in the utilitarian way—it's educational only in the broad sense."

This morning in class I show a long series of slides that I had meant to show over the last week or so. Pressure of business, and the attempt to say too much too quickly, inhibited me, so today there is a big, hour-long show with about fifty pictures. I am able to slow down the pace of the whole class in a way it has needed for the past week or two, and to go over several main themes again. The feeling I had last time of rushing through the New Deal dissipates as I show pictures of the principal figures, some Dorothea Lange and Ben Shahn photographs from the Farm Security Administration program, some Walker Evans photos that illustrated James Agee's great book *Let Us Now Praise Famous Men,* and some New Deal murals from Coit Tower in San Francisco and other public sites around the country. I have a picture from the Detroit auto-factory sit-in strikes of 1937 that shows the strikers' wives parading outside the factory. One of them carries a placard that reads: "Ladies Union Auxiliary: We Support Our Heroe's." The students know my obsessions by now and one of them actually calls out, as if on cue: "Misuse of the apostrophe!"

In the middle of the afternoon Lucas knocks on my door. He's a freshman, doing well in the class, so I am surprised to see him looking uncomfortable. He's come to tell me, in the nicest possible way, that I have blundered. It turns out that Friday, the day of the midterm, is Purim, a

Jewish festival. Is there any way, he asks, for him to be allowed to take the exam tomorrow instead? I'm the guilty party, not him—we're not supposed to schedule exams on anyone's religious holidays. So, after thinking it over for a moment, I decide that the only thing for it is to offer an alternative exam to those who don't want to be in class on Friday. Rather than write a "Jews-only" exam, however, I'll offer the choice to everyone, for reasons of impartiality. I reassure Lucas that he is justified in his request, then send out an e-mail to the whole class explaining that they can choose whether to do a take-home on Thursday or the in-class exam on Friday. Then I draft two different exams. I don't want them to be too different, because that would make the problem of comparable grading awkward. But they must not be too similar either, or else students doing the take-home will just pass along the word to students doing the in-class.

The first exam goes like this:

1. How did the United States become the world's wealthiest and most productive nation between 1870 and 1940? What problems did it encounter, and how successfully did it overcome them? (40 minutes)
2. Identify, and explain the historical significance of, four of the following (five minutes each):
   a. Theodore Roosevelt
   b. The first transcontinental railroad
   c. Anarchism
   d. The Battle of the Little Big Horn
   e. America's role in World War I
   f. Mass production

The second exam goes like this:

1. What difficulties did the United States overcome in achieving agricultural and industrial supremacy between 1870 and 1940? How widely were the benefits of this achievement shared inside America? (40 minutes)
2. Identify, and explain the historical significance of, four of the following (five minutes each)

a. Emma Goldman
b. Fundamentalism
c. Mass immigration from Europe
d. Full interchangeability of parts
e. The Hawthorne experiment
f. Populism
g. The Wall Street Crash
h. The New Deal

There are more choices for the in-class people on question 2, since they won't be able to make a last-minute check of their notes before beginning to write but after looking at the exam.

Take-Home Exam (Thursday)

Even though they are free to pick up the take-home exams any time between 8:30 and 10:00, nearly all those who are coming (eleven in all) come after 9:45. Why lose valuable sleep time? At the other end of the day, having been told that they must hand the exams in again between 4:00 and 5:00, all eleven show up between 4:50 and 5:10. When the first one arrives, breathless from fear of being too late, I tell him, "Congratulations; you're the first."

Lucas, appearing fifteen or twenty seconds before 5:00, stays to chat. We get onto the subject of *Bread Givers*. He was in Regina's section on discussion day, so I have not had the chance to talk it over with him. He says he didn't like it because if it is the only book on Judaism students read, it will give them the impression that Orthodox Judaism is tyrannical and repressive. "But," I plead, "it's such a good book on assimilation and immigrants' intra-family tensions." He and I are going back and forth on the point when the phone rings. It is Tricia, dreadfully anxious, saying she's only just come out of the clinic after an unexpectedly long visit to the doctor, must get her paper from her dorm, and will I still be there if she arrives in ten minutes? I reassure her and hang up, telling Lucas, "I was expecting a call like that. I wouldn't be surprised if any minute now someone came in with a desperate story about a failed computer. It happens every time." I am thinking of the occasion when, with one minute to go on a twenty-four hour take-home exam, a young man came staggering into the room carrying all the components of a big desktop computer, to prove to me that he really had written the exam and that he couldn't print it out.

Not a minute after I have made this prediction, in comes Marcia, cheeks mottled from crying, to say that her computer has gone wrong and that the repair people can't get to it until seven in the evening. Her inseparable friend Meredith is there too, for moral support, so I instruct her to give Marcia a supportive hug. The only way I'm allowed to express concern is by handing over the Kleenex (or, in my case, the industrial-size toilet paper roll). Marcia has a little bit more of a cry, I tell her I'll accept the midterm as an e-mail attachment after seven, and off they go. Lucas is visibly impressed by my ability to predict this event, but I disclaim all credit, since, at least in this little corner of human experience, history really does repeat itself. Not a minute later Tricia bursts onto the scene, with a desperate hacking cough, breathless after running from the remote dorm room and clutching her midterm in anxious hands. With her arrival, all eleven exams have come home again!

Twenty-Third Class (Friday)

At 10:30 the in-class exam begins for the twenty-eight students who didn't do it yesterday. Given the choice, and especially given the warning that the take-home would be graded to a higher standard, most students have made the decision I also would have made: to accept the extra day for preparation and then accept the short-term duress of doing the exam in class.

Tomorrow the midterm break begins, giving them a week off. Every year at this time, the university puts in a prominent place, usually on the grass in front of one of the dorms, a horribly wrecked car in which drunken drivers and their friends have been killed. There's one there today, and its crushed front end, shattered windows, and twisted metal, all make the don't-drink-and-drive point with graphic power. I'm nannyish enough to say, as they leave the room, "Have a great vacation everyone but drive carefully, and take a long look at the mangled red car before you leave."

Regina and I meet to discuss the grading. I xerox three exams and we each settle down to grading them independently, after making a list of things that should be included in a good answer. We grade the big question on a scale of 66, so that two-thirds of the time spent corresponds to two-thirds of the grade, and each of the short answers on a scale of 9, making a total possible grade of 102, and calling it a percentage. Regina was shocked by the low standard of the papers two weeks ago, and she's even more shocked by the low standard of the exams, but after a bit of to-ing and fro-ing we established a grading standard. I can't resist reading her a couple of little nuggets that I found while browsing the take-homes from yesterday.

Theodore Roosevelt was the author of the *Rough Riders* and also the president during the Depression up to the Second World War. He led a group of soldiers from all around the country to fight with him in the Spanish-American War of 1898. He enacted the New Deal; he had gotten polio at the beginning of his political career and was paralyzed from the waste [sic] down.

General Custer underestimated the Indians and lost, dying with his 7th Cavalry at this battle in eastern Montana. This victory by the Indians was short lived, as they were forced to scatter once again and Custer was more determined than ever to eliminate them after this humiliation.

The temptation to *not* get busy with grading the exams is pretty strong, but they're like courses on which you took a grade of "incomplete": the longer you leave them, the less appetizing they become, and the higher the mountain they represent seems to become. I'm not exactly encouraged by reading the opening sentences of the first one I turn to: "By 1940 the U.S. was a completely transformed nation from the time of 1870. Becoming an agricultural and industrial supremacy was not an easy task though . . ." but the task is inescapable.

Twenty-Fourth Class (Monday)

Midterm break is over and classes resume. We missed one of the reading assignments a couple of weeks ago because the book hadn't arrived yet at the bookstore. I asked the students to buy it before they left for the week and said we would make it the subject of our first class after the vacation. It is Melvyn Leffler's *Specter of Communism* (1994). As I was reading it yesterday evening, I realized there were going to be problems in class. I browsed it last fall when choosing books for the class but I now realize that it is too tough for many of the students to grasp. It begins in 1917 and goes to 1953. In 130 packed pages it describes the Russian Revolution and Civil War; the outcome of World War I; the American intervention with the White Russians; Lenin's New Economic Policy; the power struggle that followed his death; the rise of Stalin and the idea of Communism in one country; the rise of Hitler; the Comintern swerve of policy that led to the Popular Front; the attractions of Communism to idealistic young Americans in the 1930s, when the Depression seemed to have proved that capitalism was dysfunctional; the Spanish Civil War; the Hitler-Stalin pact; the partitioning of Poland and the beginning of World War II; the Anglo-Soviet-American wartime alliance; Stalin's anger over the slowness of a second front to develop in Western Europe; the bitter wrangling over Poland after the defeat of the Nazis; Churchill's "Iron Curtain" speech; Kennan's famous long telegram; the Berlin Airlift; NATO; the nuclear research and weapons race; and the Korean War. That's material enough to keep a class happy (or miserable) for several weeks. It is dense in the same way that a neutron star is dense—light rays positively bend toward it and are swallowed up—and here I was vainly hoping that they could read and digest the whole thing in a couple of days, immediately following sybaritic vacations on the Florida coast.

Regina and I divide the class, as usual on discussion day. Her e-mail later in the day tells me that her session was "very painful," and I am not surprised to hear it. Before I get going with my group, a man about my own age approaches me. He is there with his son, who is a prospective student, hoping to be admitted next year, and they have come along to watch a typical history course (I remember filling out a form a few weeks ago, agreeing to admit any visitors who wanted to drop in). I welcome them, borrow a copy of the book from Karen so that he and his son can follow along with the maps, at least, and then I begin class. "Maria, what is communism?" She says it is a system where everyone is equal. "Isn't that true of democracy?" "We're equal in our chances, at least in theory, but Communists say everyone should actually have the same." "Where does the idea come from?" "Karl Marx." "What do you know about him?" "Nothing, really." Vernon and Charles know that he was German, that he lived in the nineteenth century, and that he predicted the self-destruction of capitalism through the intensified immiseration of the working class until it felt it had nothing to lose and became revolutionary.

"Why did Americans dislike the Russian Communists in 1917, Marcia?" "Because Americans don't believe in Communism." "Well, until then it had never been tried on a large scale in any nation. What else was going on in 1917?" I ask. She's been on vacation a day or two too long (deep beach tan) and cannot remember. I give her a nudge. "Do you remember how, in the election of 1916, Woodrow Wilson won re-election with the slogan 'He kept us out of war'?" "Er . . . yes?" "Then what happened?" She gives the bowed-head look of absolute defeat and blank forgetfulness. Simon chimes in from the back: "He got us into war!" "Yes. Do you remember now, Marcia?" She looks upset and says yes, but with no conviction at all. I continue, "So let me ask you again: why should the Americans take such a rapid dislike to Communism?" "I don't know." "Did you read the book?" "Yes." "What did the Russian revolutionary leaders do that upset the British, French, and Americans?" More of the look. "Can't you remember that passage?" "No." That is the standard of many of their contributions today, though a handful of them, particularly the men, have tried hard at least to sort out the major issues. Foreign-policy history tends to open up a big gender gap, with the women lagging far behind, and today illustrates the point.

A bit later on in the class I ask Kathleen, "Why did some idealistic Americans join the Communist Party?" "Because they liked Russia?" Her answer is a question. "Possibly, but put yourself in the position of a student, exactly your age, and let's imagine for a moment that it's 1933. If a young Communist asked you to join the party, why might you say yes?" Long, troubled stare. "I don't like Communism." That's off the point but I go with it for a while. "Why not?" I ask. "It's unrealistic about human nature. It doesn't reward people for their hard work and so it lets everyone stop bothering to work hard." Simon chimes in again, "What about the appeal to patriotism?" I ask Kathleen, "Do you love your country?" "Yes." "Would you make sacrifices for it?" "Yes." "If your country asked you to work very hard to help industrialize it, would you do it?" She answers, "Maybe for a while, but when the people around me stopped bothering I would probably stop too." "OK. It's true that one of the commonest criticisms of Communism is that it's always been unrealistic about human motivation, and the need to let people be more self-interested if they are going to be creative and hard-working. But you haven't answered my question: why did you, a young American, join the Communist Party back in 1933?" Blank look. "What else was going on just then?" She's been on the beach a bit too long as well, and just can't remember all the way back to early March, when we studied it. Finally Roy, right behind her, hisses, "the Great Depression" in a stage whisper. Kathleen does a double take then says to me, in a loud clear voice, "the Great Depression?" Even then it's more of a question than a statement—maybe she's afraid her neighbor is a practical joker. "Oh, well done, Kathleen, yes, the Great Depression. Why should that make you join the Communists?" "Because I'm so poor." "Maybe, but quite a lot of American Communists were middle-class, rather than the desperate workers Marx had anticipated. What do you think about the Depression you're seeing all around you?" "It sucks." We continue in this way for a minute or two more.

I ask Eric about the Communist Party's frequent changes of direction in the 1930s. "That bit was too complicated for me." "Oh, yes, it is complicated. So I bet what you did was to draw a chronological chart to make sure you kept it all straight in your mind." Bashful grin. "Let me see your chart, Eric." "Actually there isn't one." "So how on earth did you keep it all straight?" "That's what I need some help with." "I'd be delighted to help you. My first piece of advice is to draw up a chart so that you get the sequence of events straight and the changing configuration of all these groups. Haven't I told you over and over in this course that chronology matters?" "Oh yes, you've certainly said that a lot!" "Right. And when I have said it what have you done?" "I've tried to be more chronological." "Show me some evidence that you tried to be chronological in reading this book." "Well, I started at the beginning, in 1917, and read right through it to the end, in Korea." "But now you can't remember one of the key passages?" "Sorry, professor, there was just too much of it." "Can you remember any aspects of the politics of the 1930s?" "Just the New Deal." "But the author scarcely mentions the New Deal. What does he think was the really big event of 1933?" "Don't know." "Barbara?" "The election of Hitler?" "Good; if you're ever looking for arguments against democracy, you can always use the fact that Hitler won an election. Now Eric, back to you for a moment: do you recall the passage on the election of Hitler and the Communist reaction to it?" "I guess." "What did Stalin think of Hitler?" "He was against him." "Why?" "Human rights?" "Why is that probably not a good answer?" "He wasn't a human rights guy either?" So it continues, with nearly every answer offered as a doubtful question in itself.

I break off from badgering him eventually to make a declaration. "Chronology matters more than ever when we're discussing these political events. Between the beginning of the Great Depression and the end of the Second World War the picture keeps changing, often very quickly, and it's easy to lose track." A few minutes later I'm nagging away at Charles in the same way. "What happened in December 1941?" "Was that when Hitler and Stalin made their deal?" "No, that had happened two years earlier, in 1939. When Hitler attacked Russia in the summer of 1941, obviously, the deal was off. But what happened the same year just before Christmas?" Blank look. "Come on, Charles, it happened on a day that will live in infamy." Gale of laughter from some of the others, and finally he blurts out, "Pearl Harbor." The class has been slow and laborious throughout—that visiting father and son can't have been very impressed. Although I make a great show of indignation at the casualness with which most of them have read the book, I also have to blame myself (not publicly) with the reflection that it really is rather hard. Its brevity is deceptive because it is the brevity of acute compression— every paragraph packed with complicated summaries and insights that are far from commonsensical.

Twenty-Fifth Class (Wednesday)

It's time for the Second World War. Bearing in mind the students' dismay and confusion on Monday, I go over several issues I have mentioned before, including the Hitler-Stalin pact, the issue of the second front, and the imperative need to get the chronology straight if you want to understand the Second World War. To give them a break halfway through the lecture, which is otherwise another work of compression and complexity, I mention that the Battle of Midway, 1942, was the first naval battle in the history of the world in which the rival fleets of ships never came within sight of each other. Instead it was fought by aircraft from the all-important aircraft carriers, which proved to be the decisive weapons of the Pacific campaign. I draw a picture of a gentle curve to represent the curvature of the Earth, explaining how the curve limits the distance we can see, and explain that the two fleets were over the horizon to one another. Nathan doesn't get the point, so I ask him if he has ever been to sea. "Yes, on a cruise." "When you saw another ship coming in the far distance, Nathan, which bit of it did you see first?" "The front?" "No, surely not." "Er . . . the side!" "Oh no! Look here," and I hand him the chalk: "Draw a ship here on the curved ocean." He draws a weird little box, and to help him out I draw a little stick figure standing on the box to represent him, looking out into the distance. "Do you see in straight lines?" "Yes." "Okay, so when you look into the distance, eventually your line of vision touches the point where the curve obscures further places from view (I draw a dotted line from the stick figure's head until it touches the curve). What's the name of that point?" "Midway Island?" (laughter).

"Come on Nathan, I know you know." There is another ripple of laughter. He feels self-conscious because he's in front of the whole class. Someone hisses in a stage whisper, "the horizon," which brightens him up considerably and prompts him to say, "The horizon." "Yes, well done, I knew you'd think of it after a minute. Now, when another ship is beyond the horizon but coming towards you, which bit of it will you see first?" I draw the other ship. He looks and looks at the board but can't work it out. To help a little more I draw a tall mast on it. At last he gets it: "The top!" "Right. Please take a seat. The thing about carrier-borne aircraft, especially when coupled with radar and radio, is that they vastly extend the distance a ship can 'see.' Aircraft from the two fleets each contacted their enemy, and attacked, without the fleets themselves being within even a horizon of each other." There was nothing lighthearted about the Battle of Midway itself, but it's become a source of merriment here, and a momentary distraction from grim tales of Stalingrad, firestorm bombing, and the Holocaust.

Also today, I assign everyone their second paper. They are required to answer this question: "Why did the United States of America take on global responsibilities between 1917 and 1990? How successfully did it manage them and in what ways did they change American society internally?" Rather than simply give them the title, I hand out a sheet of instructions, on which I've tried to alert them to at least most of the obvious conceptual and practical difficulties they will need to overcome. You can see the sheet at the back of this book (page 235).

Twenty-Sixth Class (Friday)

This morning, aware that I have been driving the class rather hard, I show them a film. It is *The Life and Times of Rosie the Riveter*, made in the early 1980s. It follows the fortunes of a group of women who worked in heavy industry during the Second World War, when the men were away in the military. Film sequences of the women describing the work, their union activity, their problems with family, male employees, child care, and social life, are interspersed with newsreel footage from the time, all drenched in patriotic sentimentality and Glenn Miller tunes. The newsreels show clearly enough that women were first manipulated into the workforce and then, when the war ended, manipulated out of it again. In a 1942 newsreel, for example, one scene shows a group of women playing cards. A stern voice on the radio announces that women are needed in the factories and shipyards. The four put down their cards, give each other guilty glances, and stand, as though resolved to get down to the factory at once. In 1945 films, by contrast, the women are told that they've got to give up their jobs so that the returning heroes can have work.

It's understandable, in a way, since it was reasonable to assume that the terrible Depression conditions of the 1930s might recur and that heads of families should have a shot at whatever work was available. Even so, it's unsettling to see the message underlined by 1945 interviews with doctors who say that a generation of neglected children is growing up and that working mothers are selfish. The actual old "Rosies" describe their experiences in the factories and shipyards. Most of them enjoyed it because they gained more skills than ever before and were much more highly paid. They became union activists and, in several instances, struggled to overcome racial and gender discrimination in their workplaces. They talk about their search for industrial work after the war and the blunt way in which they were rejected because they were women. It's a strenuously feminist film, but not heavy-handed, and I am pleased, glancing around the room, to see many of the men in class laughing and groaning in ways the director surely intended. For a course of this kind it is absolutely tailor-made.

13

A Dry Pleasure

Twenty-Seventh Class (Monday)

Today we're discussing Carey McWilliams's *California: The Great Exception* (1949). I loved it and thought it was a fine book, but it isn't long before I find the students sullen, mutinous, and resistant. It turns out they don't like all the details about squabbles over access to water, aren't interested in the skulduggery of Los Angeles as it hijacked the water supply of the Owens River Valley, and don't care about the erratic flow of the pre-Hoover Dam Colorado River. I warned them that they must learn the geography of California in order to make sense of the book, and I begin with a ten-minute in-class map quiz, which requires them to site and label various rivers, mountains, canals, and cities on a blank outline map of the state. It does nothing to mollify them, and through the course of the discussion they say they can't remember what the author said, or else they don't understand his words. I leave feeling dejected and discover that Regina has had the same experience with her half of the class. To make matters worse, she didn't like the book either. I must be slipping. It's true that the history of irrigation farming, like the history of railroads, is one of my hobbyhorses, and that it leaves nearly everyone else ice-cold with indifference. Let's hope next week's reading, about the great black migrations from the rural South to the urban North between the 1940s and the 1970s, will have enough human interest to get the blood pumping again.

It's a busy day for me because in the evening I have to give my fortnightly lecture to the senior citizens. When I arrive the group is already buzzing about the fact that I'm going to return next year to talk about Victorian Britain. Tonight, however, it's "Religion and War in the Twentieth Century." I've given this lecture two or three times previously, to student groups, but it feels different this time around because five or six of my audience are World War II combat veterans, for whom it was an existential, rather than a merely theoretical, matter. One of them flew with Claire Chennault's "Flying Tigers" in China, another sailed on Atlantic convoy escorts.

They listen courteously to my description of the theological controversy over the rights and wrongs of area bombing and the atom bomb, but each in turn assures me during the interval that they never felt better than when they heard about the atom bomb. It might well have saved their lives by sparing them the need to participate in a conventional invasion of Japan. I'm careful, as usual, to be neutral in tone, to come off neither hawkish nor dovish, and this approach (which raised some eyebrows when applied to Union and Confederacy a few weeks ago, because they would have liked me to be much more pro-Dixie) is acceptable. They laugh at my stories about Daniel and Philip Berrigan, the priests who tried various theatrical demonstrations in their efforts to stop American participation in the Vietnam War, including kneeling in the snow, fully robed, outside the Secretary of Defense's house, and pouring their blood over the draft files at the Selective Service Office in Baltimore. (Later, the Berrigans tried a similar stunt in nearby Catonsville, using homemade napalm on the files and setting them on fire.) As ever, I leave the senior citizens feeling welcomed, satisfied, and weirdly maternal. The reception here is a total contrast with the cold resistance I met in the morning from the undergraduates.

Twenty-Eighth Class (Wednesday)

Today I lecture on the beginnings of the Cold War. The students read about it in the Leffler book, but their grasp of the issues was so tenuous I decided to go over the principal issues again and to throw in a few anecdotes that Leffler didn't bother with, such as the drama of George Kennan's "X" telegram, the explosion of the bombs at Bikini Atoll, the controversy surrounding the Alger Hiss and Rosenberg cases, and the barefaced cynicism of Joe McCarthy. I do a long passage on the city of Berlin and the role it played throughout the Cold War, periodically becoming the center of the world's attention (the 1948 airlift and the 1961 wall, for example). Chris is surprised to hear me state baldly that Hiss and the Rosenbergs were found guilty without adding that they might not have been. I tell him and the others that in bygone days I also believed them wrongfully accused, but that the more I read about the two cases, the more I became convinced that they were in fact guilty. I also mention Ronald Reagan's red hunt when he was president of the Screen Actors' Guild. Most students look back at me with more or less blank faces, which reminds me that to them Reagan too is ancient history. Most of them were only about six years old when Reagan left office—too young for them to have had much impression of him. When I first taught the introductory course, back at Berkeley summer school in 1986, that bit of information set off a great clamor, thick with denunciations of the villainous, much-hated, and then-still-in-office president.

I forgot to mention here that I was unable to sleep last night, so I jumped out of bed and did the most soporific thing I could think of: I graded the map quiz. On the California outline map, I had asked the students to draw and mark the following twenty items: Central Valley, Colorado River, Sacramento River, San Joaquin River, Owens River, Death Valley, Imperial Valley, the Mohave Desert, Bakersfield, Fresno, San Francisco, San Diego, Los Angeles, Mono Lake, Lake Tahoe, the Sierra Nevada Mountains, the Coast Range, the Pacific Ocean, and Mexico. If they were right I gave a point, if they were in more or less the right area I gave them a half-point. The worst student got just two right, the best got nineteen, and most were in the seven to twelve range. Many of the students, now as always, are comically bad at geography, having no idea about basic matters. For example, I asked one in class the other day a well-known trick question: "Vernon, every river in the world flows in the same direction. What direction is that?" He thought for a moment and then said, "North to south." "What about the Nile?" "Well, apart from that one!" As usual, someone else let the cat out of the bag by hissing, "Downhill." Vernon suddenly got the point. "OK," said I, "where do rivers usually begin?" "In the mountains." "Yes, and where do they usually end?" "In another body of water." "Such as?" "A lake?" "Or?" Very long pause. "The ocean." "Right." Despite this little exchange, he and many of his classmates have contented themselves, in drawing the rivers, to short little squiggles that begin nowhere in particular and end in the same way. One of the women did not hesitate to have her own personal Colorado River beginning east of the Sierra Nevadas but finishing west of them, where, despite its heroic climb and precipitous descent, it apparently petered out somewhere near Fresno.

I thought back to a similar quiz from a few years ago, when I asked the students to name all the states on an outline map and then draw the course of several rivers. The Colorado was among them. One student correctly identified the state of Colorado, but when it came to the river she didn't quite know where to begin. Looking at the page afterward it was possible to reconstruct her frame of mind. Tentatively, she drew a squiggle in the middle of the state of Colorado, thinking it was a reasonable guess that the river began there. Then she caused it to wander about the state for a while, with some spectacular meanders. Gaining confidence that she was in the right place, but not having confidence enough to actually lead it into another state with a different name, she finally linked up the end with the beginning, to make a ragged circle. So far as I know, her Colorado is the only river to flow into itself—there should be an Escher drawing to commemorate it.

Sure enough, grading the map quiz was sufficient to summon Morpheus. After falling back into bed for a long, deep, and dreamless sleep, I awoke refreshed. I now hand back the maps, telling the students, "Anything over twelve is a pass, anything over fifteen is an A. Some of these were . . . disgraceful, others excellent!" (nervous laughter). The students begin to disperse, but Curtis comes up to petition for more points. He insists that his Mono Lake and his Coast Range both deserve a whole point instead of halves. I agree under pressure and he goes away with his A strengthened from an eighteen to a nineteen.

Another student stays to haggle over grades, but not in connection with the map. He is brandishing his midterm, insisting I was mistaken in several places when I graded it. The first use of fully interchangeable parts came, he argues, not in the bicycle industry, as I said in lecture, but in guns manufactured by Eli Whitney. I ask him to bring some documentation for this assertion—if it's true I want to know about it. Next he shows me a passage in his blue book that I had criticized but that, in his opinion, was correct. It says: "The Populists had a series of legislative successes, including the direct election of Senators, the federal income tax, Prohibition, and the federal Interstate Commerce Commission."

Me: Those reforms came later, during the Progressive era.
Him: Yes but they were Populist ideas.
Me: Well, they were ideas that some Populists and some members of various other groups espoused in the late nineteenth century, but they didn't become law until the twentieth. There had been a prohibition movement in the 1830s but surely you'd find it misleading if I said: "National Prohibition was a legislative success of evangelical Christians in the state of Maine during the 1830s."
Him: If it was their idea that's how you *should* put it.
Me: Remember that when you're writing papers and exams I expect you to write them to an audience less well informed on the subject than you. Readers who didn't already know that national Prohibition began after the First World War would be deceived into thinking that it began in the 1890s, from what you have written.
Him: Well, there wasn't much of a time delay.
Me: More than twenty years!

He's a manipulative devil and his eye-rolling and heavy sighs make me feel I must be wrong, even when I know I'm really not. For the last few weeks he has contrived to treat the class, and me, as a dreadful imposition on his life.

Honors Program Planning (Thursday)

Office hours, and I'm expecting a crowd. Sure enough, there's a line in front of my door when I arrive. Many of them are talented juniors, history majors whom the History Department has invited to participate in our Honors Program next year. If they accept the invitation, they are supposed to come and see the director of undergraduate studies (me) for more detailed information about the program, to help them make an informed decision. I round up four students and speak to them as a group rather than say the same thing again and again. Here's my little speech.

The Honors Program is the best thing we offer to undergraduates, and I hope you'll join it. To get honors, you'll need to take a special honors seminar with the most talented history majors in your year, take a graduate seminar with some of our current history graduate students, and then research and write a thesis on a topic of your own choosing. Before you leave Emory this semester, you should try to decide what the topic will be and who you would like as your advisor. Talk to the advisor and try to spend part of the summer vacation doing preliminary research. It is a time-consuming program—the research itself just eats up time, and the more you're able to make a start on it before your senior year begins, the better you'll probably do in the long run.

Instead of having the history served up to you predigested, as has been the case up to now, you will *become* real historians. Rather than accepting the fruits of someone else's research and analysis, you'll be doing the research yourself, working out what it means, and making sense of it all in writing. It is difficult, very difficult, and a quantum jump harder than anything you have done so far. But it is also gratifying. Within a few weeks of beginning the research you will have become the world's leading expert on your particular area of concentration. Your advisor can guide you, give you research advice, and warn you away from blind alleys, but you are the historian, making the decisions, compiling the information, and gradually developing mastery of your chosen area.

It can be exhausting and it's nearly always daunting, especially in the early days. You look sometimes at great boxes of papers and documents, millions of words, and feel it's too much ever for you to reduce to some kind of coherent order. You plod along anyway and you are rewarded with a few wonderful moments. Suddenly you discover a document that leads you to understand one of your principal characters' motives better than before, or that shows you that other historians' interpretations of him have been insufficient. Or else you discover that an event you'd previously not known about had taken place and changed the situation in a way no other historian has noticed. You stumble through masses of memoranda, feeling you're getting absolutely nowhere, then suddenly a revealing exchange brings everything into sharp focus. That's what historical research is like.

Some people say it's dry . . . very dry. It *is* a dry pleasure, but dry like dry wine—better than something too sweet—a real pleasure, with immensely positive psychological benefits. Some people say the writing is painful and difficult. It *is* painful and difficult, and may in fact be the toughest thing you write in your whole life, because it's the biggest project you've ever undertaken. To write a forty-page paper is more than twice as difficult as writing a twenty-page paper, and to write a hundred-page thesis (of the kind we expect in this program) is harder still. Nevertheless the rewards make it worthwhile. It's an immense confidence builder to know you can do it, and to know that here is an area of historical knowledge of which you are the master.

Now let me follow up with a few warnings. Every year this program has a high attrition rate. More people start than finish. Among your many tasks in the honors program is to make sure that you're not one of the casualties. The ones who drop out are usually those who didn't make an early start, or who permitted themselves to get discouraged when the research didn't yield up as many gems as they had hoped. Sometimes students get into a weird avoidance pattern, saying to themselves, "Yes, I must get on with my research . . . next week." I've been advisor to students who, instead of coming to see me with their research problems, stayed away because they had these problems, hiding from my summons. Don't be one of those! I and the other professors really can help.

Above all, don't be a procrastinator. Procrastination is the downfall of honors students every year. You need to be a self-motivator. You know how it is in ordinary classes: you have a deadline or an obligation almost every week? In the honors program you often go two or three months without an externally imposed deadline, because you're supposed to be systematically gathering data and we know it takes time. That means you have to stick to a schedule and impose deadlines on yourself, or get your advisor to impose a few of them on you, so that the year is structured rather than open-ended.

There's the warning, but don't let me discourage you. You wouldn't be here in the first place if you weren't good enough to do it. You've all got excellent records and have shown every sign of being the kind of people who can do this kind of work and do it well. Rise to the occasion, and cover yourselves with glory.

The flourish in my peroration makes them blush or chuckle, depending on personality, and they ask me a few administrative questions to bring us down to earth again. I can tell I've aroused their determination to do it and do it well. Each of them is thinking, "Those poor saps who can't get the whole thing done in time and start hiding from their own projects! You won't catch me in that situation." They may be right but I know from a dozen or more years' experience that probably half of them will in fact drop out sometime between October and February.

When they have gone, a gaggle of foreign-study applicants come in seeking course-equivalency approval, another of the staples of my job as director of undergraduate studies. Next I have to deal with a different kind of problem, one that I dread—a weeper! By the time she leaves I'm exhausted and it's still barely ten in the morning.

What actually happens is that this student enters and sits down, saying, "Doctor Allitt, I really want to do well in this class to try to get my grades up, and I was disappointed to get only a B- in the midterm because I worked so hard and felt sure I'd done very well." I answer, "Okay, let's have a look at your blue book: I graded so many I can't remember yours without having a look at it to remind me." She hands it over and I begin to glance through it, but as I do so I hear telltale snuffling sounds. Sure enough, when I glance up, I see big tears rolling down her cheeks and the snuffles rise to become gasping sobs. It's a sight that usually makes me freeze with horror, and before I can say a word she berates herself: "I can't believe it. I didn't come here to cry. Oh, I'm so very sorry, Doctor, so sorry." Resisting the temptation to put a paternal arm around her, I hand over the big industrial toilet roll. It's a bad case of boyfriend trouble, and before I can restrain her the whole painful story comes out.

After a while she calms down enough to ask whether we can return to studying the exam. I open it but almost at once we come to one of the short answers in which she has confused the two President Roosevelts. In fact, she admits that she thought there was only one, and was surprised in class to reflect on how old he must have been during the Depression and World War II. "But don't you remember me describing the fact that they were distant cousins and belonged to different political parties?" Rather than answer she begins to cry again. I murmur a few calming words and tell her we'll go on with this review of her exam when she's feeling better. When she's gone I have a long soothing nap on the office floor.

In the afternoon there's an orientation meeting for the people who are going to Emory's summer school in England this year. Tom Lancaster runs the meeting with his usual flair and authority; he's a great boss. This January, on the first morning of registration, seventy-five students applied for the program. There are only forty-five places, and it's been so popular in the last few years that anyone who doesn't sign up before lunchtime on the first day doesn't stand a chance. This time it was all over by ten o'clock, apparently. None of our other study abroad programs quite matches this one for enthusiastic participation. It's become semilegendary over the last decade, such that students mention to me, when we're there, escapades from former years (in which I figure), often embellished and magnified to mythical proportions as they have passed around by word-of-mouth.

Each of the faculty gives a brief presentation about what his or her class will do, and about what books students will need to buy before they leave Emory at the end of this semester. Tom goes over the rules with them, emphasizing that they must have current passports, must have tickets getting them to England on the right day, and above all that they must not break the law while they are in England. He cites a few hair-raising examples of American students who have been arrested overseas for drug offenses and have had to face the full force of local laws. Remember, he concludes, you are ambassadors for America and for Emory.

Twenty-Ninth Class (Friday)

I hate to miss class but just occasionally it has to happen. Today at ten o'clock Mrs. Allitt and I appear in a lawyer's office to "close" on a house. Among the many hectic aspects of this semester has been our search for, and now purchase of, a house, our first ever. It's a great life being a professor, but there's not much money in it; until now we couldn't afford to buy a house. It's a mixture of thrills and horrors, signing a document in which I undertake to keep on making the payments until I'm seventy-four. However, let's not get into that; the point is that my absence is the occasion for Regina to make her debut as a lecturer. Later in the day, when I check my e-mail, I find a message from her, reporting on how she got on. After preliminaries it says:

From my standpoint the lecture went well: I wasn't all that nervous and I actually came close to preparing the proper amount of material. From their standpoint, hmmmm, they were a little bored and restless. But I know my presentation will improve in time. I just needed to prove to myself that I could actually do it. The topics I covered were; the debate over dropping the A-Bomb, Truman, his proposal of an international nuclear agency, the Bikini tests, the Soviet bomb, Eisenhower and "massive retaliation," a little on the RAND corporation, Herman Kahn, Sputnik, the ICBM, the Cuba Missile Treaty, SALT I and II, nuclear winter, Reagan and SDI. In retrospect I should have organized this around some themes but I did want to cover as much ground as possible. I'm also beginning to realize that things I find amusing and wonderful about history may not necessarily be true for everyone.

How right she is on that last point; I've had the experience throughout my life as a teacher, most recently earlier this week with the book on California water politics. I send her a congratulatory e-mail in reply.

Thirtieth Class (Monday)

The last two discussion classes haven't been much good—first came the rather-too-complicated book on Communism, then came the much-hated book on California and water-politics. I'm not criticizing the books themselves—I like both of them, but I can see in retrospect that they were not ideally suited to the introductory course, most of whose members are taking it because they've got to (it fulfils a college requirement) rather than because they have a deep and abiding love of history. (Students with a deep and abiding love of history are usually excused from this course because they scored a five on their Advanced Placement test in high school.) The last two weeks' experience makes me all the more anxious that reading and discussion should go well this time, and luckily the book is just right. It is *The Promised Land* (1991) by Nicholas Lemann, a journalist writing straightforward prose, telling an important story in an intelligent way, without needless digressions or complications. I have been rereading it over the past few days with a sense of pleasure, partly for the book itself, and partly in relief at confirming its suitability for the course. We are reading just the first two long sections of the book, about 120 out of its 350 pages.

Lemann traces the great black migration from the cotton-sharecropping South to the industrial cities of the North in the years between about 1930 and about 1970. He singles out one Mississippi delta town, Clarksdale, and one destination, the South Side of Chicago, and makes them stand for the much bigger process of which they are a synecdoche. Extensive interviewing with now-elderly Chicagoans who started life in Clarksdale, along with research into Chicago politics and national "war on poverty" policy debates, enables him to weave together stories about the big picture and all its little components. He begins with the invention of the mechanical cotton picker, which became commercially viable in 1944. Until then, white plantation owners had depended on the presence of black laborers, the descendants of slaves, who worked as laborers or sharecroppers.

The sharecropping system was outrageously iniquitous. The black farmer was furnished with supplies, land, and tools on credit in return for half the value of the crop. But he was rarely literate, had no access to the plantation owner's books, no way of checking the fairness of the "settle" at the end of each season's growing, and often found himself still in debt after a year of backbreaking toil. As Lemann says, a handful of plantation owners treated their sharecroppers fairly, giving them an incentive to stay in the same place and work hard. Many others routinely cheated and exploited their sharecroppers, who retaliated by moving frequently, leaving behind unpaid debts. These itinerants, though, could often do no better on the next plantation than on the previous one because the same structural factors were in place, supported by strict legal segregation and a racial caste system.

The First World War set off an employment boom in Northern industrial cities, and employers willingly hired black migrants from the cotton South, whom they knew to be hard workers, when the European immigrant labor supply was cut off. So long as the war persisted the migration boomed, and Clarksdale blacks discovered they could earn four or five times as much in Chicago as in Mississippi. The same thing happened again in the Second World War, and this time around the migration was accelerated because the invention of the mechanical cotton picker signaled a declining need, among local landowners, for labor. Whites tried to prevent migration the first time around; by the end of World War II they were actively encouraging it, especially when they could foresee that the spread of civil rights (then just on the horizon) might eventually lead to black voters outnumbering whites in black belt counties.

The South Side of Chicago was anything but a paradise. Lemann is unsentimental in his description of the street crime, recurrent family violence, squalid poverty, and overcrowding of the district. Still, he nudges the reader toward an understanding that it was superior to the Mississippi alternative. Next he shows how postwar politics worked in Chicago, the machine system and the ethnic ward bosses. One of the great characters in the book is the wooden-legged black congressman William Dawson, who was a commanding presence on the Chicago South Side, and its representative between 1942 and 1970. Like the old turn-of-the-century bosses that Lincoln Steffens denounced in *The Shame of the Cities*, Dawson regarded politics as a transaction in which voters gave their votes in return for jobs, housing, emergency help, and favors. He corrupted the police to protect the numbers racket, and delivered the vote reliably every election day. Content with the geographical segregation of the city, he even urged President Kennedy *not* to talk about civil rights, for fear it would upset the operating agreement by which the Democratic Party's odd components (Northern workers and Southern white segregationists) held together. He was in cahoots with the Reverend J. H. Jackson, a prominent Chicago minister (who, I've read elsewhere, opposed Martin Luther King Jr.'s attempts to mobilize the black Southern Baptists behind the civil rights cause).

Lemann explains that Boss Richard Daley, the famous midcentury mayor of Chicago, blundered in his treatment of the South Side. By trying to preserve geographical segregation he first approved the building of vast public-housing tower blocks, which have since become a byword for alienation, fear, crime, and crack. Next he tried to prevent the orderly spread of the black population as it continued to grow. The result was severely overcrowded schools on the South Side, while schools in other parts of Chicago were half-empty. Eventually sheer pressure of numbers forced the black ghetto to expand. Neighborhood organizer Saul Alinsky and Catholic Archbishop Stritch make cameo appearances in this book as well-intentioned supervisors of this expansion. Neither could make a sufficient impression to prevent the white flight that followed, as areas lurched rapidly from all-white to all-black, spurred on by unscrupulous "panic peddlar" realtors. The first black family to move into a white neighborhood would often suffer physical attack and firebombing. Next, more black residents would arrive, whites would sell their houses at rock-bottom prices, and the ward bosses, often belonging to the depart- ing ethnic group, would find themselves unable to maintain their old jobs-for-votes business with the suspicious newcomers.

To my delight many of the students are as fascinated by the story as I, and the conversation around it is lively and engaging. Undergraduates here are extremely sensitive to questions of racial good manners, and so talk their way delicately around the question of family breakdown, vio- lence, and addiction. Several of them glance frequently at the only black student in my half of the class, but he is not among the enthusiasts and shows no inclination to join in except when I ask him a direct question. I try to avoid the development of an "identity politics" mood in class—by which students claim special insight into problems by virtue of their own gender, religious, or racial identity. I urge them, instead, to stick to the information actually presented in the readings. Inevitably the attempt breaks down from time to time—witness our discussion on *Bread Givers* a few weeks ago—but I still think it's worth keeping the lid on as far as possible. I know from talking to people in our Institute of Liberal Arts that it's all too easy, once identity claims get started, for class to degenerate into a more-victimized-than-thou arena of clamoring spe- cial pleaders.

I bring Nathan out in front of the class to read a key passage to us about Congressman Dawson. Recently I've been letting that hat stay on his head some days, but his reading aloud is so bad I force him to take it off and read the passage through again, "with feeling." He is better the second time through, but he still cannot understand why Dawson was opposed to civil rights. This is a problem I've bumped into a few times over the past few years, especially since Martin Luther King Jr. became, over and above his status as a national hero, a Day! Students find it difficult to grasp that he could have had opponents, not just among the white segregationists but also among black leaders, and that his rise to greatness and the Nobel Prize were not the subject of unanimous acclaim in the black community. Cross-questioning brings Nathan gradually toward the point, but he still shies away from the logic of this opposition, even though it is a principal theme of the book he has been reading.

Helen, when asked to read and comment on a key passage, singles out a set of forlorn love letters written by Lillian, one of the Clarksdale women in Chicago, to the man she loves, Ferris Luckett, who mistreats her. Their passionate reconciliations are punctuated by bitter fights, which usually end with him being sent into the other room to sleep among the children. While he is there he begins to molest Connie, one of the girls. At first the mother won't believe her daughter's account of this unwanted attention but one day,

Lillian came out of her bedroom and actually saw Ferris doing to Connie what Connie had been saying he did. She ran back into the bedroom and came out with a gun in her hand. She pointed it at Ferris's head and pulled the trigger. The bullet struck Ferris in the jaw; he was alive, but bloody and badly wounded. The apartment was filled with a sick, rotting smell. When it registered with Lillian what she had done, she burst into tears and pleaded with Ferris to forgive her, because she hadn't really meant to shoot him. (88)

She nurses him back to health, but once he's out and about again he tells the police what happened and has her arrested. Lemann's skill, to which the students respond, is his ability to blend heart-wrenching and melodramatic tales like this with an incisive explanation of machine politics, the debate over the Moynihan Report on the black family, and changing economic and technological conditions. It has been a good meeting, one I could conclude at 11:30 with a real feeling of accomplishment.

14

■ ■ ■

Vietnam as Ancient History

Thirty-First Class (Wednesday)

The Allitts are moving house but the semester doesn't stop to oblige us. After greeting the movers, haggling over the exact amount of stuff they are going to move, and for how much, I leave the capable Mrs. A. in charge and head off to campus. This morning I lecture on the Vietnam War, following my pattern, since February, of handing around a detailed outline. When I first became a teacher of American history, in Berkeley in 1979, it was quite common to have people in class who had been in the army or activists in the antiwar movement. Vietnam and the controversy it had provoked swirled through every conversation and stood front and center in the concerns of hundreds of people in Berkeley. The Cold War was still in full swing, then just heating up because of the Soviet invasion of Afghanistan, and the revived antinuclear movement was flexing its atrophied muscles. A lecture on Vietnam in those days was certain to generate controversy, and hardly a word went unchallenged for bias, emphasis, or implicit stand-taking.

How different it is now to teach on Vietnam. The students before me this morning were born ten years after the Americans withdrew and are no more concerned, existentially, about its events and meaning than they are about what really happened to *The Flying Dutchman*. None have been there (I know because I begin by asking), and when I ask who's the son or daughter of a Vietnam veteran, only one raises her hand. "Who had family in the antiwar movement?" Another one. For the rest it's just history, effectively as remote in time and place as the crusades or the War of the Spanish Succession. The disadvantage of teaching it in 1970s Berkeley was that it was sometimes difficult to get beyond the first or second sentence of your lecture before controversy erupted. The disadvantage of teaching it now is that it is so complicated when approached cold. Like all these foreign-policy issues (which we're plugging hard just now to enable students to get a good start in writing their second paper, on a foreign-policy topic), it's essential to know when things happened, how the alliances lined up, and how apparently pointless actions and decisions all made sense in context.

By pressing hard through the Japanese occupation, the French attempt to re-subdue Vietnam, Dien Bien Phu, the Geneva Accords, General Diem, the Tonkin Gulf, the "light at the end of the tunnel," Tet, the Paris talks, Cambodia, and all the rest of it, I'm actually able to get the whole thing squeezed into one fifty-minute lecture. Saigon falls and the boat people take to the waters as 11:30 strikes. It feels breathless and really needs lots more attention.

Chloe, this semester's champion puzzled-question-asker, just can't make out what the French were thinking about after World War II. I explain that demanding American help in southeast Asia was the French quid pro quo for helping America against the Soviet Union in Europe. "Didn't the French understand that we were trying to protect them from Communism?" "Yes, they understood perfectly, and they knew how to drive a hard bargain. It would have been so awkward to America not to have French cooperation in the Western Alliance and NATO, and this theater of the Cold War confrontation was so vital to them, that they were forced to give way in what they thought of as a peripheral region of the world, southeast Asia. In international politics, France has a long history of self-interested politicians, who seem uniquely bloody-minded to the Anglo-Saxons. In their own view, they were just doing what they could for themselves in an increasingly difficult world, with their recent humiliating defeat by the Nazis hanging over them. They were always good at putting a gloss of high-mindedness on Machiavellian maneuvers." Chloe gets nods of assent from many of her fellows when she retorts that Truman and Eisenhower should have gone without French help in Europe rather than violate their own anti-colonial principles in the late 1940s and early 1950s.

Curtis asks why anywhere as remote as Vietnam could really suck in so much American power and energy. It gives me the chance to re-explain the domino theory and the age-old problem of generals and policy makers trying to re-fight the previous war. "Everyone was thinking about what had happened in Europe in the late 1930s. The lesson they drew was that Britain and France could have defeated Hitler easily if they had fought him earlier, when he was still weak. By waiting, and by appeasing him, they gave him time to get stronger and harder to defeat. The lesson American politicians and policy makers drew from that experience was that it's better to strike the enemy early and far away. Otherwise you'll have to fight him later and closer to home, when he's much harder to beat." Another questioner, Simon, finds it difficult to get into the frame of mind of American war resisters like Tom Hayden and Jane Fonda, who ended up attributing exaggerated virtues to North Vietnam and went to visit Hanoi. His own generation is patriotic in a general way, and the idea of consorting with the enemy seems bizarre. He's not disgusted by it in the way that 1960s "hawks" were—he just thinks it's weird.

The best students, with questions like these, are beginning to put all the pieces of the vast Cold War puzzle together, and it's possible, here and there, to see the light of recognition dawning in their eyes. Everything does fit together, everyone was thinking logically, albeit partially, throughout those decades. It's always a temptation to think that people in earlier ages were not quite as intelligent as we are. A handful of these students have conquered that temptation and now understand that in every age brilliant people have devoted themselves to international politics, even though they have done it in ways we can no longer applaud.

Thirty-Second Class (Friday)

Suddenly it's hot, after a long mild winter. The furnace turns on without notice in Atlanta and brings with it the flowering of every tree and shrub in the area. It's an incredible spectacle, and just now there can't be many more beautiful places in the world. When Alistair Cooke came to Emory one spring and took a stroll through the campus and the grounds of the president's house, "Lullwater," he declared it was the most beautiful college in the whole of America, and at this time every year it's easy to agree with him. Everything seems to be in flower and wherever you look are immense white dogwoods in bloom and brilliant pink azaleas. Unfortunately this flowering brings pollen counts in the three to four thousand range (where one hundred is high), and allergies go haywire. I suffer, and this year the doctor has put me on not only Claritin D, but also a course of steroids that prevent congestion and uncontrollable itching of the eyes but also make it difficult to sleep and give me the feeling that my heart is racing all the time. This problem has put me on edge and today in class I lose my temper.

I'm lecturing on American foreign policy since Vietnam. I've just gotten going with a complicated description of Jimmy Carter's dilemma over not supporting human rights violators in Iran and Nicaragua, when one of the chronic latecomers comes in late. She's a graduating senior who's always just a bit too keen to let me know she already knows it all and that this introductory class is really beneath her dignity. She comes in not only late but noisily, grinds her chair as she sits down, and then, before my eyes, opens a copy of what looks like a fashion magazine, and begins to browse. I give her about thirty seconds before breaking off in mid-sentence and walking over to stand right in front of her. If she ever writes an account of the incident she'll say I "towered over her." In a high and angry voice I say, "Stop reading that magazine at once. And don't you ever again do that in my class." She hastens to obey. "Do you understand me?" She nods and a fiery blush begins, that just spreads and spreads until it covers the whole of her head.

Boiling inside, I try to regain my normal manner and to carry on as though nothing has happened. I'm wondering: perhaps I should have thrown her out altogether. (I recall that when I was a TA at Berkeley, one of our veteran professors once stopped a lecture and expelled an insolent youth who was leafing ostentatiously through the *Daily Californian*.) Well, this public rebuke has been sufficient, I think, and might make her behave better hereafter, at least outwardly. For the rest of the class she sits there stiff and awkward, holding a notebook but not writing down a word. By coming in late she missed getting the detailed outline, and mortification prevents her from coming to ask for one afterward, as some of the other latecomers do.

Thirty-Third Class (Monday)

It's book day again, and this time we're discussing Tom Lewis's *Divided Highways* (1997), on the history of the interstate highway system. It's just the kind of book I like, full of information about the history of technology, but all put into social and political context, simply and ably written by a talented journalist, devoid of jargon, and with lots of good biographical and anecdotal tidbits. I foresee that it might have the same effect on some of the students, especially the women, as my railway rhapsody, but class discloses that most of them, while not enjoying it as much as me, at least have not actively disliked it.

I begin simply by asking who liked the book, and three of the students raise their hands. Nathan says that this year, for the first time, he drove a long way on the interstate, returning here by car from his Boston home after the winter vacation. He was aware of it as a feat of engineering, but reading this book has suddenly enabled him to appreciate much more fully the magnitude of the job and the implications of freeway building, political, social, and economic. Flora says it was "boring, but in an interesting way"; Blake says he thinks the author has a good sense of humor and manages to make what *ought* to have been a boring book rather fascinating. I appoint Tracy, one of the quiet young women, as a congresswoman from Missouri (her actual home state) and ask her why, this being the year 1956, she's inclined to vote in favor of the new freeway system. With lots of prompting and pushing she finally gets to the point: The building of interstates will provide jobs to her constituents and will probably bring more money and growth into her district than it will take out in the form of taxes. That means she'll be popular in her district and will get reelected in 1958.

"Who will actually get a job?" I ask Dave, another of the quiet students. He scratches his head and can't think of anyone apart from the road builders themselves, so I bring him up to the front of the class and point out a passage he should read. Glancing at his copy of the book I can see that the first fifteen or twenty pages have got grubby edges but that the whole of the rest of it is of virginal whiteness. "What did you think of this passage on pages 86 and 87?" "Er, I can't remember exactly what was happening there?" "But you did read them?" "Oh, yes." "Did you wash your hands thoroughly after reading chapter 1?" "How do you mean?" "I . . . never mind. Start reading here."

He reads a passage that describes the employment bonanza that the interstates brought into local communities. They were financed 90 percent by the federal government, which provided a stronger incentive for localities to sign on than most of them could resist, even if it did mean tearing up the center of the cities, worsening the blight and alienation for ghetto dwellers who were unable to escape into leafy suburbs. It provided jobs for surveyors, bulldozer drivers, gravel contractors, cement and concrete men, steel reinforcement men, explosives companies, paint manufacturers, sheet metal workers (for the signs), lumber mills (for the wooden forms into which concrete is poured), the trucking industry, lighting manufacturers for urban interchanges, the food and motel business, growing numbers of engineers and technologists, salt and sand providers (for winter conditions), the police (to patrol the new roads), and many more. The passage explains that Eisenhower, though a fiscally conservative Republican in many respects, was willing to invest best part of $100 billion in the project partly because he thought it had military value but mostly because he was obsessed with the idea that the Great Depression (mercifully ended by World War II) might recur in new peacetime conditions, and that the highway-building project was a great hedge against unemployment.

Faith, in answer to another of my questions, says that the author's tone of voice is always neutral, and that it's impossible to know what he is thinking. There is, she believes, no sign of his own interests or personality anywhere in the book. I point her to a passage in which Lewis describes the federal-local partnership as a "Faustian bargain," but, on cross questioning, I find she doesn't know what that means because she hasn't heard of Faust. It's enough to make me want to brandish a copy of Allan Bloom's *Closing of the American Mind* in front of her. Instead, I ask her to read another few lines, one of which includes the declaration that local mayors had made "a pact with the Devil." "Is that an example of his neutral language?" "Yes," she says, "perhaps it really was a pact with the Devil." "I see, so are you taking this passage literally, as meaning that the Devil actually showed up in Washington to negotiate with the Highways Department?" She reddens slightly and says, "You mean it's really metaphorical?"

Thirty-Fourth Class (Wednesday)

American foreign policy since Vietnam. I started this lecture last Friday but only got as far as the early 1980s. Now I have the chance to fill in the gaps, discuss the great CND confrontations of the early 1980s, Jeanne Kirkpatrick's distinction between authoritarian regimes (OK to support them) and totalitarian regimes (beyond the pale) as a rationale for Reagan's foreign policy, the great imbroglio in El Salvador and Nicaragua, the Solidarity Movement in Poland, and then the dramatic events that heralded the end of the Soviet Empire and the breakup of the Soviet Union itself. Finally, the Gulf War, and the way in which the American military applied there the lessons it had drawn from the Vietnam experience. These lessons were:

1. Attack with overwhelming superiority, relying as much as possible on high technology as a way of reducing casualties.
2. Keep the media far, far out of the way, doing harmless stories about oil-spattered seagulls in the Gulf while the actual battles take place two hundred miles beyond TV-camera range.
3. Have limited objectives that enable you to withdraw quickly when the fighting is finished, on the assumption that wars will enjoy popular enthusiasm if they're short, sharp, and decisive. Don't invade Iraq and try to capture or kill Saddam Hussein himself—that would be, potentially, another endless quagmire.

This discussion of the Gulf War has finally introduced the students to events they can remember from their own lifetimes. Most of them were nine or ten when it happened. It's still history, but seems slightly more real than everything else because they remember family members being involved or newspaper and TV stories as it was unraveling before them.

Office Hours (Thursday)

When I arrive for office hours the lovelorn weeper from last week is first in line. She's not going to weep today and is back on an even keel. We talk about her foreign-policy paper, but as she's not yet written anything it can only be in the vaguest and most general terms. A handful of foreign-study people come in too, to get their papers signed and put in order. The other day one of them wrote me the following e-mail. "APPROVAL OF COARSES. Dear professor, I am a sophomore in the Emory College, planning to study abroad next Fall with the Emory program in Spain at the University of Salamanca. Therefore I need to approve several history coarses, which I plan on taking for my major. Could I possibly meet with you sometime before Thursday to approve these coarses?" In my reply I told her, "I am willing to approve certain history courses, but I refuse to give you credit for anything coarse." When a student comes in blushing I recall this exchange, and sure enough it is she. I tell her what a wonderful place Salamanca is. We separate on good terms, and her parting remark is that she's going to be more careful with spell-check from now on.

Thirty-Fifth Class (Friday)

The music to introduce today's lecture is Tom Lehrer, singing "Poisoning Pigeons in the Park," and then, while stragglers come in, his song version of the complete periodic table of the elements. He's a standing refutation of the idea that the 1950s were a dull decade. I've always had a soft spot for the 1950s and this seems like one harmless way of spreading the good news. Historians of my generation, too young to have been part of the "Vietnam generation," tend to get irritable at that cohort's attempt to glorify itself by denigrating the decade of their childhood. The real 1950s were full of fascination, energy, intellectual excitement, religious ferment, and rapid social change. Only polemicists could substitute for it their picture of a "lost generation" and the alleged drab conformity of the man in the gray flannel suit.

The room never fills up because today is Good Friday and many students are away for Easter or Passover. Several others have brought in friends, so there's an unusual mix of people in the room. I lecture on the affluent society, first summarizing Galbraith's argument, in his book of the same name, and quoting a few passages on "conventional wisdom" and "social balance," and then using it as a springboard to talk about why America was so rich in the postwar world. Life expectancy kept growing, infant mortality kept declining, and the total population rose rapidly. It's true that deaths from cancer and heart disease rose too, but that's because people were living long enough to contract those diseases, whereas in other ages they had died of other things first. The great paradox of post-World War II America is that so many of its problems were the problems of a successful society. There was so much food available, even for the poor, that weight *loss* became a major industry. There was so much tobacco available that learning to *stop* smoking became a worthwhile objective. Tobacco kills people only gradually, and in earlier ages there had been no mass support for the idea that giving up tobacco was a reasonable way to increase your chances of a long and healthy life. I talk about the proliferation of televisions, the rise of televangelism, and then about the ever-growing role of advertising in Americans' lives.

I move on to a passage about Las Vegas, the city above all others that represents postwar prosperity and the availability of surplus wealth—in effect, a city dedicated entirely to waste. I tell the class a few stories about Benny "Bugsy" Siegel, the originator of the Las Vegas idea and builder of the Flamingo Hotel, first of the great byzantine gambling palaces. These anecdotes make a riveting story for the students, only half a dozen of whom have actually been there. I also have a passage about highbrow consumerism, the art market, and I pause to show slides of some famous art of the postwar years. Among them are works by Willem de Kooning, Jackson Pollock ("Jack the Dripper"), Mark Rothko, and Robert Motherwell. Admirers of their work spun elaborate theories around it—all nicely skewered and satirized by Tom Wolfe in *The Painted Word*—while detractors said that abstract expressionism was the entering wedge of Communism, designed to confuse and deceive Americans out of their simple faith in what was right and true. Next comes a series of pictures of the Pop Artists and their work, particularly Andy Warhol, Robert Rauschenberg, and Roy Lichtenstein. Rauschenberg's

Monogram, the stuffed goat in an old tire, is my favorite, and it causes a wave of laughter among the students, most of whom have apparently not previous seen or heard of it.

Karen asks *why* so much of this art was so strange. I answer by explaining that photography had largely displaced the older functions of graphic art, permitting the artists to think along different lines. I have been influenced in thinking about it by Robert Hughes's *Shock of the New* (1981), and I end class today by showing some slides of great pieces of landscape art that he discusses, including Walter de Maria's *Lightning Field* (rank and file of stainless steel rods planted in the desert earth, awaiting random lightning strikes) and Robert Smithson's beautiful *Spiral Jetty* in the Great Salt Lake (now submerged due to a change in the water level). This is an area of the syllabus that clearly interests the women more than the men—several stay behind afterward to talk about galleries, artists whose work they admire, and the idea of making art out of the landscape.

Thirty-Sixth Class (Monday)

My half of the discussion class this morning is swelled by a couple of high school students who tell me they've just been accepted to Emory and have come along to see what it's like. I've already talked to another one this morning, with her mother, both generations bubbling with excitement at the prospect of being part of it all. It's odd how context can change someone's appearance. When I drop my daughter off at school in the morning the high school seniors seem huge, but when I see their exact contemporaries in my office and classroom they look oddly diminished, perhaps because of their anxious awareness of not yet belonging.

This week's reading is *Postwar Immigrant America* (1994) by Reed Ueda, which traces the rise in immigration since the Second World War. Although its subtitle is *A Social History*, it's really a bit short on the social side. A more appropriate subtitle would be something like "A Summary and Statistical History, with Graphs." There were two great periods of immigration to America in the twentieth century, one in the first twenty years of the century, and the other in the past twenty years. In terms of numbers the two eras were comparable, but since the whole American population had grown a lot in the meantime, the impact on the society as a whole, and the percentage of foreign-born people in the nation the second time around, was smaller. Among the newcomers after World War II, besides, were large numbers of highly educated people, who believed they could get more highly paid and skilled jobs in America than in their homelands—a phenomenon that had no counterpart in the early twentieth century. In the case of recent immigrants from India, for example, Ueda's charts shows that more than 60 percent are college graduates.

The legal situation has had a big effect on American immigration history. Until 1921 the gates were open to nearly everyone, though the First World War, with the draft at home and the terrors of submarine attack in the Atlantic, meant a sudden dropping off in numbers that had been running at a million or more per year since 1900. The immigration restriction laws of 1921 and 1924 were inspired by the idea that it was not the best people of Europe but the worst who were then arriving, in the steerage section of Atlantic steamers—you've all seen those folksy musical peasants below decks in *Titanic*. The laws had an openly racial bias: high immigrant quotas remained for Britons and other northwestern Europeans, whereas all Asians, Africans, and most southern Europeans were excluded or severely restricted. Throughout the 1930s far fewer people entered the United States than were entitled to do so by the terms of the acts, even though, in the same years, desperate Jewish refugees from Germany were turned away, because they belonged to an excluded group.

The law changed in the 1940s, when pre-Communist China was an American ally, reopening the door to Asians after decades of exclusion. It changed again in 1952, to encourage highly skilled immigrants, who could bring in "human capital." The most decisive legal moment came with the Hart-Celler Act of 1965. The same Congress that enacted the great Civil Rights and Voting Rights acts also transformed the immigration laws by abolishing all racial distinctions, and by setting high annual quotas for every country in the world. Since then the pattern of immigration has changed—fewer arrivals from Europe and far more from Asia. The Vietnam War and its aftermath intensified that change, as refugees from Vietnam, Laos, and Cambodia began pouring in.

When I spoke to the alumni a few weeks ago my theme was immigrants' love of America, with myself as an example. Ueda's book makes essentially the same point but with statistical verification. People from all over the world are clamoring to get into the United States, and for the most part it repays them with a generous immigration policy, letting in the best part of a million every year. That's just the legal ones, and it's no secret that vast numbers of illegal immigrants arrive every year too, most from Mexico, but good numbers from Ireland and parts of Asia too. Ueda touches matter-of-factly on each of the principal themes: the changing legal situation, the debate over whether or not immigration hurts or benefits the economy, the assimilation process, immigrants' economic vitality, the conflict of generations, "ethnic succession" in neighborhoods, and the act by which integration into American society is most clearly signaled: intermarriage.

As Ueda shows, first- and second-generation immigrants are cautious about intermarriage, but after three or four generations it becomes common. His book has a handy summary of two influential theories I've mentioned earlier to the students this semester. The first is Hansen's law, named after sociologist Marcus Lee Hansen, which says, "What the second generation tries to forget, the third generation tries to remember." In other words, the immigrants themselves tend to cling to the language, food, habits, customs, and morals of the country from which they came, and to live with one another. The second generation, their children, try to get rid of everything they can in the way of foreignness. They, after all, are going through the intensive peer pressures of public school and don't want to stand out in the crowd—their sports, hobbies, clothes, and teenage enthusiasms are directed to American things. But *their* children, the third generation, whose American status isn't in doubt, want something more than to be just generically American, and they take an interest in their grandparents' place and culture of origin, because it fascinates rather than threatens them. As I summarize this theory, Tricia Ercak, in the front row, suddenly comes alive to the way it operates in her own family. Her grandmother never learned to speak good English, relying almost entirely on Polish. Her mother refused to speak Polish, even though she understood every word of Grandma's tirades. Tricia, the third-generation child, regrets not being able to speak Polish but admits that her sense of Polishness has a kind of hobby quality.

The second of these theories is Will Herberg's, summarized in his 1955 book *Protestant, Catholic, Jew,* and influential among historians, sociologists, and students of religion—I've read and assigned it to classes often and even anthologized it in a religious history book I edited recently. His idea, which made perfect sense at the time, was that America had no single "melting pot" but three of them, one for each of the three main religions. In the first generation, Irish Catholics married other Irish Catholics. Subsequently, Irish Catholics married Polish or Italian Catholics but continued to veer away from Protestants and Jews. In other words, religious lines persisted when ethnic lines faded. The passage of another forty-five years has largely invalidated the theory, or at least shown that Herberg was witnessing another stage of the assimilation process rather than its final outcome. Sociologists in the 1970s observed high rates of intermarriage among groups whose members had earlier resisted it; like Japanese Americans and American Jews.

Luckily the class itself contains a handful of immigrants. In my half are Maria from Colombia and Rifat from Pakistan. Michael from Hong Kong, Maya from Jordan, and Blake from Canada are with Regina this morning. I'm an exhibit too, and a little way into the class I ask Nigel how he would set about estimating the degree to which I was, or was not, assimilated. "Well, you sure talk strange," he begins, to laughter from the others, "and I guess you must have grown up overseas. But then there's your clothing." "Does it look foreign?" "Not really—I guess you're American in that sense." "Compare me to Maria. Which of us is more assimilated, do you think?" "She is, because she sounds like an American." "What's the most crucial test of whether we've assimilated?" He thinks for a while and says, "What you eat?" It's true that one passage in the book mentions the role of food in assimilation and the way in which the cultural significance of particular foods changes over time. It quotes the old tale about the first hot dog in America being a German ethnic novelty, introduced in 1888, and how, by the 1970s, it had become almost the quintessentially American dish. "Food maybe, but there's something even more fundamental." Kathleen says, "Whether you'll marry an American."

I don't tell them that I did marry an American. Instead I ask Maria and Rifat whether they feel pressures, either inwardly or from their families, about who would and would not be a suitable marriage partner. Maria says her parents will let her decide but that she'd probably prefer someone from Colombia, who knows the way of life that is most familiar to her. Rifat, from Pakistan, says that her parents, Muslims, will not only require her to marry a Pakistani Muslim but will choose which one! A couple of the other class members give her looks of stricken, horrified pity; she herself takes it calmly (though I've known several Indian and Pakistani students here for whom it's been a source of terrific conflict).

The discussion in class is lively and good-natured. Suddenly the end of the semester is in sight and from here on the days and weeks will seem to accelerate as the end draws near. That's good news for those who've had enough of school and want to be out sunbathing in the warm weather. It's bad news for those who haven't yet completed their long research papers and feel the amount of time available to them fleeing at an ever-increasing rate.

CHAPTER

15

■ ■ ■

First Drafts, Draft Dodgers, and Deadlines

Office Hours (Tuesday)

A former student, Scott Saposnik, comes to visit. He graduated two years ago; after we have chatted about various memories, he says something that delights me. He was a member of my summer school class on Victorian Britain at Oxford three years ago. I told the students that one of the requirements was that they do a series of drawings of Victorian objects, and research their history. They must do ten careful drawings, no more than two of which could be the same type of object. Scott says, "I was horrified by that assignment. I hadn't done any drawing in years and it seemed like a completely futile and pointless activity. But as the summer school went on I really got into it and finally enjoyed it very much. What you said was true; having to draw objects makes you look at them really closely and carefully, with the result that you get to know them better than if you just glanced or took a snapshot." He says he often draws now, as a way of relaxing, and that he traces it back to that class. I'm pleased to hear him say it because, after two years of struggling with the drawing assignment, I abandoned it. So much criticism and complaint and so much hilariously bad drawing had come in by then that I feared it just wasn't worth the grief. I had consigned it to the same dustbin into which, last term, I stuffed the prohibition on using the word *like* in class discussion. Something tells me it may now be climbing its way out of the bin again.

I spend the best part of an hour in the afternoon talking with a history major, a senior, about the draft of her honors thesis which I have read over the past few days. Last summer she was one of the winners of our traveling fellowship, and she spent the money on a trip to South Africa to research the history of Christian missions to the Zulu and Xhosa peoples. Her thesis draft is testimony to a painful discovery that nearly all students of religion go through sooner or later. Although she's a devout member of her church, she can't avoid drawing the conclusion that the missionaries did more harm than good. They were culturally insensitive on a Wagnerian scale, and did everything they could to extinguish the traditional way of life, replacing it with their idea of what good, civilized men and women should be like. Unfortunately, having had this insight, she's been too eager to share it with the reader. Instead of saying in the introduction or conclusion that the missionaries harmed a culture they were trying to "save" or "convert," and that it was regrettable, she says it on every one of her hundred pages.

Anyone who delivers the same message that often is going to start getting it served right back. With each new splutter of rage that comes off the page, I find myself less and less willing to accept it, and as we talk over the strengths and weaknesses of the draft I explain that she must tone it down a lot. "Look at it this way. What makes you special isn't your righteous indignation. You can find that wherever you look in America today, especially when it's a question of whites tyrannizing blacks. What makes you special is that you have learned the story of exactly how they did it in a particular time and place. You know who they were, where they came from, what they wanted to do, what they actually did, and what their contemporaries thought about it. No one else, or hardly anyone else, knows all those details. You should write the story in such a way that readers, whatever their own opinion of the moral situation, can *learn* from you. Don't always be pushing your sense of outrage at the reader. Keep it in the background, with maybe just a mild adjective here and a veiled tone of detachment there. Some readers might themselves be aspiring missionaries. They might believe that since the Christian faith is true, all others are not true, and that to convert the Africans really is to offer them salvation and eternal life. Be informative to such people as well as to readers who happen to share your opinion. Otherwise, you'll lose more and more readers with the turning of each new page. It may sound strange but, really, historians' opinions are a bore. It doesn't specially matter what you think about the issue—what matters is your ability to tell the story and explain how and why it happened."

She is abashed by my remarks. "I thought we were supposed to have a strong thesis statement." "You are, but it should be an analytical thesis rather than an emotional or moral one. The thesis, 'African spirituality was consonant with the Zulus' traditional way of life, whereas Christianity was not, so that conversion often triggered cultural breakdown' would be an analytical thesis. But 'It was all dreadfully wrong' would not be." I tell her the story of a student I once taught at Berkeley, who did his senior thesis on the history of the National Rifle Association. "He was a student journalist, a good-hearted emotional liberal, and his thesis just oozed contempt for the NRA and was breathless in admiration for its opponents. It was full of editorializing too, and its last sentence read, 'The time has come for the NRA to give an inch.' I told him more or less the same thing I've just said to you: tone down the emotions and make the paper equally useful to pro- and anti-gun readers, so that both can learn history from it, rather than making it something pro-NRA people will throw away in disgust. Result? The final sentence of the final version read, 'The time has come, it seems, for the NRA to give an inch.'"

What I don't tell her is, that as an undergraduate and graduate student, I suffered from exactly the same problem she's got now—the tendency to let my emotions show when they ought to be in hiding. I learned to control it over the years, and when my first book came out in 1993 I was delighted to discover that reviewers on both sides of the issues it covered believed I was sympathetic to their own side. Taking that approach may seem a bit bloodless, but for analytical history it usually pays off. Having said that, I can't hide from myself the fact that the really great historians are highly opinionated people, whose opinions turn up right there in the text. I love the writing of Richard Hofstadter, among the Americans, and E. P. Thompson, among the Brits, both of whom leave you in no doubt about what they think on the issues they study. But they were geniuses, as were the other historians who permanently changed the shape of the entire discipline.

For us mortals, by contrast, the cool, detached style is best. I learned that truth partly from realizing, over the years, how easy it is to change your mind with the passage of time and new circumstances. Various things I used to think utterly wrong now seem to me profoundly right. I learned it also from one of my best old English friends, Stephen Kinsey. I asked him once what he thought about one of the big events of Margaret Thatcher's prime-ministerial life, to which he replied, "I don't have an opinion of it at all. I'm trying to cut down on opinions." He meant it half as a joke and half as a serious point; we live in a world overloaded with opinions, most of them poorly formed, inadequately educated, on topics that have nothing to do with our own lives, and nearly all subject to fashion and whim.

The honors student and I part after a long talk about cultural relativism. She gets the point but still can't bring herself to admit that she ought to be as culturally relativist about the missionaries as she is about the Africans. If it is right that their culture should have been preserved intact, isn't it equally right that the missionaries' culture should have been preserved intact too? Why should all our sympathies go one way, rather than both? Besides, she has passages in the paper in which she admits that while the missionaries were trying to feed, clothe, school, medicate, and convert the Africans, most of their fellow Britons, not to mention the Boers, would have preferred war to the point of annihilation. "There are relative degrees of right and wrong, aren't there?" say I. "It wouldn't take much for me to use the same evidence you've got here to paint these missionaries in a distinctly heroic light."

Thirty-Seventh Class (Wednesday)

Today's music is a couple of early love songs by Stevie Wonder and today's lecture is about the civil rights movement. I always enjoy giving this lecture; there are so many paradoxical turns of event to keep the audience off guard. First there's the irony that Earl Warren, the hero of the *Brown* case in 1954, had previously committed one of the worst civil rights violations in American history. As attorney general of California, it was he who supervised the expulsion of Japanese Americans from their California homes after Pearl Harbor and ordered their resettlement in concentration camps in California's deserts and mountains. Many lost their businesses and their property, or were forced to sell them at give-away prices—all lost their liberty. Even then the young men among them were not exempted from military service. On the contrary, they had to serve in the European theater of the war.

The next paradox is that a group of women started the Montgomery bus boycott but almost at once put it into the hands of a group of men, of whom King was soon the most famous. Rosa Parks wasn't the only one. A few years ago in this course I got the class to read *The Montgomery Bus Boycott and the Women Who Started It* (1987), by Jo-Anne Robinson, who was a little bit waspish in tone when she came to remark on the doings of the Great One. A further nice irony is the fact that white women contributed to making the boycott succeed. Another year the class read *Outside the Magic Circle* (1985), by Virginia Durr, whose husband was one of the few pro-integration whites in Montgomery at the time. She describes how white housewives, impatient at the late arrival of their black maids, would drive over to the black side of town to pick them up rather than do without the help, making it that much easier for the maids to stay off the buses. As Durr says, some white husbands gave their wives strict instructions not to help the boycott in this way, but it was advice they ignored rather than do their own housework.

Some students look at the end of segregation as an example of extreme opposition finally overcome only by extreme measures. Others, with me leaning their way, see it as a system already so rotten by the late 1950s that it only needed a couple of good pushes to bring it crashing down altogether. After all, the Southern congressional delegation's promise of "massive resistance" didn't amount to much in practice. In the whole South only one county, Prince Edward County, Virginia, actually shut down its entire school system rather than follow the *Brown* decision, and even that shutdown only lasted a couple of years. Everyone else found they just couldn't stand the pressure. It's true that desegregation moved slowly and that there have been plenty of rearguard actions—it would be mad to imply that racism and discrimination have vanished—but at least now it's morally disgraceful openly to avow racist ideas.

It's invigorating to lecture on the sit-ins and the freedom rides because it's so easy, at least from our vantage point, to distinguish right from wrong in the 1950s and early 1960s. Later on things get a lot murkier. What about the urban riots of the mid 1960s? Were they rebellions, or just opportunities (as Edward Banfield notoriously wrote) for "fun and profit" in the form of rioting and looting? What about the Black Muslims? They generally get a very good press, with an emphasis on Malcolm X in the last years of his life moving away from the nuttier aspects of Elijah Muhammad's inverted racism, and even claims that King and X would eventually have learned to work together. What about the Black Power movement, the Stokely Carmichael swagger, and Eldridge Cleaver's *Soul on Ice* macho? Things like that, and pictures of armed black students sitting-in at Cornell, began to alienate even the parts of the white middle class that had loved King. Affirmative action and busing programs made it more difficult for all the right to be obviously on one side and all the wrong on the other. When I ask Chris to summarize the arguments for affirmative action he does a good job, but Helen, the student summarizing the arguments against it, is his equal. A few years ago there would have been no volunteer to oppose it in a class like this.

Over the years I have collected more than a hundred slides on these events, so I lecture from the projector throughout the class. As usual, time runs out a little bit before I do—I hurry into a summary of later episodes (busing in Boston and the *Bakke* case) before dismissing class. Afterward Maya comes up to say that she's decided to be a history major and asks me to be her advisor. Kathleen says she's decided to take my environmental history course next term. Others crowd round to tell me anecdotes about Malcolm X, to ask whether King really did plagiarize his doctoral dissertation, and to see whether I've seen various movies and documentaries like *Malcolm X* and *Mississippi Burning*.

Draft Deadline (Thursday)

Way back at the beginning of term, I wrote on the course syllabus that 10:00 A.M. this morning was the last moment at which I would advise students on drafts of their second papers, the final versions of which are due next Monday. A couple have had the prudence and foresight to write them well ahead of time—I've already been through two versions with Curtis—but the majority leave it to the last minute, just as they leave everything else to the last minute. At 8:30 I have a counseling session with Flora, a charming student from Boise, Idaho, who has written a fine draft already. Then, between 9:00 and 10:00 about eight papers appear all at once, two clutched in the hands of their authors, who want immediate help, the others appearing as e-mail attachments. It makes me a trifle irritable to get them all at the last minute, but I have to uphold my side of the bargain, so I spend all spare moments of the day slogging through these drafts and e-mailing back to their authors. Most are pretty good (only the superior students bother with drafts at all, despite my nagging), but one is hopeless. The author thought, for example, that Japan was a Communist power when it attacked Pearl Harbor, and she wrote that, after the atom bomb attacks on Hiroshima and Nagasaki, "the commies were finally defeated." In her passage on McCarthyism, she also wrote about a thing called the "House of un-American Activities." It's a wonderful mental picture—made me think of the movie *House of Games*.

In the evening I screen *Doctor Strangelove* for the class. We've done quite a lot of work on nuclear weapons and the Cold War, so it seems like a fitting complement to the more serious side of the work. The film is nearly forty years old now but still brilliantly entertaining. Peter Sellers plays Colonel Mandrake, the hapless RAF officer advising General Ripper. He also plays the American president and Doctor Strangelove himself, the wheelchair-bound ex-Nazi who's become an American war and rocketry expert. As usual, some of the class get the point and are just rocking with laughter; others look at it with blank incomprehension and afterward ask me puzzled questions. Well, you can lead a horse to water but you can't make it drink. With each of the three feature films this term (this one, *Inherit the Wind*, and *Heartland*) there's been a blend of hits and misses. It was ever thus.

Thirty-Eighth Class (Friday)

There are only five meetings of the class left now, including today, and as usual, I'm not going to be able to get all the way to the present. Today my theme is students and youthful radicalism in the 1960s. It's another subject I know backward and forward, so I just put forty slides in the machine and lecture from them. I have a good set of pictures of the Berkeley Free Speech Movement, made when I was still at Berkeley, and many more of student demonstrations at Cornell, Columbia, and San Francisco State. Also some pictures of the great March on the Pentagon (about which Norman Mailer wrote his magnificent book *The Armies of the Night*), pictures of the Woodstock rock festival, of the Democratic Convention in Chicago in 1968 and the street fighting outside the convention center, of hippie communes, and of children smoking marijuana in Golden Gate Park.

Once again today there are several newly accepted students in class, coming along for a preview of college, and a couple of high school juniors, one with his father, another with her mother. These parents stay too, and the father tells me afterward that for him the lecture was a drenchingly nostalgic trip down memory lane, from the Joan Baez song with which I started the class onward. By now, many of the students are too young even to have *parents* who were involved in these events, but this dad's a trifle older than most and looks as though he fits squarely with the baby boomer profile. The students are fascinated—they've heard lots of "sixties" mythology—and they love to see the transformation of students' appearance between 1964 (Free Speech Movement) and 1968 (big Vietnam demonstrations) at Berkeley. "A lot happened in a short space of time," I tell them. "You could have been a freshman wearing a jacket and tie or a twin-set and pearls in the fall of 1964, and a senior in the spring of 1968 with unisex jeans, long hair, tie-dyed shirt, and Birkenstocks. By then you were probably in rebellion against the university itself, against what you alleged was the irrelevance of the courses, against grading, and in favor of severing the university's ties with the military-industrial complex. If you were one of the guys, there were places on campus where you could get advice on how to evade the draft."

Thirty-Ninth Class (Monday)

I reached the end of the Cold War, and the Gulf War, in foreign policy a couple of weeks ago, but it looks as though, in domestic matters, I'll scarcely make it to John Hinckley Jr.'s assassination attempt on President Reagan. This coming Wednesday Regina will lecture on the women's movement, and on Friday we'll be discussing the last assigned book, Tim O'Brien's *If I Die in a Combat Zone* (1975). That just leaves next Monday for tying up all the loose ends. For music today I bow to necessity and play some wet-rock from the 1970s. What could be wetter than the Carpenters' "On Top of the World"? The only students who've heard of the Carpenters are those preoccupied by anorexia.

I'm lecturing this morning on the origins and early history of the American environmental movement and the way it changed politics in the 1970s. In the fall I'll be teaching an entire course on American environmental history, so this class is something of a teaser to bring in recruits. It's common to find, at the beginning of each fall semester, half a dozen former members of the introductory class joining the environmental class, which is more advanced and more demanding than this one, in terms of length and difficulty of reading and writing assignments.

I give the quickest imaginable summary of the precursors of the movement, Thoreau, John Muir, Theodore Roosevelt, and Gifford Pinchot, outlining the nature of the dispute between the preservationists, under Muir, and the conservationists, under Pinchot, that came to a head around the building of Hetch-Hetchy dam and reservoir in Yosemite National Park. Then, with hardly time to catch a breath, we jump forward to the Sierra Club's lobbying against the building of dams in Echo Park and the Grand Canyon in the late 1950s and the early 1960s, and David Brower's clever ad campaign in which he said that flooding the Grand Canyon would be like flooding the Sistine Chapel in order that visitors might get a closer view of Michaelangelo's ceiling murals. These campaigns were triumphs for the environmentalists, which showed that a wide fund of latent support for protecting and preserving the landscape was growing in the postwar nation. Next comes a passage on Rachel Carson's *Silent Spring*. The great irony here is that the invention of DDT had at first looked like an immense breakthrough for the suppression of insect-borne diseases—the inventor got the Nobel Prize. By the time of Carson's book, 1962, DDT had become one of the great villains, moving in ominous concentrations up the food chain and threatening the health of every human baby. That was her claim, anyway, though later students have knocked some of the shine off her assertions.

In the mid-1960s, Carson's classic was followed by Ralph Nader's *Unsafe at Any Speed*, the opening salvo of the consumer advocacy movement. Next came Paul Ehrlich's *Population Bomb,* which claimed that the world was so overpopulated that by the 1970s catastrophic famines and Malthusian wars would be sweeping not just the third world, whose millions were already beyond salvation (or so he said), but America and other developed countries too. I've got an original paperback edition of that one—a tatty old thing with a lurid alarmist cover. It shows a fizzing anarchist bomb and in stop-press letters across the front declares: "While you are reading these words four people will have died from starvation, most of them children."

Much more than Carson's work, Ehrlich's has been discredited since, but the "population bomb" idea was certainly widely believed at the time, and contributed to the gearing up of the environmental movement, whose first great public event was Earth Day, April 22, 1970. Fanatical anti-Communists noted darkly that April 22 was Lenin's birthday and that environmentalism (or "the ecology movement," as it was then called) was part of the great Communist conspiracy. Most people joined in the day's zanier events with goodwill—streets in major cities closed down, kids rode horses instead of driving cars, cleaned up parks, buried gas-guzzling cars in holes in the ground, and promised to live less wasteful, less ostentatious consumer lives. It seemed like a feel-good holiday, especially by comparison with the era's bitterly divisive demonstrations over Vietnam and civil rights. Even President Nixon made a pro-environmental speech. That year Congress passed the National Environmental Policy Act and created the Environmental Protection Agency. These days, opponents of environmentalism tend to be on the right—President George W. Bush, for example, is already making a bad name for himself because of his cozy relations with the coal and oil men. In those days, by contrast, opposition came from the left, especially from people involved in the antipoverty and antiwar movements, who looked at environmentalism as a paltry, middle-class, Volvo drivers' distraction from serious matters.

I go on to describe the array of congressional laws to clean up the air and water and rescue endangered species, and then the events of 1973 that proved the first great stumbling block to the movement. The Yom Kippur War, the OPEC embargo, and the first "oil crisis" created political support for building a trans-Alaskan pipeline, despite the vigorous opposition of environmentalists, who didn't want northern Alaska opened up by oil drillers. In the short run the pipeline was a technical marvel and reasonably clean, but it laid the foundations for the *Exxon Valdez* disaster of 1989, America's worst-ever oil spill. I also do a short passage on the rise and fall of civilian nuclear power, heralded in the 1950s as the era's great "swords-into-plowshares" issue but condemned after the Three Mile Island accident in 1979 as intolerably dangerous, because the power stations couldn't be built or monitored well enough and because there was no adequate solution to disposing of the used but still toxic fuel rods.

At 11:20, after this quick sampling of the issues, I ask the class to write evaluations. I wrote the evaluation form yesterday and I'm using it to complement the official "bubble sheet" form from the college, which merely quantifies the students' reactions to the course. On the front, students are instructed, "Please evaluate the course, with reference to the teachers, teaching style, the use of audio and visual aids (music, slides, movies), the work load, and any other issues you found useful, interesting, or distracting." Two-thirds of the way down the page is the question, "What improvements would you suggest for this course?" and on the back is a list of all the books they read. For each one I'm asking them to rank out of 5 (1 meaning good, 5 meaning bad) on two scales: first, on how useful the book was and, second, on how enjoyable it was. Finally I ask whether they've read any books, biography, fiction, or nonfiction, that they think would be suitable for an introductory course of this kind—never tried this question before, so it will be interesting to see whether they answer it straight, satirically, or not at all. Professors aren't allowed to read evaluations (even though they're anonymous) until after the final exam is graded and grades handed in to the administration. I ask Blake to collect them all and take them to Becky, the undergraduate affairs administrator in the History Department office.

Another event today is the handing in of papers. The students have known since January that today is the day they must deliver them to me by five o'clock. I know from long experience that I'll actually get two things: papers, and excuses about the absence of papers. I'm not disappointed. When I began my life as a college teacher there were no word processors, and in those days the commonest reason for failure to hand in papers was the death of a grandmother (or occasionally a much-beloved dog). I'm pleased to be able to say that the death rate among grandmothers and mutts has gone down since the invention of personal computers. Unfortunately, there has been a commensurate rise in the death rate among the computers themselves, or at least in the rate at which they fall critically sick at vital moments. There is a smattering of "computer jammed" excuses, but also this letter from one of the haughtier young ladies in class:

Professor,

First off, I would just like to apologize for missing class last week. I have been horribly sick, and Friday was the first day I was well enough to come to class. All the pollen has just been upsetting my allergies. Also, I'm sorry for all the coughing and sneezing that I did in class today and last Friday.

Now to the original intent of this email. I don't know what happened, but for some reason I was thinking that the paper was due on Friday. I don't know how I marked my calendar wrong but today was the day that I was going to start it. I wish that you could grant me an extension on the paper but I know I am unlikely to receive one just because I was too ignorant to realize the due date. Had I realized that it was due today, I surely would have done it though. I will work my hardest to try to complete the paper by tomorrow, though I have to give a campus tour today and lead a BTS meeting tonight. I really wanted this paper to turn out well, considering the fact that the last one was sub-par for me. Now I'm afraid I will have to rush while writing it. I just made a mistake, and now I'm afraid it will hurt me when grades come out. Professor, please have mercy on me.

Remember when I missed a week for my family reunion April 2–6? In order to complete my paper I need the handouts from class for April 2, 4, and 6. If it is at all possible, could you send those to me attached in an email, so that I may begin work on my paper? Once again I am very sorry, and please know that this is unlike me. I appreciate your timely response in this matter.

In my big folder of excuse letters I'll have to give this one a fairly prominent place. I think I'll put it right next to the one (from a student who had just received an F) that began with the immortal sentence: "It has come to my attention that I did very badly on the paper assignment." First, the excuse itself is so astonishingly lame it's hard to believe she has the nerve to make it at all. It says right on her syllabus, which she has had since January, that today is the day. For each of the last five or six classes, besides, I've been warning them of the approach of the deadline and encouraging them to write drafts. She did miss a lot of classes, but she came to a lot too and has heard my monotonous message again and again.

What about her style? There's plenty to enjoy in the letter. I like the idea that "the pollen has just been upsetting my allergies." It's bad enough to have allergies but apparently it's a good deal worse to have pollen upsetting them! And why the "just?" Is it "just" in the sense of recently, or is it a way of saying that annoying her allergies is the only thing the pollen has been doing? Next the deliciously inappropriate use of "original intent," a lawyers' phrase if ever there was one (I bet her dad is an attorney). Usually "original intent" gives notice that we're going to hear an account of what James Madison and the other founders were thinking about when they wrote the Constitution and the Bill of Rights, prior to a denunciation of what some creative lawyer or judge has decided the Constitution means today.

I also admire "I wish that you could grant me an extension." She knows perfectly well that if I wanted to, I could. She's really saying, "I wish you would grant me an extension," but by substituting "could" she's offering a sly form of flattery, as if to say, "I realize that you're the victim of iron necessity in these matters. Wouldn't it be wonderful to live in a world where the professor was able to grant extensions to people whose memories had misfired!" That's giving me an opportunity to find unexpected reserves of magnanimity in myself and to say, casting care and iron necessity to the winds, "Yes, you may have more time."

"I know I am unlikely to receive one just because I was too ignorant to realize the due date." A well-known form of groveling here: daring the instructor to take literally an act of self-abasement. We all learn as children to contradict anyone who denigrates himself. "Oh, no, not at all, what nonsense . . ." There's another dare here, too, because she's implying that it would be rather rude of me *not* to give her an extension, since by doing so I'd be saying, in effect, "You really are ignorant, and ignorance is no excuse."

In the next sentence, while accidentally admitting that she hasn't yet started on the project (I handed out the assignment sheet three weeks ago), she describes two worthy and charitable deeds she is about to perform. These campus tours are a regular feature of life here. A dozen times every day you see little groups of ten to twenty-five parents and potential future students (or just interested passersby) going around the quad, the library, the student center, and the gym. They are led by undergraduate volunteers, usually walking in reverse and talking as they go, in order to face their audience. When I have my window open I hear, every half-hour or so, "And this is Bowden Hall, where our history and philosophy departments teach and have their offices. It is named for Henry Lumpkin Bowden, formerly head of our trustees. Ahead of us you can see the Candler Library . . ." and the voice tails off as the group shuffles on. So here's my student selflessly giving up her time to lead one of these groups while her paper lies unfinished and the hours tick away. I don't know what the BTS is, but you can be sure that I'm meant to be favorably disposed toward her on learning that she is leading one of its meetings.

As the paragraph comes to an end there's a crescendo of anxiety and misery, climaxing in a little stream-of-consciousness fragment—"I'm afraid it will hurt me when grades come out." Yes, that's what it's all about—grades. There certainly isn't a word anywhere in the letter to suggest that she has any interest in history. What really makes the letter an object of transcendent and perpetual beauty, to be treasured always, is the concluding sentence of paragraph 2: "Professor, please have mercy on me." It's a prayer. At church I often say, along with the rest of the congregation, "Lord, have mercy," but I don't think I've ever said, "Lord, please have mercy." As a child I was an Anglican choirboy. In those days, before the latest round of prayer book revisions, we used to say, in the General Confession, "Have mercy upon us miserable offenders, Spare thou them O God that confess their faults, Restore Thou them that are penitent." In the morning service we also said, "We are not worthy so much as to gather up the crumbs under Thy table. But Thou . . . in Thy great mercy . . ." I remember eventually coming to recognize in that passage the same trick as the student is trying here—we were aiming to shame God into forgiving us.

Next comes paragraph 3 and a sudden change of mood, pace, and feeling. She becomes bossy and peremptory, telling me to get on with sending her the missing materials quickly, almost as though the thing *really* holding her up is my slowness to send the materials she missed. On the reading list at the beginning of term I said that the only acceptable reason for missing class was medical. It's hard to see how the family reunion features as a medical problem. And don't you love that "I appreciate your timely response in this matter," another lawyerish locution, as if she were expecting me to respond to a summons?

Well, reader, what would you have done with this letter? Would you have granted her the extension? Or would you, in the name of equal treatment for all, have denied it? After conquering the temptation to use a little bit of sarcasm, here's what I wrote in response:

Dear Y,

Thanks for your long and sorrowful email. I will always remember that mercy is a virtue, and will try to practice it. I'm afraid, however, that I cannot send you those outlines because I always delete them from the file "Outline" as soon as it's time to write another. You'll have to ask another member of our class to lend them to you, instead.

Best wishes from Patrick Allitt.

Weasel words, of course. While seeming to claim that I'm always merciful in a general way, I refrain from saying whether I'll be merciful in this case, and I give her no help at all in the matter of the outlines. Now comes the wait, either for the paper itself or for the next installment of excuse making.

In the evening I give my final talk of the year to the senior citizens. My theme is religion and the American counterculture from the 1960s to the present. The audience is old enough that some of them had troublesome children who went over to the hippie way of life, and when I mention the People's Temple they recognize at once that it's the group whose career ended in a mass suicide in the Guyanese jungle in 1978. They're straight arrows and never previously have heard anyone talk about cults, except pejoratively. I try to make a neutral case, pointing out what followers liked about them as well as what detractors criticized, and then I put them on edge with a quotation from Harvey Cox's *Seduction of the Spirit*, in which he talks about the connection between drugs, "expanded consciousness," and youth.

I don't believe for a minute that all those terrifying "drug education" spots on TV will scare kids out of trying drugs. In fact they may have the opposite effect. Everyone longs, sometimes secretly, to experience altered states of consciousness. Adolescents are intrigued by death and danger, not repulsed. How can people lure them *into* movies with the same symbols they somehow think will *repel* them from drugs? Our drug epidemic may or may not be a serious one. But I believe it is the symptom of a deeper cultural disease—the disappearance of legitimate occasions for ecstasy, trance, emotion and feeling, and the erosion of traditional rituals. When I was a kid, people got "high" at revivals and during other religious events. Everyone needs to experience that kind of mental elation now and then.

Cox wrote that paragraph in 1973, long before Nancy Reagan's "Just say no" campaign, when Timothy Leary, one of his chums, was still a recent memory at Harvard.

I knew Harvey Cox when I was a postdoctoral fellow at Harvard and I enjoyed visiting his classes, sometimes to listen, occasionally as a guest speaker. He always thought the way to understand a new group was to get involved, and he pioneered as a participant-observer among new and Asian religions. Lots of his work from the 1960s and 1970s looks a bit dotty by now, packed with utopian yearning and self-indulgent jumps into this or that form of spiritual adventure, but it's a refreshing change from the ponderous, unimaginative sociology of religion written at the same time, and it thrives on Cox's absolute inability to feel sheepish or silly.

It's a lot to ask eighty-eight-year-olds to warm up to this stuff, but most of them do. They trust me not to lead them into temptation or at least, if I do, to deliver them from evil. By showing them the amusing as well as the terrifying side of it, I can give them a glimpse of a world they probably knew only from a grim, suspicious, external gaze at the time. As with my college class, so with this night class, there's always a sudden change in mood the moment the teaching finishes and ordinary life resumes. We all return to the present moment, to courtesies, and to the pressing and distracting stuff of everyday life. But the more absorbing I've been able to make the last two hours, the better. We say warm farewells and look forward to getting together again in the fall.

Orientation for Germany (Tuesday)

In the evening I go to a meeting at Emory's Halle Institute, in preparation for a forthcoming goodwill expedition to Germany with fourteen other professors. Tonight we're having an orientation talk about German politics, and the instructor is none other than my old chum Tom Lancaster. He leads our summer program in Oxford. I've always had a high opinion of him and never more than tonight, when, for the first time, I am part of the audience while he is teaching. One of the sad things about being a professor is that we rarely see each other doing what we do best. Each professor has more or less complete classroom autonomy, and although there are classroom exchanges now and again, we often go years at a time without seeing each other at work. Instead we usually see each other in faculty or department meetings when we've turned aside from the thing we do well (teaching and writing) and are struggling to do something most of us do badly (run things). It's a pity and sometimes leads professors to underestimate their colleagues.

Tom, as I would have expected, is great in class. In two hours he gives a wonderfully comprehensive explanation of the postwar German political system, explaining the nature of the parties, how the proportional representation system works, how the West's parties were able to dominate the East very rapidly after reunification, and how particular individuals like Konrad Adenauer and Helmut Kohl were able to modify the system. He's not flashy but has a steady rhetorical power whose effects are cumulative so that, unlike teachers who lose their audience when the novelty's worn off, he becomes more and more engaging. It's a real shame that we have to stop at nine o'clock and I feel I could have listened to as much again. Like all really confident teachers Tom is perfectly willing to take questions at any time and to weave his answers into the main fabric of his talk—occasionally he tells a questioner that he'll answer them in a minute or two, and he never forgets. Tom's a comparitivist and is always ready with a quick and useful comparison of the German system with what is happening in Britain, America, Spain, and Italy. I'm forced to admit that he's got a far better grasp of what is happening politically in Britain than I have. It's a first-rate performance that underlines my admiration for him.

CHAPTER

16

■ ■ ■

From the Hitler-Stalin Pack
to the Peace Treat

Fortieth Class (Wednesday)

Regina gives her second lecture presentation to the group. About three weeks ago I gave her a choice of subjects on which to lecture—anything that was left, essentially—and she chose recent women's history and the feminist movement. I missed her first lecture, on nuclear weapons, so I sit down with the students for the first time to see what she has to say. I can see that she's terribly nervous. She's not an expansive talker even one-on-one, and the pressure of circumstances, with thirty-nine students plus me, makes her shyer than usual. It has the effect of constricting her voice, which is almost too quiet to hear. She is undemonstrative and doesn't wave her arms or stride around the room. Being physically small already, she seems to shrink before us. Our "smart classroom" is full of ambient noises: grunts and groans, creaking chairs, machinery, ventilation fans, people outside the door and walking overhead (we're in the basement), and the students inside, with the result that it's hard to hear what she is saying, even though none of us is more than fifteen or twenty feet from her. We're literally leaning forward.

Still, the lecture itself is fine. Picking up the story with the forcible ejection of Rosie the Riveter from the factory when hubby came marching home, she describes the steady rise of women at work, the baby-boom-era cult of motherhood, Betty Friedan's "problem that has no name," the 1960s antidiscrimination legislation, the exploitation of white women in SNCC and their doubts about the benefits of the "sexual revolution," the creation of NOW and then the rise of the more radical branches of feminism, the picketing of the Miss America contest with its "freedom trashcans" for girdles, bras, and makeup, the debate over lesbianism as the logical outcome of feminism, the abortion controversy, the launching and ultimate failure of the Equal Rights Amendment, and the counterattack against feminism by Phyllis Schlafly's "StopERA." Either by coincidence or with exquisite tact she finishes just about the place where the whole course will finish, at the start of the 1980s.

Incidentally, most years, when I give a lecture along more or less the same lines, I begin by asking who in the classroom is a feminist. Usually nobody raises a hand; occasionally there is one. Last year, when no hands rose, I said to one of the women, "Why aren't you a feminist? Don't you believe in equal pay for equal work?" "Oh yes, I do believe in that." "Do you think women should have the vote?" "Yes, of course." "Do you think it's all right to advertise jobs by specifying that the successful candidate will be an attractive young woman?" "No, certainly not." "So you're taking a whole series of feminist positions." "That's not feminism. Feminists are aggressive lesbians who won't wear makeup or look nice."

Forty-First Class (Friday)

Class meets for the second-to-last time this morning. We're discussing *If I Die in a Combat Zone*, by Tim O'Brien, a thinly fictionalized version of his experiences as a soldier in Vietnam in 1969. I read it when I was a first-year graduate student at Berkeley, back in 1978, when it was relatively new (it came out in 1975). I've learned such a lot about Vietnam in the meantime, and my own views about politics have changed so much in the interim, that it doesn't strike me at all the same way now as it did then. I like it as much as ever, however, and it's a terrific read—its pages practically turn themselves, and it's easy to die to all other interests while you're in the middle of it.

O'Brien describes how he grew up in a Minnesota prairie town among veterans of the Second World War, including his father, and how reminiscences and memories of that "good war" were the stuff of everyday life as he matured. An intelligent kid, he goes off to college and increasingly has doubts about whether America is doing the right thing in Vietnam. When he graduates he is drafted and spends the summer discussing with his friends whether or not he should go. He recalls that on a college exchange program he went to Prague and there met, and talked with, a persuasive young man from Hanoi. He's increasingly convinced that America is doing more harm than good in Vietnam, but can't be sure that he isn't simply rationalizing his own fears.

When the time comes to join the army he does join, fulfilling his family's and his community's expectations. There are some graphic passages about the mortification and brutality of basic training and the attempt to dehumanize and diminish the recruits. He goes to visit the chaplain with his doubts. The chaplain tells him, "You're a soldier now and have your duty to think about." He visits his battalion commander and says, "I'm not sure this war is justified." The officer, without missing a beat, answers, "Lots of guys are just as scared as you are but you'll learn to deal with it." At the base library he researches people who have deserted to Canada or Sweden and prepares to run away. Everything is ready when he goes on leave to Seattle, but he finds, when it comes to the point, that he just can't bring himself to do it. The accumulated weight of social expectations, and his own uncertainty about the purity of his motives, keep him in the army. He goes through advanced infantry training and then heads off to Vietnam.

American troopers simply had to survive 365 days and then they were cycled out of Vietnam, the army having become convinced that battle fatigue would otherwise wear them all down to breaking point. Evocative descriptions of the heat, dirt, fear, and uncertainty of life as a patrolling infantryman follow. He's dismayed by the brutal insensitivity of many fellow-grunts and their open racism toward the Vietnamese. One by one his friends die or are wounded, mostly by horrible land-mine booby traps. He realizes that the same people who help the Americans by day in the villages are helping the enemy by night, or indeed *are* the enemy. Women, children, and old men play a key role in guerrilla war, and that knowledge tempts the American infantrymen to treat every Vietnamese person as an enemy. He witnesses atrocities and does little or nothing to stop them because he's constantly aware that the perpetrators of the atrocities are people whose help he might need at any moment to save his life. He meditates on the nature of courage and describes the variety of ways it shows up in his officers and buddies.

Since this is the last discussion class, I've kept the whole class together rather than breaking it into two. We easily get into a vigorous discussion of the book. I'm pleased to find that everyone liked it and that nearly everyone seems to have read it cover to cover. They each say what they liked: the difficulty of the moral situation he's in; his discussions of courage and fear; and the fact that he's just the same age as they are, making decisions they would have had to make if they had lived then. Some scorn him for being weak, for not having the courage of his convictions when he wants to desert. Others sympathize with his dilemma and argue that it's sometimes right to go against your conscience for the sake of obeying the law and the community. That gives me a chance to make a comparison with the civil rights movement, whose leaders insisted that's just what you mustn't do. The compromisers at once do an about-face and agree that if it's a matter of protesting against segregation it's right to break the law, but they're not so sure when it's a matter of serving your country during an unjustified war. There are a couple who deny that the war was a bad cause (though that view seems to be getting steadily scarcer, even among rock-ribbed Republicans).

We compare O'Brien with Sara Smolinsky in *Bread Givers* and with Emma Goldman in *Living My Life*, two other first-person narratives we've all read this semester. The best comparison from this term's work, however, is with Theodore Roosevelt's *Rough Riders*. What a difference. According to TR the men couldn't wait to get into combat and positively relished the experience of being shot at by the enemy. When wounded they would, he claims, sneak out of the hospital to get back to the front lines. O'Brien's account of men at war couldn't be more different. The only things he describes with relish are some purely imaginary patrols his platoon undertook, complete with calling in artillery fire on imaginary enemy contacts, all with the connivance of their officers, to save them the fear, anguish, and futility of actually going out on patrol. He also mentions a couple of cases of men killing, or threatening to kill, officers and sergeants who were too gung ho.

There are no remarks of piercing insight today, but the generally high level of interest and involvement makes the class a pleasure from start to finish. As we wind up I ask them whether the class, next year, should have more books of this sort, first-person tales, and they chorus a big yes. "But aren't you fascinated by books on irrigation systems and books filled with immigration statistics?" Big shout of no! "But if I don't assign such books when will you ever read them?" Curtis grins and says, "That's what you're there for, professor, to lecture to us about the stuff that would be too boring for us to read about, and to find a way of making it bearable."

We'll meet for the last time on Monday. Just as I predicted, from starting the semester ugly and same-ish they've become beautiful and different. I'll miss them—not the annoying minority of chronic latecomers and excuse makers but the big pleasant middle and the exceptional few at the top.

However, there's no surer way of keeping the sentimental nostalgia at bay than actually reading their final papers, and I've been wading through three or four a day since Monday. There's the usual dismaying clutter of grammatical mistakes, the grievous misunderstandings, the imperfect sequencing of events, and the inability to make an argument. The student who wrote the heartbreaking plea for mercy really did hand her paper in, a day and a half later, and it's good. I'm pleased by her improvement since last time, but sorry to say that it's nowhere near so entertaining as her first paper, which contained a wonderful succession of accidental howlers. She's obviously taken to heart my injunction to edit carefully. But some of the other student papers more than make up for it. Here's one, for example, making a surprising claim: "The United States did not get any direct material advantage out of becoming involved in World War I, except death." This author shares the misconception, familiar among inexperienced history students, that a society can only do one thing at a time and have one opinion at a time. If I taught foreign policy one week and the civil rights movement the next, then that must be what happened in history itself. Hence: "But by the end of the 1960s, nuclear strategists stopped their work and the country began focusing on other issues, such as the Civil Rights Movement." The student also appears to think that everyone was keen on anti-Communism until they all suddenly became ardent civil rights advocates, then they all became hippies, then they all joined the women's movement.

Students' writing about Hitler nearly always gives rise to accidental comedy, and he plays a major role in these papers. One student has somehow got it into his head that Hitler was a Communist and that the war against Hitler was the main source of American anti-Communism. His girlfriend's paper, meanwhile, tells me in a tone of shocked innocence that: "Hitler made another tricky move and invaded Russia. It was obvious that this Fascist and imperial ruler was not trustworthy." Why did the Germans vote for Hitler? "Hitler was very popular with Germans because he promised to get Germany out of their depression, out of debt, and back into the eyes of the world." Another of the men writes about Hitler as though he would have been all right except that he had a lot of annoying personal habits: "The Americans fought against Germany under Adolf Hitler, who had taken to invading countries and attempting to establish a dictatorship throughout Europe." Last time I nagged this one about grammar and about careful editing. If anything he seems to be getting worse rather than better, and at one point, in what looks like a failed grammar exercise by an EFL student, he writes, "A year later, the sinking of an British ship containing many Americans led to a upsurge of anti-German sentiment."

We have the usual array of mixed metaphors: "The donning of an isolationist stance by the United States was understandable," and "The tensions built up between the U.S. and Russia steered the way into great technological advances." There is the usual lovely transformation of words due to carelessness, or misuse of words that have been heard but not seen. "The war was handled well, but the peace treat was not." "At the outset of the Second World War the world shuttered with fear." "Stalin refused to believe that Hitler would go back on their pack and therefore did not prepare his troops to fight." "After the droppings of the atomic bombs, the world knew the Americans' strength." The author of that one gave me a couple more smiles when he described the early days of the Cold War: "Even though the threat of world war no longer lurked in the corners, the world was now forced to deal with the Cold War."

"America entered the nuclear arms race with gumption." He also knows a lot about the economic consequences of the military-industrial complex: "There was an economic boom, and supply and demand was in full swing." Sorting out domestic from foreign issues in the assignment played havoc with some of these authors: "The American policymakers were afraid that if they did not permanently militarize Western Europe, Communism would keep spreading and would eventually dominate the world, which was known as the 'red scare.'"

The best paper has been written by one of the most annoying members of the class, who thought herself too good for the rest of the students, often skipped class, and was rarely on time if she did appear. After losing my temper with her in class when she came in and began reading a magazine, I had a conciliatory chat with her the other day and discovered that she's going off to anthropology graduate school. There's no question about it—she can write. Coming from anyone else I'd suspect that the paper she turned in was plagiarized, but I believe that she really did write this accurate and economical paragraph, and others like it:

Meanwhile, with the destruction of the pre-war European empires, America found itself in the position of leading half of a bipolar international community. The US completely abandoned its pre-war policy of international restraint, and sought to engage the USSR on every possible front. Espionage, arms buildups, proxy wars, propaganda, and international alliances characterized this point in the Cold War, and continued to escalate for much of the next four decades. The effectiveness of these tactics remains to be judged conclusively by history. Although the US ultimately won the Cold War, it is doubtful whether the war itself was necessary for the defeat of Communism. While such tactics may have hastened the end of the Soviet Union, it was ultimately the economic fallacies of communism that led to the system's collapse.

Almost alone among the class's thirty-nine students she knows how to cover a lot of material in a short space. She has some nice paradoxical turns of phrase, too: "After the USSR caught up with the USA in the nuclear arms race by detonating its own atomic bomb in 1949, the prospect of total war between the two sides appeared both more frightening and less likely." The assignment required between fifteen hundred and two thousand words. Nearly every paper has actually run longer than two thousand and a few are pushing three thousand. In a shade under two thousand, this student has been twice as informative as many of the long-winded ramblers.

Forty-Second Class—Last Meeting

It is the last day of classes. I follow a tradition I began the first time I used music in class by playing them a track from the Indigo Girls. Why? Because the Indigo Girls are Emory graduates who became local celebrities, then went on to have a fairly major career in the pop music business. They're still much loved here, and as "Closer to Fine" is playing I can see two or three of the women lip-synching along. Sure enough, when I ask, there's a great chorus of recognition. Next I ask who's graduating and about eight of the thirty-nine raise their hands. For Bill this morning's class is his absolute last as a college student.

I begin with an apology about not getting all the way to the year 2000. Rather than spend the class on winding up and reiterating earlier themes, however, I carry on, outlining the political events of the 1970s: Watergate; the Carter campaign; his "malaise" speech; the bruising Democratic primaries of 1980, in which doomed Jimmy Carter and doomed Ted Kennedy tore each other to pieces, while Reagan, hardly able to believe his good luck, put together a winning campaign. I describe the new religious right and the role of Jerry Falwell, quote a few of his words, and explain why abortion, school prayer, and the profamily agenda were such resonant issues that year.

It's such a thrilling lecture that Blake falls fast asleep, slumping over alarmingly to one side and looking as though he might fall out of the chair completely. I stop, stare at him, everyone else's eyes follow mine, until I say, with slow emphasis, "Are you with us, Blake?" At first there's no reaction, but then something in his reptilian cortex must be sending a signal and he suddenly straightens up, widens his eyes, and gives me a quizzical look, as if to say, "Why are you staring at me? All I did was blink." There's some suppressed tittering from the women at the back and a lot of nudging. A minute later I discover that Eric is also having a snooze. I accidentally catch my foot against his desk and he too lurches back into the land of the living. The last day of classes is notoriously a tough day for teachers, because the students are nearly all trying frantically to finish papers. (Sure enough, after class Blake comes back to the classroom to apologize, explaining that he was up all night finishing his paper for another course.)

Reagan got lots of help from the religious right. When it came to the point, however, he wasn't really prepared to put much political energy into enacting their profamily agenda. The other half of the Republican Party was much more interested in getting government out of citizens' lives, and didn't want it becoming more embroiled, as "profamily" policies would have required. As it played out in practice, the early years of the Reagan revolution were mainly a matter of stimulating business, rubbishing environmentalism, and offering the difficult blend of less taxes and more expenditure for the arms buildup.

As usual I run short of time, this time in the midst of an elaborate description of the Democrats' dilemma in 1984 over the Rainbow Coalition and the candidacy of Jesse Jackson. Determined to give them at least some sort of peroration, I end by summarizing the growth of social inequality in the 1980s and 1990s and warn the students that it's an issue they'll have to deal with in their own adulthood. They're members of the privileged minority, with immense opportunities for good and evil in their future lives. It's up to them to improve their world. Then the clock announces that the last minute of the last class meeting has expired. Several students pause to say thanks as they leave.

There's a special feeling in the air at end of the spring semester. Everywhere are signs of change and a sense of expectation. The big stage is going up across the quadrangle, on which the VIPs, honorary degree recipients, and top administrators will stand on graduation day. In the next day or two, thousands of chairs will be arranged in careful rows, radiating out from this big covered stage, in such a way that no one's sight line will be blocked by trees and that everyone will be able to move. It's a mob scene outside my window every graduation day—I usually take it in from my elevated perch and wave to the students I know who are graduating. Everywhere now you can hear students discussing travel plans for the summer and work plans for next year and already the first hugs and farewells among friends. But you can also hear descriptions of harrowing all-nighters, angry professors, unreasonable TAs, work unfinished, and disagreements over whether requirements have been fulfilled.

The ending of the semester is always a bit depressing. I love the rhythm of teaching three times a week, around which everything else has been structured since January. I've come to know the students well and to like most of them. Now and then I'll have little farewell conversations with them, but the class as an entity is dispersing. I'll see them together for the last time when they take the exam, then never again. They're such a powerful group, taken all together; a wonderful mixture of ability, energy, youth, vitality, wealth, beauty, utopianism, hope, nuttiness, muscle, energy, laziness, and willpower, it's hard to believe so much raw material all fitted into that room. I know I'll see some of them again in later classes, which in turn will take on their own collective identity, but this group as a whole will quickly fade, and within a year I'll have forgotten at least half of their names. (I've written far more about this group than about any other class, though, so perhaps I'll have a longer memory of them than of their predecessors. And why on earth didn't I think to get a group photograph, since I've written an entire book about them?!?)

Another aspect of the depression comes from the fact that, as the semester draws to its end, I don't have the reward of meditative, nostalgic chats with the good members of the class. Instead I have sharp struggles of the will with students who didn't do what they were supposed to do. To make matters worse I'm also, as director of undergraduate studies, dealing with the hopeless cases from other courses, those who didn't fulfil their assignments, or who plagiarized, and are now casting about angrily for someone to blame.

17

Inflated Grades and Sentiments

More "Appreciation" (Tuesday)

It's a great life being a professor, and one of the many little perks that come along at the end of the semester is invitations to "faculty appreciation days" at the sororities. Last week I found in my mailbox a bag of chocolate chip cookies and a little scroll. It read: "You have been selected as a favorite teacher of Alpha Delta Pi. Thank you for all your hard work and dedication while teaching us this past school year. We greatly appreciate all that you do to make our classes interesting, challenging, and enjoyable. Thanks for being such a great teacher!!!" In wiggly writing at the bottom was the signature, "The sisters of Alpha Delta Pi." Jeff Lesser and I ate the cookies and found them excellent. Today I'm off to a faculty appreciation tea party with the Thetas. It turns out that no fewer than five members of my class are sisters in this house: Tricia, Maria, Faith, Elizabeth, and Chloe, all five as cheery and amiable as you can imagine. At the tea party I can also see half a dozen familiar faculty faces (the same ones who were at most teaching-related events this term) and a smattering of young women I've taught in former years.

As a teenager, and especially as an undergraduate at Oxford, I had a terrible feeling of social inferiority. If British colleges had had sororities I would have quaked even to enter. However, my social status took an immense upward bound when I came to America. By now I'm a middle-aged geezer and can enter such places without too much social dread, especially since the residents call me "Doctor" and treat me as a remote and elderly object of veneration. Everyone's on their best behavior and I have half an hour of little chats with women who seem dauntless in their wealth, confidence, sporting ability, intellectual achievements, and beauty. They tell me about the tennis tournaments they have won, about the worldwide journeys they are about to undertake this summer, and about their plans for future careers.

Did I mention, earlier, that one of the characteristics of our students is that they have grown up in the lap of luxury, have extremely high incomes and expectations, and are familiar with far bigger sums of money than their teachers? Compare their motor cars with ours. Walk with me around the Emory parking lots and let me show you first to the faculty area. There we discover the most broken-down Buicks, tottering Toyotas, superannuated Subarus, and even representatives of brands that no longer exist, like dowdy old Datsuns. It wouldn't surprise me to come upon rusting Studebakers, Packards, and Edsels either.

Now let me escort you to the student parking area, where we encounter a magnificent fleet of the best vehicles currently on sale anywhere in the world: haughty Mercedes Benzes by the dozen, stately Lexuses, fleet little BMWs, zesty sports cars from Italy and Japan, and monstrous SUVs with zip codes of their own. I always found the experience of seeing slim American college women driving these giants something half-erotic, half-spiritual. You know what I mean—the way these people whom you know from class to be ungrammatical, poorly read, yawning, "like"-burbling youngsters are turned into Amazons of the road behind the wheels of their mighty Explorers, Expeditions, and Exorbitants.

Pre-Exam Review Session (Wednesday)

Perceptible relaxation at the prospect of not having to get ready for class three times a week for a while. On the other hand, there's still the exam to get ready. I also have to prepare a speech to give at the Free University of Berlin (and I mustn't forget to learn how to speak German in the next ten days before we go), another speech that I'm scheduled to give in London in early July, an entire course of lectures to write on Britain and the two world wars (for summer school), a book review commissioned almost a year ago, a handful of encyclopedia articles, and all the usual bills to pay, internship papers to grade, and the other undergraduate business that never stops.

For an hour in the middle of the day, I give a review session to students who are feeling anxious about the exam, which is to be held next Monday from 8:30 – 11:00. It's a voluntary review and about half the class shows up; exactly the half I would have expected. Most of them are the ones who don't need it and will do well anyway.

I never write the exam before doing the review session—it's hard not to show your hand if you already know what you've written. We go over the Korean War, the Progressive Era, the causes of the failure of Prohibition, some of the immigration material, the California water politics, the difference between the two Roosevelts (!), and the student uprisings of the 1960s. I throw in a few of my exhortations, like: "To understand American history you've got to take an interest in agriculture. By now only about three percent of the American people actually live and work on farms but without them the whole society would fall to pieces at once. Making the food grow is the foundation for everything else." I praise dates, maps, and graphs for their precision and powers of compression (looks of distaste from all round) and try to argue that the alleged "dryness" of history is part of its great beauty. Faith starts laughing at me when I get into the question of whether it's better to be wet or dry, so I wind up with a few encouraging words and a good-luck wish.

After this session, the exam is on my mind so I sit down and write it. Since the students have already had to write a couple of analytical papers and an essay-based midterm, and since it's an introductory class, I've decided to try a different approach to the exam, one that demands exact knowledge of what happened, where, when, and why, with a relative minimum of interpretive work. Here it is: see how well you can do after not taking the course.

1. Explain, in one sentence, the historical significance of the following.
   a. The election of 1896
   b. The election of 1928
   c. The American Federation of Labor
   d. The Agricultural Adjustment Act
   e. The Gulf of Tonkin Resolution
   f. The Inchon landings
   g. The immigration reform acts of 1921 and 1924
   h. The Rough Riders
   i. Anarchism
   j. *Plessy v. Ferguson*
   k. Watergate
   l. The Hoover Dam
   m. The *Lusitania*
   n. John Kenneth Galbraith
   o. Geraldine Ferraro
   p. Mario Savio
   q. D-Day
   r. Malcolm X
   s. Earl Warren
   t. The Tet Offensive
   u. Mutual Assured Destruction
   v. Three Mile Island
   w. Betty Friedan
   x. Albert Pope
   y. Anzia Yezierska

2. When did the following events take place (just give the year or years)?
   a. The election of President Kennedy
   b. The first moon-walk
   c. Supreme Court's decision in *Roe v. Wade*
   d. Failed presidential election campaign of Wendell Willkie
   e. The atomic bombing of Hiroshima
   f. The Voting Rights Act
   g. The Montgomery Bus Boycott
   h. The Russian Revolution

     i. The Scopes Monkey Trial

     j. The Battle of Midway

     k. The fall of the Berlin Wall

     l. FDR's "court-packing" plan

     m. The Berlin Airlift

     n. The resignation of President Nixon

     o. The death of President McKinley

     p. The assassination of President Diem of South Vietnam

     q. Frederick J. Turner's speech "The Significance of the Frontier in American History"

     r. The attempted killing of Henry Clay Frick

     s. The Battle of the Little Big Horn

     t. The invention of the mechanical cotton picker

3. In what state did the following events take place?

     a. The completion of the first transcontinental railroad line

     b. The building of Las Vegas

     c. The bombing of Pearl Harbor

     d. The building of America's longest oil pipeline

     e. The diversion of the Owens River

     f. The Battle of the Little Big Horn

     g. The construction of the Ford Motor Car factories

     h. The birth and early political career of Theodore Roosevelt

     i. The election of Woodrow Wilson as governor in 1910

     j. The illegal liquor operations of Al Capone

     k. The first "sit-ins" at segregated lunch counters

     l. The first successful test of an atomic bomb

     m. The launch of the first American space vehicle to carry an astronaut

     n. The building of the first profitable high-speed turnpike

     o. The Dust Bowl storms of the 1930s (five different states are admissible here)

     p. The New Deal's biggest flood-control scheme

     q. The 1915 refounding of the Ku Klux Klan

     r. The Three Mile Island accident

     s. The prepresidential political career of James Earl Carter

4. Who did the following?

     a. Conducted the Hawthorne experiment

    b. Ran for president from a jail cell in 1920

    c. Wrote *The Jungle*

    d. Led the American military forces in World War I

    e. Lost the presidential election of 1932

    f. Wrote *If I Die in a Combat Zone*

    g. Sat in the "whites only" section of the segregated Montgomery bus

    h. Was first head of the U.S. Forest Service

    i. Signed the Camp David Peace Accords on behalf of Egypt

    j. Was the last Communist leader of the Soviet Union

    k. Commanded U.S. Navy forces in the Pacific, 1942–45

    l. Led the Sioux and Cheyenne at the Little Big Horn (either of two admissible here)

    m. Ran the black South Chicago districts on behalf of the Democratic Party in the 1950s

    n. Was head of the federal Highways Department between 1920 and 1950

    o. Tried to kill Henry Clay Frick

    p. Was convicted of nuclear espionage and killed in the electric chair (either of two)

    q. Tried to win the Democratic nomination on behalf of the "Rainbow Coalition"

    r. Was president in 1903

    s. Starred in the movie *Modern Times*

5. On the attached outline map of the United States, mark the location of the following.

    a. Chicago

    b. New Orleans

    c. The place where the Wright brothers' aircraft first flew

    d. Yosemite National Park

    e. Lake Erie

    f. The course of the Missouri River

    g. The course of the Tennessee River

    h. Pittsburgh

    i. Houston

    j. Promontory Point

    k. Detroit

l. Montgomery, Alabama

m. Levittown, New York

n. Alamagordo

o. Write the initials LRS in the state which has the lowest annual rainfall

p. Write the intials CM in a state with a long history of coal mining

q. Write the initials IOM in a state with a long history of iron ore mining

r. Write the initials LI (low immigration) in three states with populations that were less than 1 percent foreign born in 1986

s. The course of the Columbia River

6. Choose four of the following and write a paragraph in answer to each.

a. Why did the Great Depression not recur after World War II?

b. Why did the Americans fail in Vietnam?

c. Why did Prohibition fail?

d. Was the New Deal a success?

e. Why did Martin Luther King Jr. become a national hero?

f. What factors made environmentalism popular in the 1960s and 1970s?

g. Why were college students so confrontational in the 1960s?

Anyone who paid attention and came to class regularly should be able to get close to 100 percent (in an ideal world, but not in this one). The dates will cause the most protest and misery, I expect, closely followed by the "who did the following" section and the challenge to draw the course of the Missouri River. The first and last sections, especially the last, give a bit of scope to the most intelligent to flex their brain muscles a little. I expect most students will finish with plenty of time to spare, whether or not they get many questions right. You, reader, may look in the appendix for the answers to sections 2, 3, and 4. I prepare the students for the exam with an e-mail, explaining in detail the form of the exam and offering sample questions and answers.

Grading

Who's in favor of grade inflation? Nobody. Who practices grade inflation? Everybody. It's an example of Gresham's law. Bad (inflated) grades drive out the good. A teacher who is determined to hold the line and give students the grades they deserve, as opposed to the grades they want, is like a bull in a china shop. The first thing he will discover is that he is bitterly hated by the students, who feel as though they have been cheated of something that is rightfully theirs. The second thing he'll discover is that he is equally bitterly hated by the students' parents, who feel as though they've been cheated out of something for which they just paid $120,000. The third thing he'll discover is that his own colleagues and the associate deans will soon be putting pressure on him to stop it. Otherwise enrollments in the department will go down, storms with students' families will rage, and the quiet professorial life will be just a memory.

Look at the students I've been teaching this term. In an ideal world I would give about a quarter of them Fs. Why? Because they have no aptitude for history, no appreciation for the connection between events, no sense of how a historical situation changes over time, they don't want to do the necessary hard work, they skimp on the reading, and can't write to save their lives. That's grounds enough for an F, surely.

Will I give them Fs? No. Most of them will get B- and a few really hard cases will come in with Cs. The only person who's going to get an F this term is the one to whom I sent the threatening mid-semester e-mail. Briefly she began showing up for class, but soon her deep, deep propensity for not bothering reasserted itself. She missed nine classes in a row and failed to hand in the second paper. Her I can fail with a clear conscience, in the knowledge that everyone else around here would fail her too. Let her parents rage all they want: I'll just refer them to their own dear girl for explanations and, if necessary, to my little attendance book. All the others, one way or another, are going to scrape through.

Where do grades come from? Out of my head, but in a rich social context. On my reading list this term it says the grade consists of the following:

Quizzes	10 percent
Class participation	26 percent
Midterm	15 percent
Papers	24 percent
Final	25 percent

There's a feeling of precision about that list, but it's belied by the human realities on every side. First, I hardly ever actually gave quizzes, and it would be unreasonable to make two little map tests comprise 10 percent of the whole grade. In reality, then, those ten are going to have to be distributed elsewhere. The idea of 26 percent for class participation as opposed to 24 for the papers, instead of a straight 25 for each, is my way of saying that it's important for everyone to read the materials and join in discussion. Even so, many of them didn't really do the reading properly, or else they just caused their eyes to pass rapidly over the lines of words on the page. I could write a hundred thousand words on the difficulty involved in making students really *read* an assignment in such a way as to understand it fully. One day I'll make a week's reading assignment just one paragraph, with the proviso that it has to be scrutinized in all its fullness and complexity! Until that day I'm always going to have exchanges like this one:

Me: Did you read the assignment?
Student: Yes.
Me: What does the author say about the changing immigration laws?
Student: I can't remember.
Me: Did you take notes on the important issues?
Student: Yes.
Me: Did you think the legal situation was an important issue?
Student: Yes.
Me: Do you have the notes you took on the legal changes?
Student: Yes, they're on my computer at home.
Me: Can you remember what they say?
Student: No.
Me: Can you say anything at all about American immigration law?
Student: People were allowed to come from other countries to America.
Me: And . . . ?
Student: That's about all I know.

How do you grade class participation on the basis of this exchange? It is possible that the student did read the assignment hastily. It's possible that he made hasty and sketchy notes. It's equally possible that he did neither, and he's certainly been uncommunicative. It's one of those many places where you might think the perfect solution lay with the letter F, but the student's memory of this exchange will be that he and I had a long class conversation about immigrants and that he showed a real engagement with the issue.

Then there are students like the one who, throughout the term, never once volunteered a word and would speak only if asked a direct question. When asked, she would answer correctly but in the fewest possible words, with every sign of shrinking distaste and giving away the minimum of information. Cross-questioning would elicit one or two additional nuggets of fact but no sign of engagement or interest. For her everything was just such a chore. How do I decide on a score out of 26 for her?

The midterm, paper, and final grades are a bit more objective, although since we give the papers letter grades and the exams percentages we have to find a way of turning their numerical scores into appropriately corresponding letter grades. It's at least partly a subjective process. Students don't always know *how* subjective, but they get a sense that in the end every grade is based not only on objective criteria but also on the teacher's judgment. Teachers *decide* grades, and canny students try to do everything they can to influence their teachers' decision making. Think about those sorority parties. Is it entirely a coincidence that they take place just before finals, in the middle of marathons of paper grading? When it comes to deciding about hospitable young ladies, how will the memory of their kindness the other day affect my judgment of borderline cases?

There's a long-running debate about grading for effort. What do you do in the case of a poor student who works flat out to keep up, who devotes hours more to the readings than his nonchalantly talented contemporaries, struggles with the words and the meaning, makes painstaking drafts of papers, and seeks advice and guidance every step of the way? We're not made of stone; it's hard to slap a discouraging C on such people—you find yourself being tempted up to at least a B. But then a jaundiced awareness of the tricks people play makes you ask: suppose he's just pretending to be a plucky struggler? Am I letting myself be taken in?

Here's something to keep squarely in mind: everyone wants an A for every course, and no student has ever, in my twenty-odd years of teaching, reproached me for grading too generously (even though I do). Emory's full of eager strivers, often with a parental knuckle in their backs, eager to get into business school, law school, medical school, or graduate school. They know that only big GPAs and big test scores are going to get them there, and the prospect of a low grade makes them desperate, so much seems to hang in the balance. That doesn't mean they all go after it honestly, but there's no doubting the emotional seriousness and intensity of their desire.

The aftermath of distributing grades every semester, accordingly, is a series of visits from the students who didn't get straight As. Some of them come in a contrite spirit, asking, "Could you go over the exam with me and explain what I did wrong?" You go over it with them and they contest every point, decorously but remorselessly. Others arrive in a belligerent spirit, declaring, "I'm a straight-A student. Why didn't I get that A?" You go over it with them too and they huff and snort derisively. I've always found it difficult to stand up to their browbeating. I'm the teacher and they're the students, admittedly, but it doesn't quite feel that way. Students of both sexes are equally good at making this professor, at least, feel sheepish and mean-spirited—they make me wonder if it really was spite or insufficient appreciation for their greatness that caused my pen to write a B+ in the box where the A was supposed to be.

It's happened so often, however, that I've developed tactics of resistance. I say to them, "I'm not going to change the grade, because I'm convinced it is right. However, I see that you are not satisfied, and I'm willing to hand your papers and exams to one of my colleagues for a second opinion." Usually they grudgingly give up at this point, because somewhere inside they know they're wrong. Occasionally they are full enough of self-righteousness to accept the offer.

I know from years of experience that the possibility of an upward shift in the grade from one of these second opinions is vanishingly unlikely. First, my colleague rarely knows the student in question and feels none of the human sympathy that has developed over the course of the semester (if only the student knew it, he or she has already been given an unreasonably *high* grade because I'm so soft-hearted). He's more likely to grade the student lower rather than higher because he can see with a purely objective eye what's wrong with the work. Second, the colleague can't help being aware that a complaining student has brought about this request for help. He has whiners too and knows what they're like—a gigantic pain in the neck. A sense of professional respect also restrains him—sooner or later he'll be asking me to return the favor. And, of course, this is the time of year at which he's got fifty big papers of his own to grade; the last thing he wants is another one.

In our department some professors offer students a second opinion with hazards attached. If the second professor thinks the original grade was too low he'll raise it, as the student hopes, but if the second professor thinks the original grade was too *high* he'll lower it, and the student will be obliged to accept that outcome too. There's a deterrent! I'm too weak to do that—I hold out to them the prospect of an increase without the threat of a decrease. In practice the real outcome is the same—the grade is not changed.

Grades and letters of recommendation are comparable. Both are conspiracies of exaggeration; we make ridiculous, dizzying claims in our letters of recommendation, knowing that if we don't we're dooming our candidates' chances, since other candidates against whom they are competing will certainly have exaggerated letters of their own. We inflate their grades too, to help them along in their quest to join professional schools, graduate programs, and to get good jobs. It happens all over the country, at every level—I saw the other day that the *average* grade at Stanford is A-.

I remember that about ten years ago some states began introducing basic literacy tests as prerequisites for graduating from high school. Kids with all-but-perfect GPAs began *failing* these tests, showing that their teachers had been giving them As even though they couldn't read and write. In one deep South state (not Georgia, for once) a good number of the *teachers* failed these tests too. There was a lot of indignant spluttering in the media over this discovery. Any professor who searched his soul and thought about what goes on in college as well as school cannot have been too deeply surprised.

On the question of student papers, incidentally, I was chatting last weekend with a friend who teaches music theory and music appreciation at a nearby community college. We were discussing plagiarism, and I explained my long-running struggle against it. He said, "Quite frankly,

I'm content to see students plagiarizing. It shows they've opened a book and read through a few passages before copying it out. Half the papers I get are completely unreadable, they're so bad; but the plagiarists' work flows nicely and is a pleasure to read!" He was kidding, but not by all that much.

18

■ ■ ■

Finals and Farewells

Final Exam (Monday)

The exam begins at 8:30 and everyone is there. I've fielded about twenty-five e-mails over the last two or three days, some from students trying to work out exactly what's on the exam and some asking me to remind them about who did what at Inchon, Anzio, and so on. They get right to work on the exam after I've given them a brief reminder about the honor code and the need to apportion their time wisely. As usual, several have forgotten to bring blue books and are panicky about whether they can use loose sheets ("Yes, but make sure your name's on every one"). Others haven't got a pen or pencil. Others again, however, have brought in twenty or thirty new pens, ready for every contingency, and can be persuaded to lend to their less provident fellows. I wait for a few minutes as they read through the exam to make sure everything is clear, then leave the room (in accordance with the honor code, which specifies that professors should not be in the room during exams) and go back to my office. Those who finish early, which should be most of them, are free to leave as soon as they are done.

After about two hours one of the women comes to find me and complains bitterly. She says the exam is all nit-picking detail and that although she has learned everything in this course, the exam hasn't given her the opportunity to demonstrate her learning or her analytical skills. "No, no," I answer, "there's nothing nit-picking about it. Every question is based squarely on important issues, events, and personalities that we addressed in the course—things every course member should know. You can't write a conceptually convincing paper if you don't even know the factual basics, and this exam is easy because it requires *only* the basics, except in its first and last sections." She knows, and I know, that exams of this kind leave students with nowhere to hide if they don't know the facts. I'm willing to give them half a point if they're close on the dates, but with the states, the individuals, and the map question, they've simply got to know what's what and who's who. It's pretty clear from her presence here and her anguish that she doesn't know. I tell her, "Well, let's wait and see how you got on. I haven't seen your exam yet so I can't judge how well you did. By Friday I will have graded it so check back with me then." She then repeats that I have been unfair and says that she's afraid her grade, which would have been an A- or B+, will now be a C. That's a common stunt, too—telling the teacher that you were "going into the exam with an A for the course"—and it's usually delusionary.

When I get back to the classroom at 10:50 there are only four or five students left, and they keep going to the bitter end. Regina, as arranged, comes in as the last one leaves and I show her the exam for the first time. She says, "I talked to a group of the women last night and they were freaking out." "Why?" "Because having to know the facts puts them so much on the spot." We go over the map questions together and I give her a master copy with answers because she says she would otherwise get most of it wrong! We'll grade them tonight and tomorrow, then meet on Wednesday morning to figure out final grades.

Exam Grading (Tuesday)

The grading marathon is not so arduous as usual, partly because I have a TA and partly because much of the exam is mechanical. There is a wide spectrum of grades among them, as I expected. Some students have obviously prepared carefully, systematically learning all the main points including the names, dates, places, and issues. Others have a good grasp of some issues and only a tenuous hold on others, and some are hopelessly confused all the way through. Hardly anyone gets more than half the questions on the map right, and only one out of thirty-nine can trace the course of the Missouri River even approximately.

On the initial twenty-five questions most students do well, though a few of the identifications are obviously too hard. Only two out of the thirty-nine can remember Mario Savio, even though I showed a sequence of slides of him standing on the Berkeley police car roof during the big Sproul Plaza free speech demonstration in 1964 and read a few passages from one of his speeches. One thinks Savio was a McCarthyite in the 1950s. Another writes that "Mario Savio, in response to the first major oil crisis, became very weary of shortages in general, feeling that eventually there would be nothing left." A third says, "Mario Savio was a political machine that helped the impoverished immigrants in exchange for votes and political support." In yet another student's view, "Mario Savio was an Italian man who may have killed Robert Kennedy."

They have trouble with economist John Kenneth Galbraith too, around whose *Affluent Society* I based a lecture on postwar prosperity. Here is some of the *un*conventional wisdom about Galbraith's historical significance (with, in brackets, my guess about who they were really talking about):

John Kenneth Galbraith was a major student leader during the civil rights movement in 1960s, specifically the Free Speech Movement on Berkeley's campus. [Mario Savio!!!]

John Kenneth Galbraith tried to kill Henry Clay Frick. [Alexander Berkmann]

John Kenneth Galbraith is an economist who argued that raising oil prices is good for the economy. [????]

John Kenneth Galbraith made paintings of Yosemite National Park and sent them back east. He was a product of manifest destiny—the idea that white Europeans were to spread Christianity and the word of God to the west. [Albert Bierstadt?]

John Kenneth Galbraith ran for president against Franklin Roosevelt in the 1940 election and lost. [Wendell Willkie.]

John Kenneth Galbraith studied labor and work and connected psychological and sociological aspects of work and productivity. [Understandable: this one has confused him with Frank Gilbreth, the efficiency expert who wrote *Cheaper by the Dozen*.]

John Kenneth Galbraith wrote about the "germ theory." In it, whites are the dominant race and should not interbreed with anyone of "lesser caliber" for fear of diminishing the white race. [A nifty mix of Herbert Baxter Adams and Madison Grant.]

John Kenneth Galbraith was a scientist during the Cold War era who helped construct a bigger nuclear bomb. [Edward Teller.]

D-Day got a few nice variations too. I like the one that makes the Allied Expeditionary Force sound like a really ardent group of holiday makers, who are just determined to have their own way on the beach: "D-Day was the day American troops crossed the English Channel and took the French beach with a decisive but bloody victory." "D-Day was in 1944 when we entered World War II through the weak under belly of Europe to fight the Germans." For pure muddle, you can't do much better than this one: "D-Day was when Germany invaded France at the shores of Normandy, and another reason for the US joining the Second World War." There's a lovely, understandable slip in this description of Albert Pope (actually a pioneer bicycle manufacturer): "He was the first Catholic presidential candidate."

By the end of the day, pestering e-mails are flowing in from students wanting to know their grades, but for the moment I put them off.

Winding Up

Regina and I meet, compare grades, and then fill out the grade sheet. I assign grades for class participation, based on notes I've taken throughout the semester and her remarks, and then work out from all the components (papers, midterm, final, participation) what the final grades will be. The act of writing down some of these grades is physically painful because I know, the instant the pen makes the mark, that it is the prelude to a long and ugly argument. Luckily I'm going abroad next Tuesday, but I'll be blessed indeed if I can escape three or four angry confrontations before then. Some will be with students who got an A- and who will tell me that I've ruined their hitherto perfect GPAs of 4.00. Others will be with students who got a C+ and would really much rather have a B+. Surly Bs, the most common grade, will be campaigning for an A-. Lots of students these days regard the grade you give them as a bargaining point. Just as used-car dealers set the initial price too high, knowing the customer will haggle them down, so (the students think) the professor sets the initial grade too low, expecting the student will haggle them up. None of them will welcome the truth that I've really been generous in grading and that they might easily have scored lower.

On the final, they got an initial grade out of 187. To each score I have added 13 points, then divided the resulting score by two to give a percentage. In view of the fact that most of these percentages are in the sixties and low to mid-seventies I have decided to let an A be anything above 80. I then descend in five-point increments, to let 75–79 be A-, 70–74 be B+, and so on. If I had made 85 or 90 the A point, everyone's grade would be worse. What do you think, reader? Here is the spread of the thirty-nine final grades

A	4
A−	7
B+	7
B	12
B−	4
C+	2
C	1
C−	1
F	1

It's not exactly the work of a ruthless hanging judge, is it? In theory, A is supposed to mean outstanding, B good, C average, and D poor. A fair number of these people were poor, but ask them if *they* think they were poor. I've clearly made B mean average, rather than C (the old "gentleman's C" is now the "preprofessional's B," attainable by the ordinary, moderately idle frat boy). Incidentally, to further soften the blow on the lower end of this grade chart, several of the lower grades went to people who are actually taking the course S/U. In other words, their letter grade won't show up on the final grade roll, which will simply report that their performance was satisfactory.

I give Becky, our administrator, the grade sheet—she'll check it and pass it along to the registrar—and in return she gives me the evaluations that the students wrote during the last week of classes. They are a pleasure to read on the whole, with lots of praise for the lectures, music, slides, and films, but there are a few brickbats too. Many students say how glad they were not to have a textbook, in view of texts' dreadful dullness and high cost, but a few say they would have liked one, to help them prepare for the final (never mind that the library—which they seem to regard as mysteriously inaccessible—is bursting with them). Here are a few of the harsher comments on me and on the readings:

Every week we had to read another novel and although some of the reading was tedious and soporific, I found many books to be quite interesting [for "novel" read "book"].

Some of the books were so boring and factual that they were very hard to read. I guess everything can't be fun to read, though . . . Professor Allitt just talks so fast that it's hard to keep up with him. It is also hard to know what is not important.

Books assigned for reading should be changed. I think historical fiction, for example Margaret George's novels, would be something you would remember after the course ends, rather than *Divided Highways*.

Drop the California river book in the river!

Reconsider which books we read for the course. Some of them (like the California river book) seemed useless and I felt so bored reading it that I couldn't even pay attention.

I glow with pride on reading this next one, which you must pardon me for quoting at length:

It's always wonderful to have a professor as energetically interested in the subject matter as Professor Allitt. In addition to being masterfully well-prepared and inventive, he's also a captivating orator, capable of keeping my interest high even on the driest of topics during the course. The mix of media only complements his wonderful teaching style, together making the class one of my most educational and enjoyable ones.

I'll draw a veil over what this otherwise excellent person had to say about the California river book. Poor old Carey McWilliams—I still think he's a good writer, but I doubt whether he'll see the light of day in my courses ever again. I had it in mind to assign his *Factories in the Fields* next time but I'd better not. Maybe a romance by Margaret George instead.

Conclusion

That's the whole story. Next Monday is graduation day. Next Tuesday I'm off to Germany for three weeks, then back in America for the month of June before returning to Europe for six more weeks as a teacher in our British Studies Program at Oxford. As always, I feel sad to have reached the end of the semester, sad to think that this wonderful class, with all its quirks, delights, and oddities, will never meet again.

As I predicted, the students became far more attractive with the passage of time, far more varied, and far more obvious in their vulnerability. Some learned a lot, some picked up a handful of ideas and insights, a few improved their writing, and nearly all learned (more or less willingly) a cluster of facts. As my quotations from papers and exams demonstrate, however, not all the students were able to banish misunderstanding; a few remained, apparently, in outer darkness throughout. The Catholic Church used to use the expression "invincible ignorance" to describe someone who had never heard about Christianity and therefore could not be criticized for not being a Christian. Professors everywhere can find another use for this delicious phrase.

I hope, however, that I haven't given the impression that the students were dim or hopeless. In the nature of things you have to spend more time dealing with the problem cases than with the successes, and even the problem cases are often doing excellent work in other courses, whatever their blind spot for history. Besides, it's no fun quoting the good ones' papers; they're just accurate and matter-of-fact; hardly any rise to actual literary merit. And there are so few opportunities to meet and talk with the good ones, because they're just steadily doing everything right and feeling content with the way things are going. Most will just fade into the background, to be seen occasionally on campus, names forgotten until they ask me, two or three years from now, for letters of recommendation.

The end-of-term feeling of nostalgia is intensified by the knowledge

that these days are, for a quarter of our students, their last days of college. Already students all over campus, finished with exams and unin-
volved with graduation, are loading up cars, hugging friends goodbye,
and driving away. Three thousand chairs have been laid out on the
quadrangle, all facing the VIP graduation stand, and the feeling of imminent ending is in the air. The big motors will crank up again at the end
of August, but it doesn't feel that way just now.

It's a great life being a professor: the benefits are major, the irritants
minor. It isn't easy keeping a distance from the students, especially in
the syrupy emotional atmosphere of graduation week. The temptation
to befriend the students, to yield to their pleas for better grades, and to
mother them before they go out into the world is so strong that I find
myself, almost, forgetting my own first rule, the one embodied in the
great decree, "I'm the teacher, you're the student."

Appendix

THE SYLLABUS

Requirements: Two papers, a midterm, occasional quizzes, and a final.

Attendance at all class meetings is required. If you are unable to attend due to illness, please notify me beforehand. No eating, drinking, or wearing hats in class. Please turn off beepers and mobile phones before entering the classroom.

The honor code is in effect at all times. Any attempt to use the work of others as your own is grounds for failing the course and expulsion from Emory. In researching and writing papers, please do not use Internet Web sites unless I have previously approved them in writing.

Most Fridays will be devoted to discussing assigned readings. Read them carefully so that you are able to discuss them intelligently. Always use a dictionary to discover the meaning of words you cannot define, and keep a book of words you have learned and their definitions. I will call on you directly, by name, during class discussions.

Grades

Quizzes	10 percent
Class participation	26 percent
Midterm	15 percent
Papers	24 percent
Final	25 percent

First Reading	John Neihardt, *Black Elk Speaks* (entire)
Second Reading	Richard Etulain, ed., *Does the Frontier Experience Make America Exceptional?*

Third Reading	Theodore Roosevelt, *The Rough Riders* (entire)
Fourth Reading	Emma Goldman, *Living My Life*, vol. 1, chaps. 7–13
Fifth Reading	Anzia Yezierska, *Bread Givers* (entire)
Papers	First paper due by 5:00 in the box beside my office door
Sixth Reading	Nicholas Lemann, *The Promised Land*, pp. 1–107 and 341–53
Exam	Midterm exam, please bring a blue book
Spring Break	No assignment (midterm break)
Seventh Reading	Melvyn Leffler, *The Specter of Communism* (entire)
Eighth Reading	Carey McWilliams, *California: The Great Exception* (foreword by Lewis Lapham, then chaps. 6, 7, 15–18)
Ninth Reading	Tom Lewis, *Divided Highways*, chaps. 1–6
Tenth Reading	Reed Ueda, *Postwar Immigrant America* (entire)
Final Reading	Tim O'Brien, *If I Die in a Combat Zone* (entire)
Papers	Second paper due by 5:00
Last Monday of Class	Last class meeting
Exam-Week Monday	Final exam, 8:30–11:00, same room

HANDOUT FOR THE SECOND PAPER

Please use the question as your title.

Why did the United States of America take on global responsibilities between 1917 and 1990? How successfully did it manage them, and in what ways did they change American society internally?

1,800–2,000 words, due by 5:00 P.M. on Monday, April 23 in the box outside my office door. Late papers will be graded down one letter grade per day.

Write as though you are addressing someone who knows less about the subject than you.

Your job is to:
1. inform the reader of what happened;
2. explain to the reader why it happened;
3. persuade the reader that your way of looking at the issue is right.

Start work on the paper early so that you do not have to write it all at once. I will read drafts and help you with them up to 10:00 on Thursday, April 19. Before handing in your paper, edit it carefully to get rid of spelling and grammatical errors. Make sure you are consistent in the use of verb tenses and in the use of singular and plural. Use a dictionary when in doubt about any vocabulary.

Things to Think About

The assignment asks you to answer three questions:
1. Why did America take on the responsibilities?
2. How successfully did it manage them?
3. How did they change America internally?

Make sure that you answer all three.
Make sure that you explain to the reader what these responsibilities were, and how they changed over time.

Be chronological.

Note that the second part of the question asks you to make a judgment. There is no right or wrong answer to this section of the question, but however you decide to answer it, make sure you justify your judgment.

You *must* make reference to the following:
1. the First World War;
2. the Second World War;
3. Communism and anti-Communism;
4. the Cold War;
5. nuclear weapons;
6. Korea and Vietnam;
7. the events of 1989–91.

ANSWERS TO SECTIONS 2, 3, AND 4 OF THE FINAL EXAMINATION

2. When
   a. 1960
   b. 1969
   c. 1973
   d. 1940
   e. 1945
   f. 1965
   g. 1955–56
   h. 1917
   i. 1925
   j. 1942
   k. 1989
   l. 1937
   m. 1948
   n. 1974
   o. 1901
   p. 1963
   q. 1893
   r. 1892
   s. 1876
   t. 1944

3. Where
   a. Utah
   b. Nevada
   c. Hawaii
   d. Alaska
   e. California
   f. Montana
   g. Michigan
   h. New York
   i. New Jersey
   j. Illinois
   k. North Carolina

      l. New Mexico

      m. Florida

      n. Pennsylvania

      o. Kansas, Texas, Oklahoma, New Mexico, Colorado

      p. Tennessee

      q. Georgia

      r. Pennsylvania

      s. Georgia

4. Who
   a. Elton Mayo
   b. Eugene Debs
   c. Upton Sinclair
   d. General John J. Pershing
   e. Herbert Hoover
   f. Tim O'Brien
   g. Rosa Parks
   h. Gifford Pinchot
   i. Anwar Sadat
   j. Mikhail Gorbachev
   k. Admiral Chester Nimitz
   l. Crazy Horse, Sitting Bull
   m. William Dawson
   n. Francis Turner
   o. Alexander Berkmann
   p. Julius and Ethel Rosenberg
   q. Jesse Jackson
   r. Theodore Roosevelt
   s. Charlie Chaplin

Index